interactive SCIENCE

Butterflies do not have noses. They smell with their antennae.

PEARSON

Glenview, Illinois • Boston, Massachusetts • Chandler, Arizona • Upper Saddle River, New Jersey

Authors

You are an author!

You are one of the authors of this book. You can write in this book! You can take notes in this book! You can draw in it too! This book will be yours to keep.

Fill in the information below to tell about yourself. Then write your autobiography. An autobiography tells about you and the kinds of things you like to do.

Name ....

School ....

Town, State ....

Autobiography ....

....

....

....

....

....

....

My Photo

ISBN-13: 978-0-328-52098-5
ISBN-10: 0-328-52098-5
20   18

ON THE COVER
Butterflies do not have noses.
They smell with their antennae.

Program Authors

DON BUCKLEY, M.Sc.
*Information and Communications Technology Director,
The School at Columbia University, New York, New York*
Mr. Buckley has been at the forefront of K–12 educational
technology for nearly two decades. A founder of New York City
Independent School Technologists (NYCIST) and long-time chair
of New York Association of Independent Schools' annual IT
conference, he has taught students on two continents and
created multimedia and Internet-based instructional systems
for schools worldwide.

ZIPPORAH MILLER, M.A.Ed.
*Associate Executive Director for Professional Programs
and Conferences, National Science Teachers Association,
Arlington, Virginia*
Associate executive director for professional programs and
conferences at NSTA, Ms. Zipporah Miller is a former K–12 science
supervisor and STEM coordinator for the Prince George's County
Public School District in Maryland. She is a science education
consultant who has overseen curriculum development and staff
training for more than 150 district science coordinators.

MICHAEL J. PADILLA, Ph.D.
*Associate Dean and Director, Eugene P. Moore School of
Education, Clemson University, Clemson, South Carolina*
A former middle school teacher and a leader in middle school science
education, Dr. Michael Padilla has served as president of the National
Science Teachers Association and as a writer of the National Science
Education Standards. He is professor of science education at Clemson
University. As lead author of the *Science Explorer* series, Dr. Padilla
has inspired the team in developing a program that promotes student
inquiry and meets the needs of today's students.

KATHRYN THORNTON, Ph.D.
*Professor and Associate Dean, School of Engineering
and Applied Science, University of Virginia,
Charlottesville, Virginia*
Selected by NASA in May 1984, Dr. Kathryn Thornton is a veteran
of four space flights. She has logged more than 975 hours in space,
including more than 21 hours of extravehicular activity. As an
author on the *Scott Foresman Science* series, Dr. Thornton's
enthusiasm for science has inspired teachers around the globe.

MICHAEL E. WYSESSION, Ph.D.
*Associate Professor of Earth and Planetary Science,
Washington University, St. Louis, Missouri*
An author on more than 50 scientific publications, Dr. Wysession
was awarded the prestigious Packard Foundation Fellowship and
Presidential Faculty Fellowship for his research in geophysics. Dr.
Wysession is an expert on Earth's inner structure and has mapped
various regions of Earth using seismic tomography. He is known
internationally for his work in geoscience education and outreach.

Instructional Design Author

GRANT WIGGINS, Ed.D.
*President, Authentic Education,
Hopewell, New Jersey*
Dr. Wiggins is a co-author with Jay McTighe
of *Understanding by Design, 2nd Edition*
(ASCD 2005). His approach to instructional
design provides teachers with a disciplined
way of thinking about curriculum design,
assessment, and instruction that moves
teaching from covering content to ensuring
understanding.
UNDERSTANDING BY DESIGN® and UbD™
are trademarks of ASCD, and are used
under license.

Planet Diary Author

JACK HANKIN
*Science/Mathematics Teacher,
The Hilldale School, Daly City, California
Founder, Planet Diary Web site*
Mr. Hankin is the creator and writer
of Planet Diary, a science current events
Web site. Mr. Hankin is passionate about
bringing science news and environmental
awareness into classrooms.

Activities Author

KAREN L. OSTLUND, Ph.D.
*Advisory Council, Texas Natural Science
Center, College of Natural Sciences,
The University of Texas at Austin*
Dr. Ostlund has more than 35 years of
experience teaching at the elementary,
middle school, and university levels. She
was Director of WINGS Online (Welcoming
Interns and Novices with Guidance and
Support) and Director of the UTeach | Dell
Center for New Teacher Success at the
University of Texas at Austin. She served as
Director of the Center for Science Education
at the University of Texas at Arlington,
President of the Council of Elementary
Science International, and on the Board of
Directors of the National Science Teachers
Association. As an author of *Scott Foresman
Science*, Dr. Ostlund was instrumental in
developing inquiry activities.

ELL Consultant

JIM CUMMINS, Ph.D.
*Professor and Canada Research Chair,
Curriculum, Teaching and Learning
Department at the University of Toronto*
Dr. Cummins focuses on literacy development
in multilingual schools and the role of
technology in learning. *Interactive Science*
incorporates research-based principles for
integrating language with the teaching of
academic content based on his work.

Reviewers

Program Consultants

William Brozo, Ph.D.
Professor of Literacy, Graduate School of Education, George Mason University, Fairfax, Virginia.
Dr. Brozo is the author of numerous articles and books on literacy development. He co-authors a column in The Reading Teacher and serves on the editorial review board of the Journal of Adolescent & Adult Literacy.

Kristi Zenchak, M.S.
Biology Instructor, Oakton Community College, Des Plaines, Illinois
Kristi Zenchak helps elementary teachers incorporate science, technology, engineering, and math activities into the classroom. STEM activities that produce viable solutions to real-world problems not only motivate students but also prepare students for future STEM careers. Ms. Zenchak helps elementary teachers understand the basic science concepts, and provides STEM activities that easy are to implement in the classroom.

Content Reviewers

Brad Armosky, M.S.
Texas Advanced Computing Center
University of Texas at Austin
Austin, Texas

Alexander Brands, Ph.D.
Department of Biological Sciences
Lehigh University
Bethlehem, Pennsylvania

Paul Beale, Ph.D.
Department of Physics
University of Colorado
Boulder, Colorado

Joy Branlund, Ph.D.
Department of Earth Science
Southwestern Illinois College
Granite City, Illinois

Constance Brown, Ph.D
Atmospheric Science Program
Geography Department
Indiana University
Bloomington, Indiana

Dana Dudle, Ph.D.
Biology Department
DePauw University
Greencastle, Indiana

Rick Duhrkopf, Ph. D.
Department of Biology
Baylor University
Waco, Texas

Mark Henriksen, Ph.D.
Physics Department
University of Maryland
Baltimore, Maryland

Andrew Hirsch, Ph.D.
Department of Physics
Purdue University
W. Lafayette, Indiana

Linda L. Cronin Jones, Ph.D.
School of Teaching & Learning
University of Florida
Gainesville, Florida

T. Griffith Jones, Ph.D.
College of Education
University of Florida
Gainesville, Florida

Candace Lutzow-Felling, Ph.D.
Director of Education
State Arboretum of Virginia &
  Blandy Experimental Farm
Boyce, Virginia

Cortney V. Martin, Ph.D.
Virginia Polytechnic Institute
Blacksburg, Virginia

Sadredin Moosavi, Ph.D.
University of Massachusetts
Dartmouth
Fairhaven, Massachusetts

Klaus Newmann, Ph.D.
Department of Geological
  Sciences
Ball State University
Muncie, Indiana

Scott M. Rochette, Ph.D.
Department of the Earth Sciences
SUNY College at Brockport
Brockport, New York

Ursula Rosauer Smedly, M.S.
Alcade Science Center
New Mexico State University
Alcade, New Mexico

Frederick W. Taylor, Ph.D.
Jackson School of Geosciences
University of Texas at Austin
Austin, Texas

Chapter 1

Unit A
Science, Engineering, and Technology

Unit A
Science, Engineering,
and Technology 1

The Nature of Science

This scientist is recording her observations.

myscienceonline.com

 **Untamed Science**
Watch the Ecogeeks as they learn about the nature of science.

Got it? 60-Second Video
Take a minute to review what you learned.

Envision It!
See what you already know about the nature of science.

Investigate It! Simulation
Do this lab online!

I Will Know...
See how the key concepts of the nature of science come to life.

Chapter 2

Technology and the Design Process

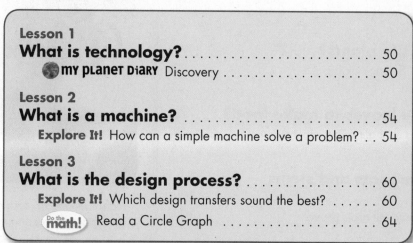

Engineers can look inside this digital audio player to learn about its design.

myscienceonline.com

Untamed Science
Ecogeeks answer your questions about technology and the design process.

Got it? 60-Second Video
Review each lesson in 60 seconds!

Explore It! Animation
Watch this lab online!

Investigate It! Virtual Lab
Try this lab in an interactive virtual lab environment!

● **MY PLANET DIARY**
Discover fun facts about technology.

Chapter 3

Plants

Plants need food, air, water, and space to live and grow.

myscienceonLine.com

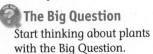

Watch the Ecogeeks learn about plants.

Got it? 60-Second Video
Review what you learned about plants in 60 seconds.

Explore It! Animation
Watch your lab online!

Envision It!
See what you already know about plants.

The Big Question
Start thinking about plants with the Big Question.

Living Things

A young antelope inherits characteristics from its parent.

myscienceonline.com

UntamedScience
The Ecogeeks answer your questions about living things.

Got it? ⏱ **60-Second Video**
Take a minute to learn about living things.

Investigate It! Virtual Lab
Try this lab online!

I Will Know...
See what you've learned about living things.

Memory Match
Practice vocabulary with an interactive matching game.

5

Unit B
Summary

Ecosystems

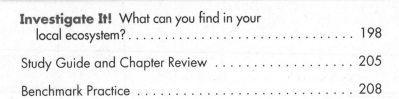

*Box turtles interact with other
living and nonliving things in
their ecosystems.*

myscienceonline.com

Untamed Science
Go on a science adventure
with the Ecogeeks!

Got it? 60-Second Video
Review what you learned
about ecosystems in
60 seconds.

Explore It! Animation
Watch your lab online!

? **I Will Know...**
A fun way to review what
you've learned about
ecosystems.

Vocabulary Smart Cards
Mix and match vocabulary
practice.

Unit C
Earth Science

Chapter 6
Earth and Weather

Tools, such as rain gauges,
help scientists measure and
describe weather.

myscienceonline.com

Untamed Science
Watch the Ecogeeks learn
about Earth and weather.

Got it? **60-Second Video**
Review what you learned
in 60 seconds.

Investigate It! Simulation
Interact with the lab and see
what happens!

Envision It!
See what you already know
about Earth and weather.

MY PLANET DIARY
Learn fun and interesting
science facts.

A telescope can help you see objects in space that you could not see with your eyes alone.

myscienceonline.com

Untamed Science™
Ecogeeks answer your questions about Earth and our universe.

Got it? 60-Second Video
Take a minute to learn about Earth and our universe.

Explore It! Animation
Watch your lab online!

The Big Question
Start thinking about Earth and our universe with the big question.

my pLaneT DiaRY
Connect science to your life.

Unit D
Physical Science

Chapter 8

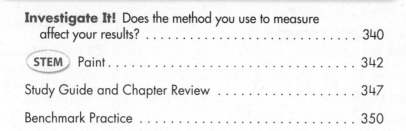

Matter

These objects are matter and have properties such as size, color, texture, and hardness.

myscienceonline.com

UntamedScience
Go on an adventure with the Ecogeeks to learn about matter.

Got it? **60-Second Video**
Review each lesson about matter in 60 seconds!

Envision It!
Interact with science to see what you already know about matter.

I Will Know...
See what you've learned about matter.

Investigate It! Virtual Lab
Try this lab in an interactive virtual lab environment!

Chapter 9

Energy and Its Forms

The siren on this fire truck produces sound energy by causing matter to vibrate.

myscienceonline.com

Untamed Science
Watch the Ecogeeks as they learn about energy and its forms.

Got it? 60-Second Video
Review each lesson about energy in 60 seconds.

Envision It!
Interact with science to find out what you know about energy and its forms.

Explore It! Animation
Watch your lab online!

Memory Match
Practice vocabulary with an interactive matching game.

Chapter 10

Unit D Summary

Forces and Motion

The speed of a roller coaster changes as it moves.

myscienceonLine.com

UntamedScience
Go on an adventure with the Ecogeeks to learn about forces and motion.

Got it? 60-Second Video
Take a minute to learn about forces and motion.

I Will Know...
See what you've learned about forces and motion.

my planet Diary
Jump into an interesting world of science online.

Investigate It! Virtual Lab
Try this lab online!

interactive SCIENCE

Big Question

At the start of each chapter you will see two questions—
an **Engaging Question** and a **Big Question**.
Just like a scientist, you will predict an answer to the
Engaging Question. Each Big Question will help you
start thinking about the Big Ideas of science. Look for the
symbol throughout the chapter!

The Water Cycle and Weather

Chapter 7

Try It! How can water move in the water cycle?

Lesson 1 What is the water cycle?

Lesson 2 What is the ocean?

Lesson 3 What is weather?

Lesson 4 How do clouds and precipitation form?

Lesson 5 What is climate?

Investigate It! Where is the hurricane going?

It has not rained, but after spending the night resting, this fly was covered with droplets in the morning.

Predict Where do you think this water came from?

How does water move through the environment?

WHERE did these drops come from?

Let's Read Science!

You will see a page like this toward the beginning of each chapter. It will show you how to use a reading skill that will help you understand what you read.

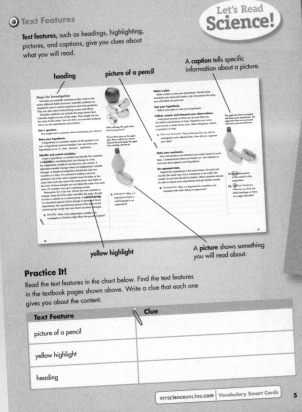

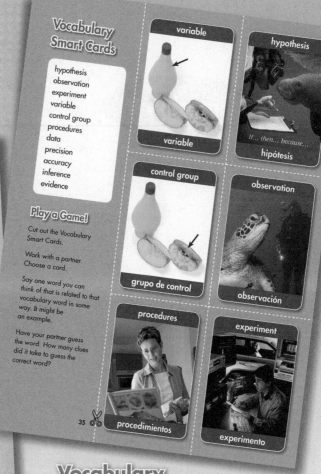

Vocabulary Smart Cards

Go to the end of the chapter and cut out your own set of **Vocabulary Smart Cards.** Write a sentence, draw a picture, or use a vocabulary strategy to learn the word. Play a game with a classmate to practice using the word!

Look for **MyScienceOnline.com** technology options.
At MyScienceOnline.com you can immerse yourself in virtual environments, get extra practice, and even blog about current events in science.

"Engage with the page!"

interactive SCIENCE

Envision It!

At the beginning of each lesson, at the top of the page, you will see an **Envision It!** interactivity that gives you the opportunity to circle, draw, write, or respond to the Envision It! question.

Lesson 1
What are forces?

Envision It!

Tell why the metal ring on the string does not fall.

I will know some forces that cause objects to move.

Words to Know
force
contact force
friction
non-contact force
gravity

MY PLANET DiARY

You may have seen video clips of astronauts floating around in a spacecraft. People often think astronauts have no weight at all in space. In fact, they do. Most astronauts work just 300 km above ground. This is relatively close to Earth. At that height, they are only a few pounds lighter. They seem to float because their spacecraft is moving along with them. However, the spacecraft and the astronauts are both in fact falling, just like a skydiver. They don't crash because they are also moving forward fast enough to follow the curvature of the Earth.

Which everyday activities do you think would be easier in orbit?

/// **MISCONCEPTION** ///

Forces

When one object pushes or pulls another object, the first object is exerting a force on the second one. A **force** is a push or pull that acts on an object.

Every force has a strength, or magnitude. This strength is measured in units called newtons (N). A force also has a direction. The direction of a force can be described by telling which way the force is acting. The dog is pushing the ball with a force of around 2 N.

Forces can change the way objects move. When an object begins to move, it is because a force has acted on it. When an object is already moving, forces can make it speed up, slow down, or change direction.

1. ◉ **Main Idea and Details** Use the graphic organizer below to list two details and the main idea found in the last paragraph of the text.

Detail	Detail

Main Idea

The direction of the arrow shows that the dog is pushing, not pulling.

myscienceonline.com my PLANET DIARY 464

myscienceonline.com | Envision It! | 465

MY PLANET DiARY

My Planet Diary interactivities will introduce you to amazing scientists, fun facts, and important discoveries in science. They will also help you to overcome common misconceptions about science concepts.

After reading small chunks of information, stop to check your understanding. The visuals help teach about what you read. Answer questions, underline text, draw pictures, or label models.

The Inner Planets

The eight known planets are divided into inner and outer planets based on their distances from the sun. The four inner planets are Mercury, Venus, Earth, and Mars. The inner planets have some things in common. They are the planets closest to the sun, and they all have rocky surfaces. But they have many differences too.

6. **Compare** Read the descriptions of the planets. What is one way Mercury and Venus are alike?

The Outer Planets

The outer planets are Jupiter, Saturn, Uranus, and Neptune. The outer planets are very different from the inner planets. Unlike the rocky inner planets, the outer planets are huge and made mostly of gas. They are called gas giants. Their surfaces are not solid. These planets have thick layers of clouds and strong winds. They also have rings around them. Jupiter's rings are hard to see.

7. **Main Idea and Details** What is the main idea of the paragraph?

Mercury
Mercury is the closest planet to the sun. Because of this, the surface of Mercury is dry and very hot. Mercury is also the smallest planet. It is less than half the size of Earth. Mercury has no moons.

Venus
Venus is the second planet from the sun. Like Mercury, Venus is a very hot, rocky planet. It has craters, mountains, and valleys. Thick clouds cover the planet and trap the sun's energy, making it very hot. Venus has no moons.

Earth
Earth is the third planet from the sun. Water covers almost three-fourths of Earth's surface. Earth is the only planet in our solar system that supports life. It has the conditions living things need, including mild temperatures, liquid water, and an atmosphere.

Mars
Mars, the fourth planet from the sun, is about half the size of Earth. Mars is called the "red planet" because its surface is reddish-orange. Temperatures on Mars are too cold for liquid water. Mars has volcanoes and deep canyons. It has two moons.

Jupiter
Jupiter is the fifth planet from the sun and the largest planet. It is over 11 times the size of Earth. Jupiter is covered with thick clouds. It has more than 60 moons. Jupiter's Great Red Spot, shown below, is actually a huge storm.

Saturn
Saturn is the sixth planet from the sun and the second largest planet. Saturn's most famous feature is its rings. The rings, shown below, are made of chunks of ice and rock that circle the planet. Saturn has more than 60 moons.

Uranus
Uranus is the seventh planet from the sun. It is smaller than Saturn or Jupiter but about four times the size of Earth. Uranus is unlike other planets because it rotates on its side. It has 27 moons.

Neptune
Neptune is the farthest planet from the sun. It is so far away that its orbit around the sun takes 165 Earth years. Neptune is slightly smaller than Uranus. It has 13 moons. Neptune's blue color is caused by gases in its atmosphere.

284   285

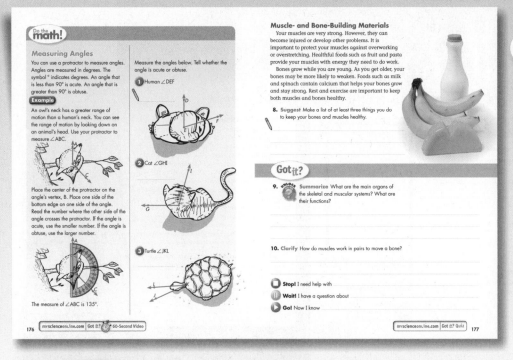

Do the math!

Measuring Angles

You can use a protractor to measure angles. Angles are measured in degrees. The symbol ° indicates degrees. An angle that is less than 90° is acute. An angle that is greater than 90° is obtuse.

Example

An owl's neck has a greater range of motion than a human's neck. You can see the range of motion by looking down on an animal's head. Use your protractor to measure ∠ABC.

Place the center of the protractor on the angle's vertex, B. Place one side of the bottom edge on one side of the angle. Read the number where the other side of the angle crosses the protractor. If the angle is acute, use the smaller number. If the angle is obtuse, use the larger number.

The measure of ∠ABC is 135°.

Measure the angles below. Tell whether the angle is acute or obtuse.

1 Human ∠DEF

2 Cat ∠GHI

3 Turtle ∠JKL

Muscle- and Bone-Building Materials

Your muscles are very strong. However, they can become injured or develop other problems. It is important to protect your muscles against overworking or overstretching. Healthful foods such as fruit and pasta provide your muscles with energy they need to do work.

Bones grow while you are young. As you get older, your bones may be more likely to weaken. Foods such as milk and spinach contain calcium that helps your bones grow and stay strong. Rest and exercise are important to keep both muscles and bones healthy.

8. **Suggest** Make a list of at least three things you do to keep your bones and muscles healthy.

Got it?

9. **Summarize** What are the main organs of the skeletal and muscular systems? What are their functions?

10. **Clarify** How do muscles work in pairs to move a bone?

Stop! I need help with

Wait! I have a question about

Go! Now I know

176   mysclenceonline.com | Got it? | 60-Second Video   mysclenceonline.com | Got it? Quiz   177

At the end of each lesson you will have a chance to evaluate your own progress! After answering the **Got it?** questions, think about how you are doing. At this point you can stop, wait, or go on to the next lesson.

Scientists commonly use math as a tool to help them answer science questions. You can practice skills that you are learning in math class right in your *Interactive Science* Student Edition!

"Have fun! Be a scientist!"

interactive SCIENCE

Try It!

At the start of every chapter, you will have the chance to do a hands-on inquiry lab. The lab will provide you with experiences that will prepare you for the chapter lessons or may raise a new question in your mind.

Inquiry — Try It!

How are weight and volume affected when objects are combined?

1. Fill a graduated cylinder with 25 mL of beads. Record the volume on the chart.
2. Hold up the spring scale with the bag. Set the scale to zero. Now the spring scale will only show the weight of what is in the bag.
3. Put the beads in the bag and weigh them. Record. Pour the beads into a cup.
4. Repeat Step 1 and Step 3 with sand. Pour the sand into the cup with the beads.
5. Mix the beads and sand with a spoon. Repeat Step 1 and Step 3 with the mixture of beads and sand.

Measurements of Matter

Objects	Volume (mL)	Weight (g)
beads		
sand		
beads and sand		

Explain Your Results

6. **Interpret Data** Did the total volume or weight change after mixing? Explain.

7. **Infer** What did you learn about volume?

Materials
graduated cylinder, beads, plastic cup, plastic spoon, spring scale with bag, sand

Inquiry Skill
When you interpret data, you can make an **inference.**

414

Lesson 5
What is climate?

Envision It!

What do you think the climate is like here? **Tell** how the house is protected against some features of the climate.

I will know that different climate zones have specific characteristics.

Words to Know
climate
latitude
elevation

Inquiry — Explore It!

How does a thermometer work?

1. Use the Make a Thermometer sheet. Make a thermometer. Will it work like a regular thermometer? Discuss.
2. Place your thermometer in warm water. **Observe.**
3. **Predict** what will happen if you place your thermometer in cold water. Tell how you made your prediction. Test your prediction.

Explain Your Results

4. **Communicate** Explain how you think your thermometer might work.

Materials
plastic jar
metric ruler
room-temperature water
red food coloring
Make a Thermometer
clay
plastic straw
plastic bowl with very warm water
plastic bowl with very cold water

Be careful! Do not use dangerously warm water.

Average Weather

The words *weather* and *climate* do not have the same definitions. Weather is made up of all the conditions in one place at a single moment. Weather changes very often. **Climate** describes the weather conditions over a long time, at least thirty years. Climate includes things such as the average amount of precipitation, the average temperature, and how much the temperature changes during the year. Climates do not change as much as the daily weather does.

Giant sequoia trees grow naturally in a small area of California, in the western Sierra Nevada. The climate of this area is generally humid, with mostly dry summers and snowy winters. Some giant sequoias have been alive for thousands of years.

1. **Infer** How do you know this is a good climate for giant sequoias?

Sequoias are able to live for thousands of years because the climate remains nearly steady where they grow.

myscienceonline.com | Explore It! Animation   282

myscienceonline.com | Envision It!   283

Explore It!

Before you start reading the lesson, **Explore It!** activities provide you with an opportunity to first explore the content!

Design It!

The **Design It!** activity has you use the engineering design process to find solutions to problems. By identifying the problem, doing research, and developing possible solutions, you will design, construct, and test a prototype for a real world problem. Communicate your evidence through graphs, tables, drawings, and prototypes and identify ways to make your solution better.

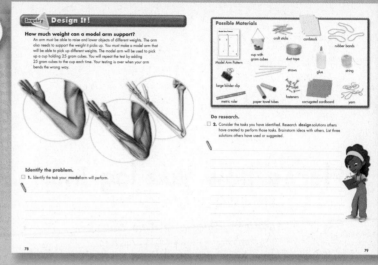

Investigate It!

At the end of every chapter, a Directed Inquiry lab gives you a chance to put together everything you've learned in the chapter. Using the activity card, apply design principles in the Guided version to Modify Your Investigation or the Open version to Develop Your Own Investigation. Whether you need a lot of support from your teacher or you're ready to explore on your own, there are fun hands-on activities that match your interests.

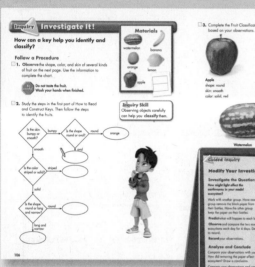

Apply It!

At the end of every unit, an Open Inquiry lab gives you a chance to explore science using scientific methods.

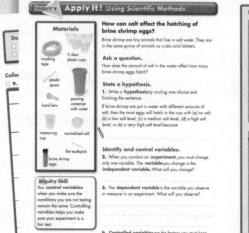

"Go online anytime!"

interactive SCIENCE

Here's how you log in...

1 Go to **www.myscienceonline.com**.

2 Log in with your username and password.

Username: _____

Password: _____

3 Click on your program and select your chapter.

Check it out!

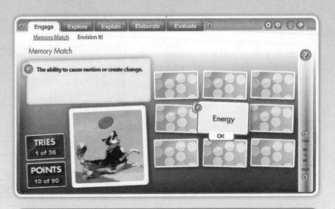

Watch a Video!

 Untamed Science™ Join the Ecogeeks on their video adventure.

Got it? ⏱ **60-Second Video** Review each lesson in 60 seconds.

Go Digital for Inquiry!

Explore It! Simulation Watch the lab online.

Investigate It! Virtual Lab Do the lab online.

Show What You Know!

Got it? Quiz Take a quick quiz and get instant feedback.

❓ Benchmark Practice Prepare for the "big test."

❓ Writing for Science Write to help you unlock the Big Question.

Get Excited About Science!

❓ The Big Question Share what you think about the Big Question.

my planet diary Connect to the world of science.

Envision It! Connect to what you already know before you start each lesson.

Memory Match Play a game to build your vocabulary.

Get Help!

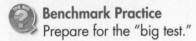 **my science COACH** Get help at your level.

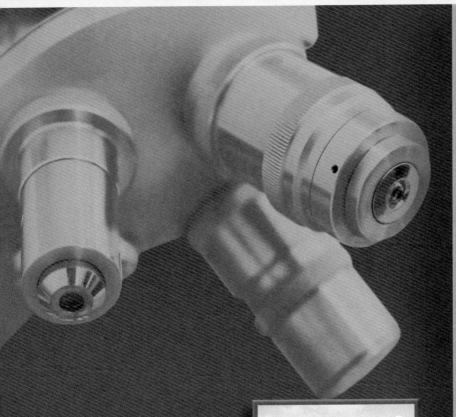

Science, Engineering, and Technology

Chapter 1
The Nature of Science

 What is science?

Chapter 2
Technology and the Design Process

How can technology affect our lives?

What can you **ask** about lake water?

The Nature of Science

 Try It! Why is it important to communicate clearly?

Investigate It! How does a microscope help you make observations?

These student scientists are studying the quality of lake water. They are using tools and recording their observations. They could analyze their data in the boat or back at school.

 Predict What type of observations about water do you think they are making?

....

....

THE BIG ? **What is science?**

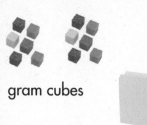

Materials

gram cubes

folder

Why is it important to communicate clearly?

☐ **1.** Work with a partner. Take 6 cubes each. Set up a folder so that you cannot see each other's work.

☐ **2.** **Design** and build a simple structure.

> **Inquiry Skill**
> Scientists **communicate** when they explain how to do something.

☑ **3.** **Communicate**   Tell your partner how to build your structure.

☑ **4.** Take the folder down. Compare the structures.

☐ **5.** Trade jobs and repeat.

Explain Your Results

6. **UNLOCK THE BIG ?** Think about the words you used in **communicating** your **design** to your partner. List the words that were most helpful in communicating clearly.

....

7. Why was it important to communicate clearly with your partner? **Infer** why it is important for scientists to communicate clearly with one another.

....

....

Let's Read
Science!

⊙ Text Features

Text features, such as headings, highlighting, pictures, and captions, give you clues about what you will read.

A **heading** tells what the content that follows is about.

A **picture** shows something you will read about.

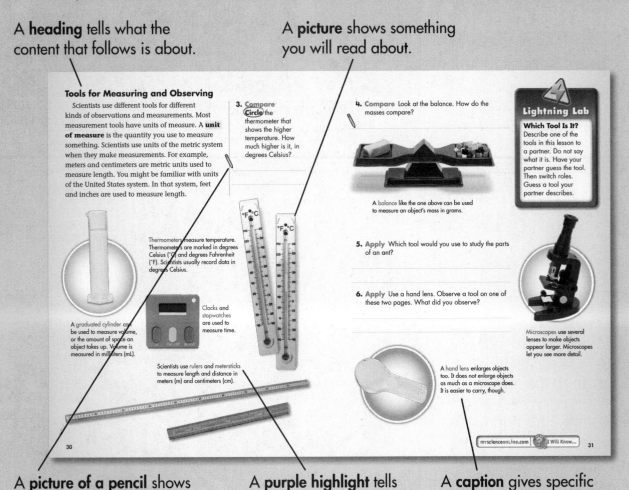

Tools for Measuring and Observing

Scientists use different tools for different kinds of observations and measurements. Most measurement tools have units of measure. A **unit of measure** is the quantity you use to measure something. Scientists use units of the metric system when they make measurements. For example, meters and centimeters are metric units used to measure length. You might be familiar with units of the United States system. In that system, feet and inches are used to measure length.

Thermometers measure temperature. Thermometers are marked in degrees Celsius (°C) and degrees Fahrenheit (°F). Scientists usually record data in degrees Celsius.

A graduated cylinder can be used to measure volume, or the amount of space an object takes up. Volume is measured in milliliters (mL).

Clocks and stopwatches are used to measure time.

Scientists use rulers and metersticks to measure length and distance in meters (m) and centimeters (cm).

3. **Compare** Circle the thermometer that shows the higher temperature. How much higher is it, in degrees Celsius?

4. **Compare** Look at the balance. How do the masses compare?

A balance like the one above can be used to measure an object's mass in grams.

5. **Apply** Which tool would you use to study the parts of an ant?

6. **Apply** Use a hand lens. Observe a tool on one of these two pages. What did you observe?

A hand lens enlarges objects too. It does not enlarge objects as much as a microscope does. It is easier to carry, though.

Lightning Lab

Which Tool Is It? Describe one of the tools in this lesson to a partner. Do not say what it is. Have your partner guess the tool. Then switch roles. Guess a tool your partner describes.

Microscopes use several lenses to make objects appear larger. Microscopes let you see more detail.

myscienceonline.com I Will Know...

30   31

A **picture of a pencil** shows where you will write something.

A **purple highlight** tells that a word is important.

A **caption** gives specific information about a picture.

Practice It!

Read the text features in the chart below. Write a clue that each one gives you about the content.

Text feature	Clue
picture	
caption	
heading	

Lesson 1
What questions do scientists ask?

Tell a question that a scientist could ask about these orange trees.

my planet diary

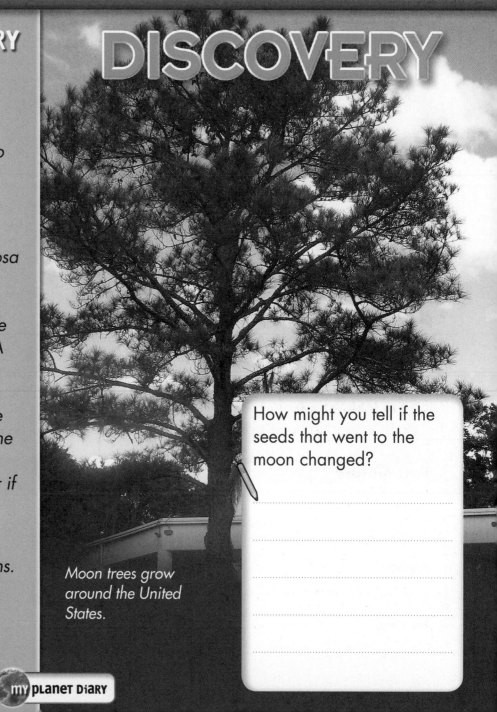

DISCOVERY

Have you ever heard of moon trees? Moon trees do not come from the moon. They are trees grown from seeds taken to the moon.

NASA astronaut Stuart Roosa took seeds to the moon on the Apollo 14 mission in 1971. When he brought the seeds back to Earth, NASA scientists examined them. Scientists wanted to learn if space travel changed the seeds. Then they planted the seeds. No one knew what the trees would look like or if the seeds would grow.

As the seeds grew, NASA scientists made observations. These observations helped scientists learn how space travel affects seed growth.

Moon trees grow around the United States.

How might you tell if the seeds that went to the moon changed?

....

....

....

....

....

mYscienceonLine.com | **my planet diary**

Words to Know

scientist   inquiry
investigate

Scientists

What type of soil works best to grow corn and soybeans? That is a question a scientist might ask. A **scientist** is a person who asks questions about the natural world. Scientists collect observations in an organized way to investigate their questions. To **investigate** means to look for answers. Then scientists explain their answers.

Everyone can be a scientist. You are a scientist when you ask questions and investigate. What questions do you ask about the natural world?

1. ◉ **Text Features** Look at the text features on this page. Identify two text features and the clues they give you.

This scientist is studying crop fertilizers. He might ask a question about what kind of fertilizer will help plants grow the largest.

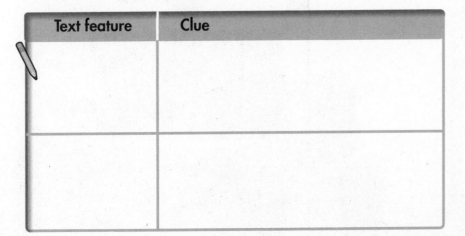

Text feature	Clue

Questions

Science begins with inquiry. **Inquiry** means the process of asking questions. Scientists ask questions that they can investigate. The questions might come from something scientists observe or a problem they know. What type of soil works best to grow corn and soybeans? How can I grow bigger crops? How can I keep insects from eating crops? These are some questions scientists might ask.

Questions That Science Cannot Answer

Some questions cannot be answered by investigating. What is the prettiest flower? What juice tastes best? The answers to these questions are opinions. You might think apple juice tastes best. Another student might think orange juice tastes best. Collecting observations would not help a scientist decide which of you is right. Science cannot answer questions about tastes or personal opinions.

2. Identify
Underline the question below that science cannot answer.

Do plants need water to grow?

Is baseball a better sport than basketball?

3. Generate What other question might the boy in the picture ask?

Which soil works best?

How much water do these plants need?

Lightning Lab

Questions and Answers

Think about something you would like to investigate. List the questions you would ask. Talk with a partner. How would your questions help you look for answers?

myscienceonline.com | Got it? | 60-Second Video

Alone or in Teams

Sometimes scientists work alone, but sometimes scientists can learn more by working together. When scientists work together they can share information and discoveries. Scientists who are investigating how to keep insects from eating crops might each try different methods and then compare their results. Scientists might take turns caring for their crops.

These students use hand lenses to observe.

4. Describe What is another way scientists might work together?

....

....

Got it?

5. Draw Conclusions If you were acting like a scientist in class, what would you be doing? Write three things.

....

....

6. UNLOCK THE BIG ? A student asks the question, "What is the best color for a bike?" Can science answer this question? Explain.

....

....

Stop! I need help with ....

Wait! I have a question about ....

Go! Now I know ....

Lesson 2
What skills do scientists use?

Look at the time-elapsed photo of a hurricane.
Tell what you can observe about hurricanes.

Inquiry **Explore It!**

How can observations help you make an inference?

☐ **1.** Place the clear blue sheet over the color wheel. **Observe.**

☐ **2.** Repeat Step 1 with the clear red sheet and then the clear yellow sheet.

☐ **3.** Discuss the changes you observed.

Materials

red sheet

blue sheet

yellow sheet

Explain Your Results

4. Infer How are blue, red, and yellow different from purple, orange, and green?

....

....

5. Tell how your **observations** helped you make your inference.

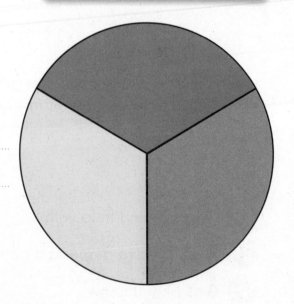

myscienceonline.com **Explore It!** Animation

I will know how to use process skills such as observation, prediction, and measurement.

Word to Know

infer

Science Skills

Scientists use process skills to learn about objects, places, or events. Observation is a process skill. When you use your five senses to find out about something, you observe. Your senses include sight, hearing, touch, taste, and smell.

Scientists often use tools to make observations. A satellite is a tool that helps scientists observe Earth's weather. Data from satellites are often displayed on weather maps. The weather map below shows hurricanes, which are strong storms.

1. **Observe** Look at the picture below. What is one observation you can make?

....

....

....

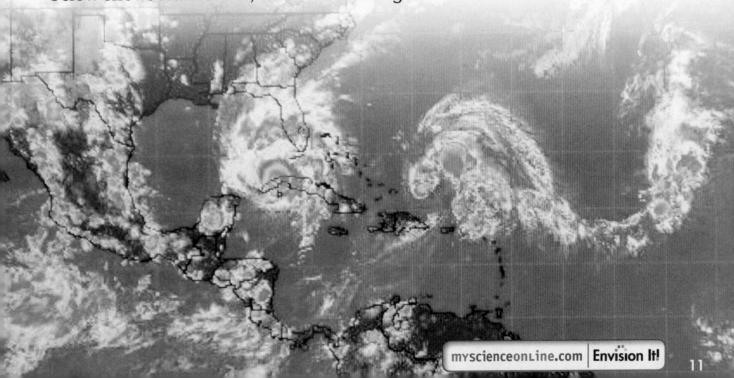

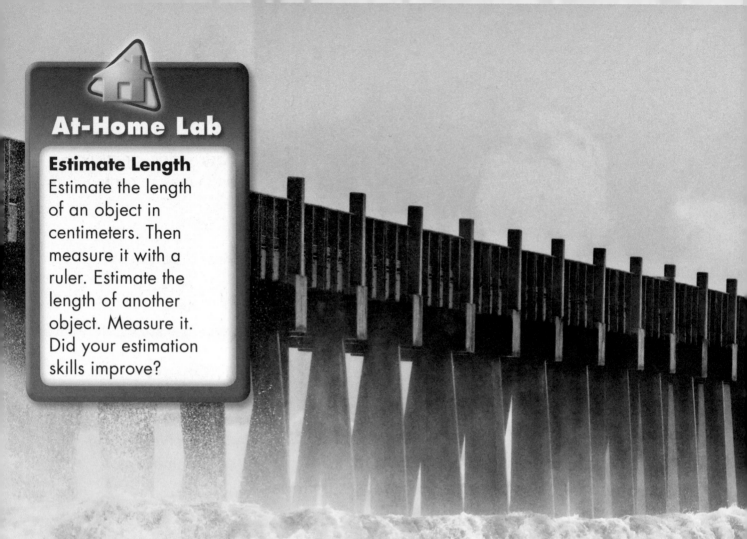

Estimate and Measure

Scientists sometimes estimate when they make observations. To estimate means to make a careful guess. A scientist standing on the pier in the picture might feel the wind pushing hard against his body. He might estimate that the wind is blowing about 70 or 80 kilometers per hour.

To find the exact wind speed, the scientist would make a measurement. A measurement is a number that tells how much or how many. Scientists often use tools to measure. An anemometer is a tool that can measure the speed of the wind.

2. [CHALLENGE] Suppose the pier in the picture is 20 feet high. Explain how you could use this information to estimate the height of the waves.

....

....

....

....

anemometer

Infer and Predict

Some data and observations are facts. For example, the statement "The wave crashed into the pier" is a fact. You can use facts to **infer**, or draw a conclusion. Scientists infer what they think is happening based on what they observe or based on prior knowledge. For example, a scientist observing the waves in the picture might infer that a hurricane is coming on shore.

Observations also can help you to predict. When you predict, you tell what you think will happen in the future. For example, a scientist might predict that the waves will get bigger as the hurricane gets closer to shore.

3. Predict What is another prediction you could make based on your observations of this picture?

....

....

....

....

Classify

Classify means to sort objects, events, or living things based on their properties. When you classify, you put similar things into groups or categories. Scientists use the Saffir-Simpson Hurricane Scale to classify and compare hurricanes. The scale groups hurricanes into categories according to wind speed.

Saffir-Simpson Hurricane Scale		
Category	**Wind Speed**	
	miles per hour	**kilometers per hour**
5	more than 155	more than 249
4	131–155	210–249
3	111–130	178–209
2	96–110	154–177
1	74–95	119–153

1. **Classify** A hurricane has a wind speed of 158 kilometers per hour. What is the hurricane's category?

2. **Compare** Hurricane A has a wind speed of 137 kilometers per hour. Hurricane B has a wind speed of 135 miles per hour. Are the two hurricanes in the same category? Explain.

3. **Analyze** The graph below shows wind speeds for Hurricane C in miles per hour (mph). How did the hurricane change on Day 4? Use the word *category* in your answer.

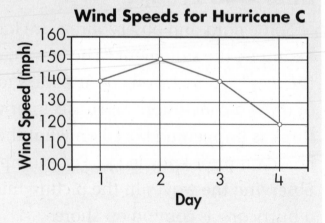

Interpret and Explain Data

Scientists work together to interpret their data and form scientific explanations. A good explanation uses observations, inferences, prior knowledge, measurements, and data from an investigation. Scientists use all this information to explain how things happen naturally.

For example, scientists are trying to develop the ability to forecast when hurricanes will form. They use observations, weather data, and their knowledge of past storms to predict where hurricanes will strike and how strong they will be. This information can help people stay safe.

4. Underline five things that a good explanation uses.

Got it?

5. **Apply** Name a process skill. How can it help scientists learn about hurricanes?

....

....

6. **Predict** What might happen if a person building a house estimated but did not measure the length of a piece of wood?

....

....

....

⬜ **Stop!** I need help with ....

⏸ **Wait!** I have a question about ....

▶ **Go!** Now I know ....

How do scientists answer questions?

Envision It!

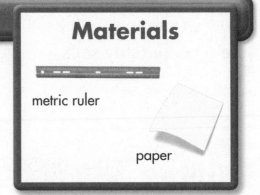

Tell how you think this model can help scientists answer questions.

Inquiry **Explore It!**

How can a model help answer questions?

☐ **1.** Spread out your fingers and put your hand flat on a piece of paper. **Measure** the length of the longest finger. Measure its height. **Record.**

☐ **2. Make a model** by tracing your hand. Measure the length of the longest finger on your model. Measure its height. Record.

Explain Your Results

3. Scientists use models to help them answer questions, but models have limitations. Does your **model** account for all your **observations** of your real finger? Explain.

....

....

....

....

Materials

metric ruler

paper

Measurements

	Length (mm)	Height (mm)
Finger		
Model of a finger		

myscienceonline.com | **Explore It!** Animation

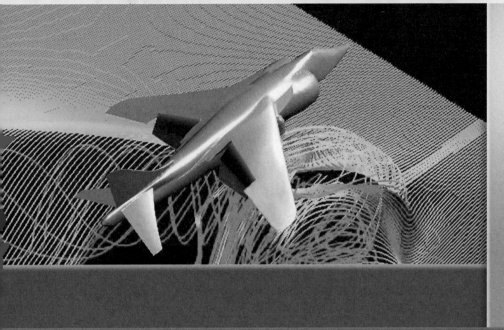

I will know how scientists use experiments and other types of investigations to answer questions.

Word to Know

model

Kinds of Investigations

Scientists are like detectives. They investigate, or look for answers, using organized steps. Different questions require different kinds of investigations. Some investigations involve observing and describing things or events. Other investigations may involve collecting samples or building models. An investigation can be any organized way of looking for answers.

An experiment is an investigation carried out under carefully controlled conditions. A scientist might do an experiment to find out if a new medicine works better than an old medicine.

1. ◉ **Text Features** What does the heading tell about this page?

....

....

....

2. **Analyze** These students are observing and describing flowers. Write what question you think they are investigating.

....

....

....

....

Scientific Methods

Suppose you want to classify animals by how they keep warm. You might do an experiment to test fur's ability to keep heat in water. When scientists do an experiment, they use scientific methods. Scientific methods include the steps shown below.

3. Hypothesize Write another hypothesis for the question.

....

....

....

....

....

....

4. [CHALLENGE] How do you know your answer to question 3 is a good hypothesis?

....

....

Ask a question.

You might have a question about something you observe.

What material is best for keeping heat in water?

State your hypothesis.

A hypothesis is a possible answer to your question. Hypotheses can be tested.

If I wrap the jar in fake fur, then the water will stay warm the longest because fake fur will keep heat in.

Identify and control variables.

Variables are things in an experiment that can change. For a fair test, you choose just one variable to change. Keep all other variables the same.

Test other materials. Put the same amount of warm water in other jars that are the same size and shape.

Test your hypothesis.

Make a plan to test your hypothesis. Include multiple trials by doing your test many times. That way, if one measurement is off, the data you collect will still be useful. Gather materials and tools. Then follow your plan.

Collect and record your data.

Keep records of what you do and find. Records can be notes, pictures, charts, or graphs.

Interpret your data.

Organize your notes and records.

State your conclusion.

Your conclusion is a decision you make based on your data. Communicate what you found. Tell whether or not your data supported your hypothesis.

Fake fur kept the water warm longest because fake fur kept the heat in. My data supported my hypothesis.

Go further.

Use what you learn from your experiment to do more experiments. Think of new questions to test.

5. 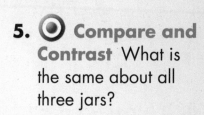 **Compare and Contrast** What is the same about all three jars?

....

....

What is different?

....

....

6. **Identify** (Circle) the tool that is used in this experiment.

7. **Apply** Use the results of this experiment to ask another question that could be tested.

....

....

....

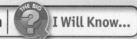

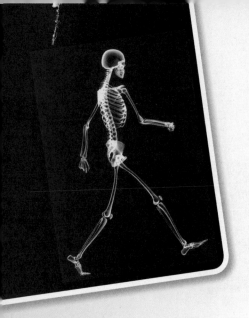

This computer model shows how the skeleton moves as the human body walks.

Models

Another way scientists investigate is with models. A **model** is a copy of something. Models help scientists understand how things work. Models also help scientists study things that are very small, large, or difficult to understand.

Some models are built out of materials such as paper and plastic. Other models are made using a program on a computer. For example, scientists have used computers to build models of the human body. These computer models help scientists better understand how different parts of the body, such as the heart and the skeletal system, work. The models can also be used to train doctors.

Models are useful, but they are not the same as the real thing. For example, a computer model might show how a person's body fits together. But it might not show how well the body will function.

8. **Infer** How do you think this model of the human body can help scientists?

....

....

....

9. **Explain** How can this model help you understand the real solar system?

....

....

....

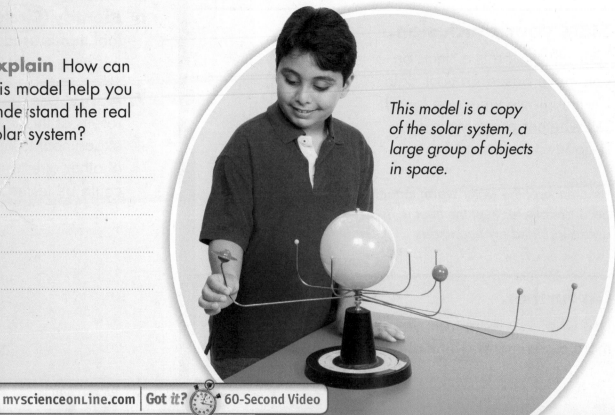

This model is a copy of the solar system, a large group of objects in space.

mYscienceonLine.com | Got it? ⏱ 60-Second Video

Surveys

Scientists also use surveys to investigate. A survey is a list of questions or choices. Scientists can give the list to many people and learn from their answers. For example, scientists give surveys to patients to learn about their symptoms. Then scientists can interpret the data and draw inferences. The surveys and data can help scientists make new medicines.

10. **Infer** How are surveys a type of investigation?

Go Green

Recycling Survey
Write a survey to find out what materials people recycle in their homes. Ask about materials such as paper, plastic, glass, and metal cans. Ask your survey questions to ten people. Record the results. Do you see a pattern in the data?

Got it?

11. **Summarize** Name three ways scientists investigate.

12. **Investigate** Grass does not grow well under a tree. Write a hypothesis that explains why this might be true. How can you test your hypothesis?

Stop! I need help with

Wait! I have a question about

Go! Now I know

Lesson 4

How do scientists communicate?

Tell how keeping records can help these scientists share information.

Inquiry **Explore It!**

How can scientists communicate what they learn?

☑ **1.** Conduct a survey. Think of a question you want to ask, such as "What is your favorite color?"

☑ **2.** Write your question in the chart.

☑ **3.** **Record** your data. Use tally marks.

☑ **4.** **Communicate** Make a bar graph using your data. Share this with your class.

Explain Your Results

5. How did your bar graph help you **communicate** what you learned?

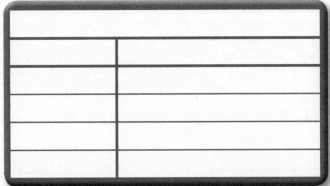

Bar Graph

UNLOCK
THE BIG
?

I will know how to
describe a procedure
and record data. I will
know how scientists
communicate.

Words to Know

procedure   bar graph
chart

Communication

Communication is an important part of science investigations. Scientists communicate with each other to share what they learn. They also question and check each other's work. When scientists share information in this way, their explanations are more thorough and better informed.

One way scientists check each other's work is to replicate, or repeat, an experiment. A good experiment can be repeated. For this reason, scientists must keep careful records of their experiments. Other scientists can repeat the same procedure if they know exactly how it was done.

1. **Infer** The scientists in the picture are investigating algae, a group of living things usually found in water. What kind of records do you think the scientists are keeping?

....

....

....

....

2. Identify Look at the procedure. (Circle) the units that were used to make measurements.

3. Analyze The person who wrote this procedure knew that warm water loses heat over time. What was the person trying to find out?

....

....

....

4. Describe What words could be added to help describe the procedure?

....

....

....

....

Plan an Experiment

When you plan an experiment, you write a procedure. A **procedure** is a plan for testing a hypothesis. It describes the materials you will use and the steps you will follow. Write the procedure clearly so someone else can follow your steps and get the same results. Tell what units you will use in your measurements.

As you plan an experiment, think carefully about the question you are trying to answer. Figure out what you know and what you want to find out.

A procedure describes exactly how an experiment is done.

Question: What material is best for keeping heat in water?

Hypothesis: If I wrap a jar in fake fur, then it will keep the water warm the longest.

Materials: 1 jar covered in fake fur, 1 jar covered in brown paper, 1 jar covered in blue paper, warm water, 3 thermometers, plastic wrap, 3 rubber bands, clock

Procedure:
1. Label the jars A, B, and C.
2. Add a thermometer to each jar.
3. Fill each jar with the same amount of warm water.
4. Quickly cover the jars with plastic wrap and rubber bands.
5. Measure the starting temperature in degrees Celsius.
6. Measure and record how many minutes it takes for the temperature to change in each jar.
7. Empty the jars. Repeat steps 2 through 6.

Keep Records

When scientists investigate, they do the same experiment several times. Each time is called a trial. Scientists keep careful records of their results for each trial.

You can keep records in many ways. You can use numbers or words. Sometimes an easy way to record what happens is to draw a picture or a map. A chart is a way to organize what you record. A **chart** is a kind of list. You can also use a graph to organize data. A **bar graph** is a graph that helps you compare data and see patterns.

5. **Explain** Why are there two rows for each type of material in the chart below?

....

....

....

....

6. **Express Data** Use your science notebook to draw pictures and write about the experiment.

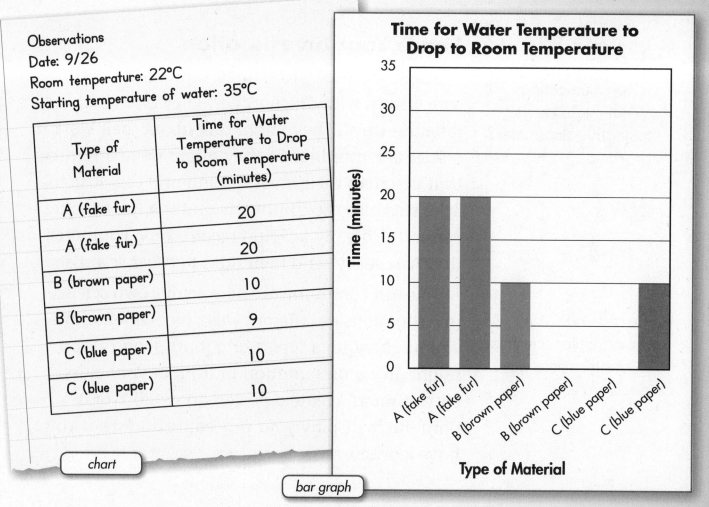

Observations
Date: 9/26
Room temperature: 22°C
Starting temperature of water: 35°C

Type of Material	Time for Water Temperature to Drop to Room Temperature (minutes)
A (fake fur)	20
A (fake fur)	20
B (brown paper)	10
B (brown paper)	9
C (blue paper)	10
C (blue paper)	10

chart

Time for Water Temperature to Drop to Room Temperature

bar graph

7. **Communicate Data** Complete the missing bars in the bar graph above.

8. Interpret The boy in the picture is communicating. What might he be telling his classmates?

....

....

....

....

9. Recall Why is it important for scientists to communicate with each other?

....

....

....

....

Share Your Investigation

Scientists share procedures, data, and conclusions with one another. They do this in different ways. They might talk about their work at a scientific meeting. Or they might write an article that describes their investigation and conclusions. Scientists also use computers and the Internet to communicate. By keeping records on a computer, they can easily send their data to other scientists.

You can communicate about your own science investigations in different ways too. For example, you might write a report or a journal entry. You might give a presentation in front of your class. Or you might create a poster, an exhibit, or a portfolio to display your procedure and what you have learned.

myscienceonLine.com | Got it? 60-Second Video

Repeat an Investigation

Scientists check each other's work. One scientist will repeat another scientist's experiment so they can compare evidence and explanations. An explanation is only considered true if another person can follow the procedure and get similar results.

If two scientists follow the same procedure and get different results, they can discuss why. They can use this information to make the procedure better for the next scientist.

10. Analyze Why would scientists want other scientists to repeat their experiment?

....

....

Lightning Lab

Construct a Chart
Go outside. Look at plants you see. Classify the plants in two ways. Make a chart to record your data. Discuss your chart with a partner.

Got it?

11. Summarize Name four ways scientists keep records.

....

12. Describe What information should a procedure include?

....

....

....

⬛ **Stop!** I need help with ....

⏸ **Wait!** I have a question about ....

▶ **Go!** Now I know ....

How do scientists use tools and stay safe?

Envision It!

Tell how you think microscopes help you view small objects, such as insects.

Inquiry **Explore It!**

How can a tool help scientists observe?

☑ **1.** Find how much water is in a cup.
First, **measure** 50 mL of water from the cup into a graduated cylinder.
Record the measurement.

Then, empty the graduated cylinder into the second cup.
Repeat until you have measured all the water from the first cup.

☑ **2.** Calculate the total amount that was in the first cup at the start.

Materials

funnel

graduated cylinder

plastic cup

plastic cup with water

Volume in Cup (mL)	
Measurement	**Volume (mL)**
1st	
2nd	
3rd	
Total	

Explain Your Results

3. Compare your total with the amount other groups **measured.** Are the totals the same? Discuss.

4. How did the graduated cylinder help you make your comparisons?

....

....

myscienceonline.com | **Explore It!** Animation

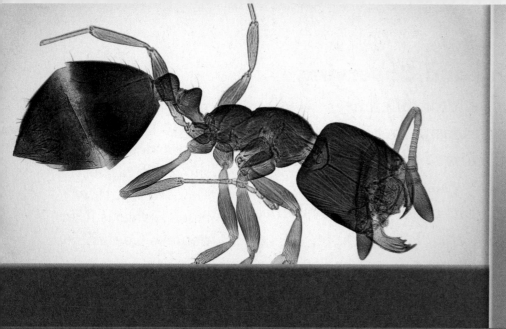

Words to Know

tool
unit of measure

Science Tools

Scientists use many different kinds of tools. A **tool** is an object used to do work. You can use tools to observe. Tools can help you measure volume, temperature, length, distance, and mass. Tools can help you collect and record data. Data are facts and information that you observe. You can record data on a computer. Computers can also help you share observations with others and find new information. Taking pictures with a camera is another way of using a tool to record data.

Some tools you use to observe make objects appear larger. Binoculars are a tool that helps you see things that are far away. For example, binoculars help you see birds nesting in trees.

1. **Underline** four things you can do with tools.

2. **Apply** How might you use binoculars like these?

Tools for Measuring and Observing

Scientists use different tools for different kinds of observations and measurements. Most measurement tools have units of measure. A **unit of measure** is the quantity you use to measure something. Scientists use units of the metric system when they make measurements. For example, meters and centimeters are metric units used to measure length. You might be familiar with units of the United States system. In that system, feet and inches are used to measure length.

3. Compare
(Circle) the thermometer that shows the higher temperature. How much higher is it, in degrees Celsius?

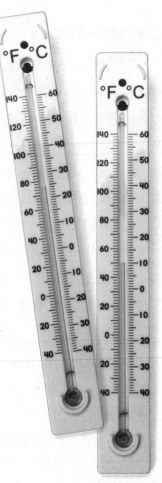

Thermometers measure temperature. Thermometers are marked in degrees Celsius (°C) and degrees Fahrenheit (°F). Scientists usually record data in degrees Celsius.

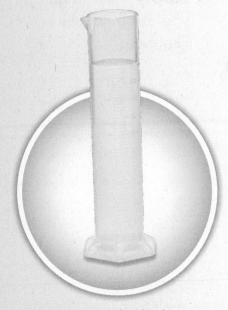

A graduated cylinder can be used to measure volume, or the amount of space an object takes up. Volume is measured in milliliters (mL).

Clocks and stopwatches are used to measure time.

Scientists use rulers and metersticks to measure length and distance in meters (m) and centimeters (cm).

4. Compare Look at the balance. How do the masses compare?

A balance like the one above can be used to measure an object's mass in grams.

5. Apply Which tool would you use to study the parts of an ant?

6. Apply Use a hand lens. Observe a tool on one of these two pages. What did you observe?

Microscopes use several lenses to make objects appear larger. Microscopes let you see more detail.

A hand lens enlarges objects too. It does not enlarge objects as much as a microscope does. It is easier to carry, though.

Safety

You need to be careful when using tools or doing other scientific activities. Some tools, such as safety goggles, help protect you. Below is a list of safety rules to remember.

- Listen to your teacher's instructions.

- Read each activity carefully.

- Never taste or smell materials unless your teacher tells you to.

- Wear safety goggles, wear gloves, and tie hair back when needed.

- Handle scissors and other equipment carefully.

- Keep your workplace neat and clean.

- Clean up spills immediately.

- Tell your teacher immediately about accidents or if you see something that looks unsafe.

- Wash your hands well after every activity.

- Return all materials to their proper places.

7. Explain Why is it important to wash your hands?

....

....

....

8. Elaborate Write a new safety tip to add to the list.

....

....

....

....

....

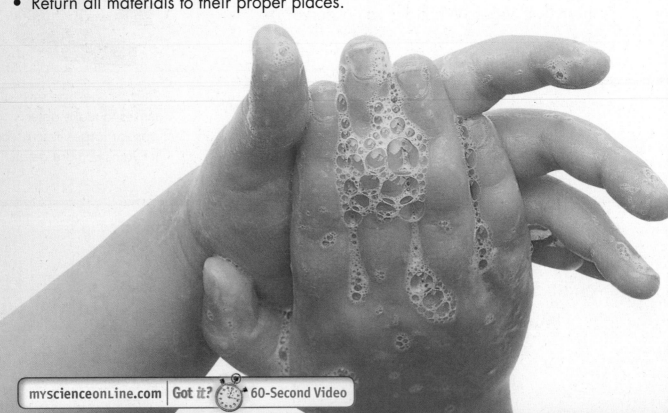

mySCienceonline.com | Got it? | 60-Second Video

Investigating Safely

When scientists explore underwater, they need certain tools to stay safe. The scuba divers need tanks filled with oxygen to breathe and wet suits to protect their skin.

9. Suggest What equipment do you use to stay safe when you play outside?

....

....

....

Got it?

10. Infer Why do you think it is important to tell your teacher about accidents immediately?

....

....

11. Explain Choose one tool from this lesson and explain why it is important to scientists.

....

....

⬛ **Stop!** I need help with ....

⏸ **Wait!** I have a question about ....

▶ **Go!** Now I know ....

How does a microscope help you make observations?

Follow a Procedure

☐ **1. Observe** a piece of yarn and a photo from a color newspaper.
Record your observations.

☐ **2.** Observe the yarn and the photo with a hand lens. Record your observations.

Materials

hand lens

microscope

yarn

color newspaper

Inquiry Skill Scientists use tools to make **observations.**

Be careful! **Handle microscopes with care.**

Observations			
Item	**No Tool**	**Hand Lens**	**Microscope**
Yarn			
Photo			

3. Observe using a microscope. First, place the yarn on the stage of the microscope. Then, look through the eyepiece. Record your observations.

4. Repeat Step 3 with the photo.

Analyze and Conclude

5. Communicate   How were your **observations** different when you used different tools?

....

....

6. Draw a Conclusion   How does a microscope help you make observations?

....

....

7. Infer   When might a hand lens be more useful than a microscope?

....

....

....

8. UNLOCK THE BIG ? **Investigate**   List two other objects a scientist might observe with a microscope.

....

....

Observe
Insect
Behavior

You can practice observing by watching insects. Go outside with an adult and look at insects on tree trunks, on leaves, under rocks, or in cracks along sidewalks. Do not touch any insect. Bring a notebook to draw an insect. Observe it for several minutes. To keep records, write down observations about how it acts. Compare observations with the adult who is with you.

Illustrate Draw the insect.

Observe Record what you observe about how the insect acts.

Infer Use the evidence you observed to make an inference. What do you think the insect was doing?

Vocabulary Smart Cards

scientist
investigate
inquiry
infer
model
procedure
chart
bar graph
tool
unit of measure

Play a Game!

Cut out the Vocabulary Smart Cards.

Cover the words on the front of each card with sticky notes.

Use the list of words above to guess which word goes with each picture. Write the word on the sticky note.

Then remove the sticky note to see if you were correct.

infer

inferir

scientist

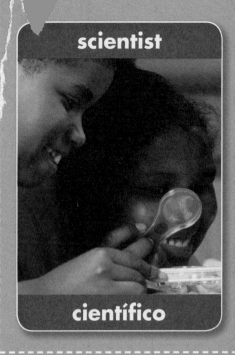

científico

model

modelo

investigate

investigar

procedure

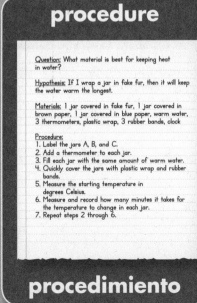

Question: What material is best for keeping heat in water?

Hypothesis: If I wrap a jar in fake fur, then it will keep the water warm the longest.

Materials: 1 jar covered in fake fur, 1 jar covered in brown paper, 1 jar covered in blue paper, warm water, 3 thermometers, plastic wrap, 3 rubber bands, clock

Procedure:
1. Label the jars A, B, and C.
2. Add a thermometer to each jar.
3. Fill each jar with the same amount of warm water.
4. Quickly cover the jars with plastic wrap and rubber bands.
5. Measure the starting temperature in degrees Celsius.
6. Measure and record how many minutes it takes for the temperature to change in each jar.
7. Repeat steps 2 through 6.

procedimiento

inquiry

indagación

person who asks questions about the natural world

Write a sentence using this word.

....

....

....

persona cuyo trabajo implica hacer preguntas sobre el mundo y la naturaleza

---

to draw a conclusion

Write the noun form of this word.

....

....

....

....

sacar una conclusión

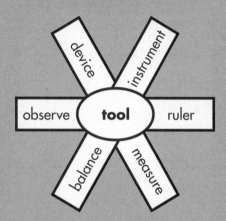

Make a Word Wheel!

Choose a vocabulary word and write it in the center of the Word Wheel graphic organizer. Write synonyms or related words on the wheel spokes.

---

to look for answers

Write the noun form of this word.

....

....

....

....

....

buscar respuestas

---

a copy of something

Draw an example.

copia de algo

---

the process of asking questions

Write a sentence using the verb form of this word.

....

....

....

proceso de hacer preguntas

---

a plan for testing a hypothesis

Use a dictionary. Write the verb form of the word.

....

....

....

plan que se usa para poner a prueba una hipótesis

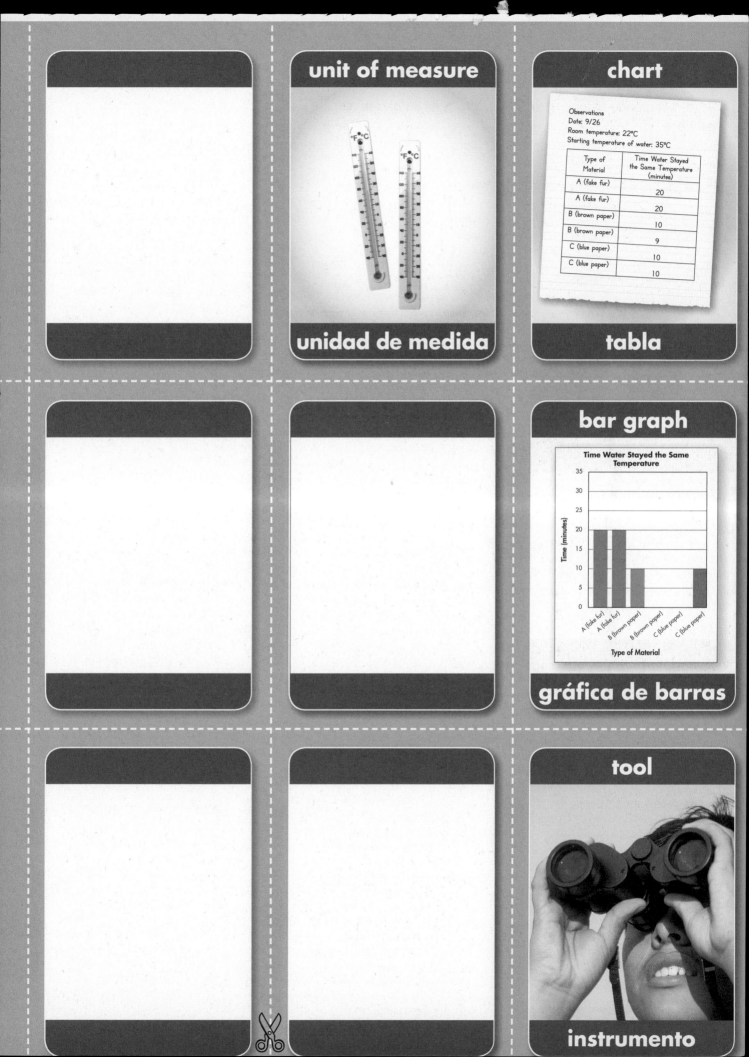

unit of measure

unidad de medida

chart

Observations
Date: 9/26
Room temperature: 22°C
Starting temperature of water: 35°C

Type of Material	Time Water Stayed the Same Temperature (minutes)
A (fake fur)	
A (fake fur)	20
B (brown paper)	20
B (brown paper)	10
C (blue paper)	9
C (blue paper)	10
	10

tabla

bar graph

Time Water Stayed the Same Temperature

Time (minutes)

35
30
25
20
15
10
5
0

A (fake fur)
A (fake fur)
B (brown paper)
B (brown paper)
C (blue paper)
C (blue paper)

Type of Material

gráfica de barras

tool

instrumento

a kind of list

Write a sentence using this word.

....

....

....

....

tipo de lista

quantity you use to measure

Write three examples.

....

....

....

....

cantidad que se usa para medir

a graph that helps you compare data and see patterns

Draw an example.

gráfica que ayuda a comparar datos y ver patrones

object used to do work

Write three examples.

....

....

....

....

objeto que se usa para trabajar

Lesson 1

What questions do scientists ask?

- Scientists ask questions about the natural world.
- Scientists ask questions that can be answered through investigations.

Lesson 2

What skills do scientists use?

- Scientists observe by using their five senses.
- Scientists infer and predict based on observations.
- Scientists use their results to form explanations.

Lesson 3

How do scientists answer questions?

- Scientists answer questions using experiments and other kinds of investigations.
- Scientific methods are organized steps for investigations.

Lesson 4

How do scientists communicate?

- Scientists communicate to share what they learn.
- When scientists investigate, they write a procedure.
- Good records include words, charts, and graphs.

Lesson 5

How do scientists use tools and stay safe?

- Scientists use tools to observe, to measure, and to collect and record data.
- Safety is important when doing science.

Chapter Review

REVIEW THE BIG ?

What is science?

Lesson 1

What questions do scientists ask?

1. **Vocabulary** Someone who asks questions about the natural world is a(n) _____.
   A. engineer
   B. model
   C. scientist
   D. teacher

2. **Apply** What is a question that cannot be answered through an investigation?

Lesson 2

What skills do scientists use?

3. **Observe** What five senses do scientists use when they make observations?

4. **Name** List three things a good investigation needs.

Lesson 3

How do scientists answer questions?

5. **Write About It** Suggest two ways a model could help you better understand the solar system.

6. **List** What are three steps that a good experiment should include?

7. **Conclude** You measure your heart rate at 70 beats per minute after resting and 100 beats per minute after exercising. Over several days you take more measurements and get similar results. What can you conclude?

Lesson 4

How do scientists communicate?

8. **Text Features** How do graphs help you communicate the results of an experiment?

....

....

....

....

....

....

Lesson 5

How do scientists use tools and stay safe?

9. **Determine** Name this tool. Tell how you could use it.

....

....

....

10. **APPLY THE BIG ?** **What is science?**

....

Think about scientists. How do they work? Use the vocabulary words *tool*, *investigate*, and *model* in your explanation.

....

....

....

....

....

....

....

....

....

....

....

....

....

....

....

Chapter 1
Benchmark Practice

Science,
Engineering,
and
Technology

Fill in the bubble next to the answer choice you think is correct for each multiple-choice question.

1 Which could you measure with the tool shown in this picture?

- Ⓐ the mass of a rock
- Ⓑ the length of a pencil
- Ⓒ the temperature of the air
- Ⓓ the volume of a liquid

2 A scientist is collecting data on the number of times a cricket chirps per minute. What sense is the scientist most likely using to make observations?

- Ⓐ hearing
- Ⓑ smell
- Ⓒ sight
- Ⓓ touch

3 Which helps scientists understand very large objects?

- Ⓐ a survey
- Ⓑ a hypothesis
- Ⓒ a procedure
- Ⓓ a model

4 Which question can best be investigated by a scientist?

- Ⓐ Should I buy a red shirt or a green shirt?
- Ⓑ Does chocolate milk or plain milk taste better?
- Ⓒ Does a plant need sunlight to grow?
- Ⓓ Which feels softer, cat fur or dog fur?

5 It is important for scientists to keep accurate records during an investigation. Describe three ways scientists can communicate their findings.

....

....

....

....

....

Cary Fowler

Cary Fowler helped run the Global Seed Vault project.

Cary Fowler was born in Tennessee and spent his summers on a farm. Later he became a plant scientist. Fowler became worried about the plants we use as crops. Through history, people have used more than 10,000 different types of plants for food. Now there are only 150 types left. Fowler asked, "What if we lose even more?" Diseases, natural disasters, and war can all wipe out plants.

Fowler moved to Italy to help run a project called the Global Seed Vault. The Global Seed Vault is a tool used by plant scientists. It is a giant freezer buried in the ground near the North Pole in Norway. The vault is used to save different types of plant seeds from all over the world. The vault is big enough to hold more than 2 billion seeds.

The goal of the vault is to save seeds for thousands of years. Then, even if we lose a type of plant, we can use the seeds to plant more!

REVIEW THE BIG ? What did Cary Fowler infer about the crops we have left?

_____

_____

Where can this tiny robot fly?

Technology and the Design Process

Try It! How can you design a parachute?

Lesson 1 What is technology?

Lesson 2 What is a machine?

Lesson 3 What is the design process?

Investigate It! What makes a bridge strong?

This is an image of a piece of technology that is still being developed. Some scientists think that in the future, the robotic fly will be able to locate people who are trapped in a collapsed building. It can fit in tiny places where a person may not fit.

Predict Why do you think the robot was designed to look like a fly?

....

....

How can technology affect our lives?

How can you design a parachute?

☑ **1. Design** a parachute that will slow the fall of a metal washer dropped from a height of 2 meters.

☑ **2. Communicate** Draw and label your design.

☑ **3.** Build your parachute. Ask your teacher to test it 3 times. **Record.** Compare your results with others.

☑ **4.** Evaluate your design. Improve it. Repeat Step 3.

Materials

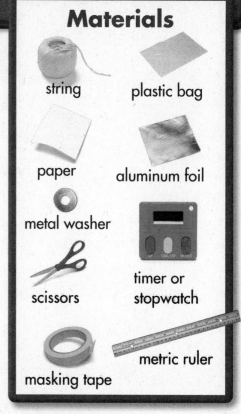

string

plastic bag

paper

aluminum foil

metal washer

timer or stopwatch

scissors

metric ruler

masking tape

> **Inquiry Skill**
> You **infer** when you use your information to draw a conclusion.

Parachute Trials Results			
Parachute	**Trial 1** (s)	**Trial 2** (s)	**Trial 3** (s)
1			
2			

Explain Your Results

5. **UNLOCK THE BIG ?** **Communicate** Which parachute dropped most slowly?

6. Infer Why did this parachute work better than the others?

Main Idea and Details

- The **main idea** is the most important idea in a reading selection.
- Supporting **details** tell more about the main idea.

Technology and Energy

Technology has changed the way we get energy. A water-powered mill uses technology to get energy from the flowing water of a river. A solar panel can be placed on the roof of a house. It gathers energy from the sun. Energy from the wind can be captured by wind turbines. This energy helps to produce electricity. Technology allows us to recycle energy, which helps protect the environment.

Practice it!

Complete the graphic organizer below. Use it to help you list the main idea and details from the paragraph you read above.

wind turbine

Main Idea

Detail   **Detail**   **Detail**

What is technology?

What do you think the technology in the picture is?
How do you think it works?

my planeT DiaRY

DISCOVERY

Sometimes technology becomes useful in unplanned ways. In 1946, Percy Spencer was working to improve radar. He was performing tests using microwave energy.

One day Spencer stood near the microwave energy. He noticed that a candy bar in his pocket melted. Curious, he put popcorn kernels near the microwave energy. They rapidly popped into fluffy pieces.

Spencer found that the microwave energy could quickly cook foods. He made a drawing that led to the first microwave oven.

Why was it important for Percy Spencer to keep asking questions after his candy bar melted?

....
....
....

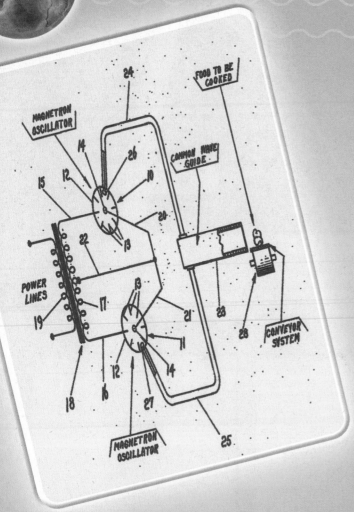

Percy Spencer's sketch helped him build the first microwave oven.

I will know how technology solves problems and provides solutions.

Word to Know

technology

Problems and Solutions

Science helps people understand the way the world works. Technology helps people solve problems and improve their lives. **Technology** is the use of science knowledge to invent tools and new ways of doing things.

Discoveries in science are helping people solve some big problems. For example, people use energy for many things. They use energy to cook food and heat their homes. But we may be running out of some energy sources. The discovery of how to use solar energy may help solve this problem. Solar energy is energy that comes directly from the sun. Solar panels gather the sun's energy. Next, they change this energy into electricity.

Solar panels provide a new way of getting energy.

1. **Underline** the definition of technology.

2. [CHALLENGE] Solar panels work well in some places but not others. Explain why this is true.

Signals from satellites can track the exact location of a car.

Scientific Discoveries and Technology

Scientific discoveries usually are made by scientists. Engineers use this knowledge to develop technologies that change and improve the way people live. Here are some examples.

Transportation

People on ships once had to figure out where they were by looking at stars. Now sailors can use Global Positioning System (GPS) technology. This technology relies on space satellites that send signals to Earth. Each ship's GPS computer uses the signals to figure out the ship's location.

3. ◉ **Main Idea and Details** What is the main idea of the paragraph above?

....

....

Medicine

X rays were discovered more than 100 years ago. For the first time, doctors could look inside the body without touching it. Today, doctors also use digital technology to look inside people's bodies.

Scientists discovered that viruses and bacteria cause disease. This led to the development of vaccines. Vaccines are medicines that protect you from disease. Vaccines are a type of technology.

4. **Interpret** This child is receiving a vaccine, a type of technology. What is another technology that you see in this photograph?

....

myscienceonline.com | Got it? ⏱ 60-Second Video

Computer Technology

A computer stores information. Computers also process and send information with great speed. Computer technology is everywhere. A digital watch tells time with a computer chip. Calculators, cameras, appliances, and cars all use these chips.

Computer chips are being made smaller and smaller. Music players, game players, and phones can process as much information as whole desktop computers once could.

5. **Predict** How would your life be different if computer technology did not exist?

Computer chips can send and receive huge numbers of electronic data signals very quickly.

Got it?

6. **Give Examples** Name two technologies. Tell how they have changed people's lives.

7. ◉ **Draw Conclusions** How can one technology lead to the development of other technologies?

■ **Stop!** I need help with

❚❚ **Wait!** I have a question about

▶ **Go!** Now I know

Lesson 2

What is a machine?

 Envision It!

Tell how the pole helps this vaulter jump higher.

Inquiry ▶ **Explore It!**

How can a simple machine solve a problem?

Pat and Chris want to know whose clay ball is heavier. All they have is a ruler and a pencil.

☐ **1. Design** a way to solve this problem. Use a simple machine.

☐ **2. Communicate** Draw your solution.

☐ **3.** Test your design. Which clay ball is heavier?

Materials

2 clay balls of different weights   unsharpened pencil

ruler

(handwritten) measher the widthe holdit

Explain Your Results

4. Name the simple machine you used.

5. Draw a Conclusion What is another way you could use your simple machine?

I will know some simple machines and how they help people do work.

Words to Know

work   inclined
wheel and   plane
  axle   pulley
wedge   screw
lever

Work

Is kicking a soccer ball work? To a scientist it is. In science, **work** means the use of a force to move an object across a distance. You do work when you rake leaves, pedal a bike, or kick a soccer ball.

It may be hard to solve a math problem. But it is not work. You may push hard to move a large rock. But it is not work if the rock does not move. You only do work when you move an object. The amount of work you do depends on how much force you use and how far you move the object.

1. ⊙ **Main Idea and Details** Complete the graphic organizer below. Write details about work.

Main Idea

Work is the use of a force to move an object across a distance.

You do work when you move an object.

Detail   **Detail**   **Detail**

A **wheel and axle** is a round object attached to a post called an axle. Turning the wheel causes the axle to turn. The axle turns a small distance as the wheel turns a greater distance.

Simple Machines

Do you recognize any of the objects in the pictures? They are all simple machines. Simple machines have just one or two parts. These machines do not lessen the amount of work you do, but they help make work easier. Six kinds of simple machines help you do work. They are the wheel and axle, wedge, lever, inclined plane, pulley, and screw.

A **wedge** is a simple machine made from two slanted sides that end in a sharp edge. As a wedge is pushed through material such as wood or food, it cuts or splits the material.

2. Identify You want to cut a piece of cake or pie. What is the common name for the kitchen wedge you use?

A **lever** is a stiff bar that rests on a support. A lever is used to lift and move things. When you push down on one end, the other end lifts up.

56

3. Apply Look at this shape ▼. Draw an ✗ on the simple machine that has this shape. How does the shape help this machine work?

....

....

4. Identify Which simple machine would you use for each task below?

A. Raise a flag on a pole. ....

B. Pry open a can of paint. ....

C. Cut an apple. ....

A **screw** is an inclined plane wrapped around a center post. Screws can be used to hold things together and to raise and lower things.

5. Apply Tell how a jar lid is a screw.

....

....

A **pulley** can make work easier in two ways. It can decrease the amount of force needed to move an object. It can also change the direction that the force is applied.

An **inclined plane**, or a ramp, is a slanted surface. It connects a lower level to a higher level. Less force is needed to move an object over a longer distance.

Complex Machines

Simple machines are often put together to do bigger jobs. These complex machines are made up of simple machines that work together.

The can opener below is a complex machine. Find the simple machines that it is made of. These simple machines work together to grip, turn, and slice through a can lid.

The bicycle is a complex machine too. What simple machines make it up? How does each simple machine help make the bicycle work?

6. **Exemplify** List three complex machines that you used yesterday.

....

....

....

....

The sharp edge that cuts the top of the can is a wedge.

The winding handle is an axle that turns the gears.

The handles are made of levers.

myscienceonline.com | Got it? 60-Second Video

7. Illustrate Draw a line from each simple machine to its correct part on the bicycle.

A. lever

B. pulley

C. wheel and axle

Got it?

8. Synthesize How do you know when a simple machine has done work?

....

....

9. Summarize Write a sentence that summarizes how simple machines are useful. Give examples.

....

....

⬛ **Stop!** I need help with ....

⏸ **Wait!** I have a question about ....

▶ **Go!** Now I know ....

Lesson 3

What is the design process?

Tell how these two computers are different.

Explore It!

Which design transfers sound the best?

☐ **1.** Use 2 of the cups and 3 meters of string. Thread the string through the hole in the bottom of the cup. Make a big knot.

☐ **2.** Test your model by talking into the cup. Have your partner listen. The string must be tight. **Record** how well you hear the sound.

....

☐ **3.** Change at least one of the cups in your model. Repeat Step 2.

....

Materials

2 paper, 2 plastic, and 2 foam cups (each with a hole)

string

Explain Your Results

4. Infer Think about your redesign and that of others. Which material works best for transferring sound?

....

mYscienceonLine.com | **Explore It!** Animation

UNLOCK
THE BIG
?

I will know how to conduct an investigation using the design process.

Words to Know

design   prototype
  process
research

Design Process

When people design something new, they follow the steps of the design process. The **design process** is a step-by-step method used to solve a problem.

People use the design process to find a solution. A solution is an answer to a problem. The design process allows engineers to produce and test possible solutions. An engineer is any person who designs new technologies.

1. **Identify** Why is it important for engineers to follow the steps of the design process?

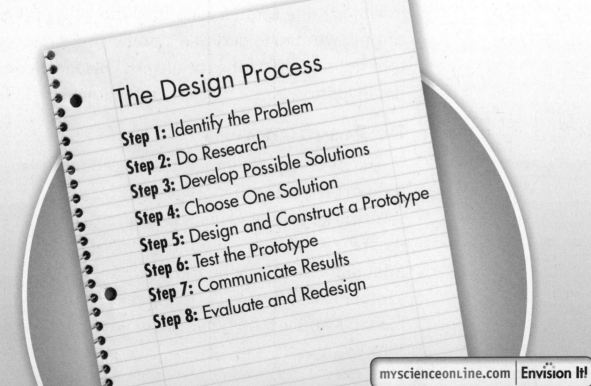

The Design Process

Step 1: Identify the Problem

Step 2: Do Research

Step 3: Develop Possible Solutions

Step 4: Choose One Solution

Step 5: Design and Construct a Prototype

Step 6: Test the Prototype

Step 7: Communicate Results

Step 8: Evaluate and Redesign

People may read books to research.

2. **Describe** How do you think Kramer researched the problem?

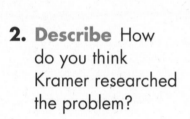

Identify the Problem

Engineers identify the problem during the first step of the design process. Before producing a design, engineers consider if there is a need for it. In 1979, there were only large music players that needed tapes or records to play music. British inventor Kane Kramer identified this as a problem. Kramer wanted to design a smaller music player that did not need tapes or records. His idea led to the invention of the digital audio player.

Do Research

The next step is to research the problem. **Research** means to look for facts about something. People can research problems in different ways. Some engineers research by talking to other people and reading articles. Kramer researched ways to make a digital audio player. Kramer took notes about what he learned.

 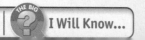

Develop Possible Solutions

After doing research, engineers think of possible solutions. They consider what designs would best meet the needs of the problem. Kramer considered different materials that were available. He knew he needed to use materials that would produce a player people would use. It had to be small enough to fit in a pocket. He made different sketches of how the player could look.

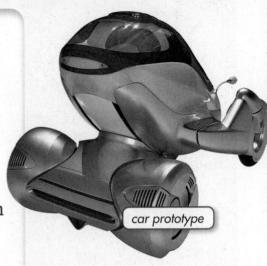

car prototype

Choose One Solution

People consider many things in order to choose the best solution. They think about how they will build the solution. They also think about what kinds of materials will work. Kramer chose the best solution. His player would be made of strong materials and be small in size.

4. Determine How can this car prototype help engineers?

Design and Construct a Prototype

After sketching the digital audio player, Kramer constructed, or built, a prototype. A **prototype** is the first working product that uses a design. Kramer made the player small and easy to use.

Someone may test an inner part of a computer to see how well it works.

Test the Prototype

Engineers test a prototype to determine if it meets their expectations. They perform multiple tests to get accurate results. Kramer tested the prototype to see how well it worked.

3. Suggest What do you think Kramer learned from his test?

This is what the inside of a digital audio player looks like. Showing it to others can help them understand the design.

Communicate Results

Engineers communicate results about their tests to people working with them. Engineers may share how they designed and built the prototype. They also explain how the experiment was carried out. After testing it, Kramer sent a report of his invention to a group of people. He hoped the people would invest money in his invention. The report described the way his invention worked. It also explained how the player could change the way people listened to music.

5. **Predict** What would happen if engineers did not communicate their evidence with others?

Do the **math!**

Read a Circle Graph

Mark's digital audio player can hold 1,000 songs. Look at the circle graph below. It tells you what types of music are on Mark's player and how many songs are in each type.

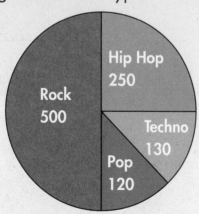

1 What type of music does Mark have the most of?

2 How many techno and hip hop songs does Mark have?

3 **Solve** How many more hip hop songs are there than pop songs?

myscienceonline.com | Got it? | 60-Second Video

Evaluate and Redesign

The final step is to evaluate and redesign the prototype. Evaluate means to find out how well something works. People try to make a prototype better by redesigning it. When people heard about Kramer's idea of the digital audio player, they designed their own version. The first digital audio player became available to the public in 1997. It could play about one hour of music. Newer digital audio players can hold enough music to play for more than 100 days!

6. **Contrast** Look at the images to the right. How has the design process changed digital audio players?

....

....

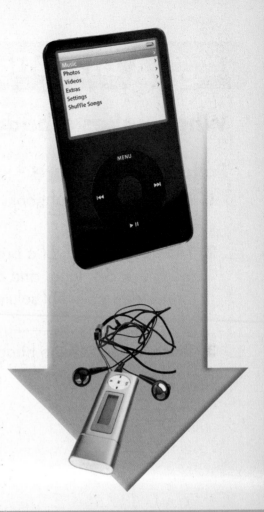

Got it?

7. **Infer** How can the design process help someone invent something?

....

....

8. **Clarify** Why is it important to test a design multiple times?

....

....

■ **Stop!** I need help with ....

❚❚ **Wait!** I have a question about ....

▶ **Go!** Now I know ....

What makes a bridge strong?

Follow a Procedure

☐ **1.** Place two stacks of books 25 centimeters apart.

☐ **2. Make a model** of a bridge between the books.
Use stir sticks, tape, and a note card.
Brainstorm potential solutions.

☐ **3.** Place the cup on the bridge.

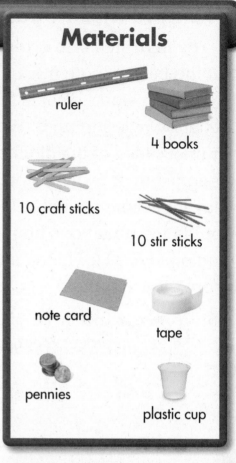

Materials

ruler

4 books

10 craft sticks

10 stir sticks

note card

tape

pennies

plastic cup

Inquiry Skill Scientists **make a model** to help them understand how something works and predict results.

4. Predict how many pennies the bridge will hold.
Record your prediction.

5. Put pennies in the cup one at a time. Record how many pennies the bridge holds before it falls.

Model	Number of Pennies	
	Prediction	Count
Stir sticks		
Craft sticks		

Which Bridge Is Stronger?

6. Repeat Steps 2–5. Use craft sticks this time.

Analyze and Conclude

7. **Infer** How did this scientific **investigation** help you determine which bridge was stronger?

....

....

....

....

8. How are your **models** like real bridges? How are they different?

....

....

....

....

....

Science
Technology
Engineering
Math

STEM

Lawn Mowers

Engineers design and develop large and small machines. These machines are made of simple and complex machines. A simple machine can be a lever, wheel and axle, pulley, wedge, inclined plane, or screw. Simple machines are often put together to make a complex machine, such as a lawn mower. It is made of different parts. Some of these parts are simple machines, such as a wheel and axle. A wheel and axle is used in a lawn mower to help it move. A screw is another simple machine. Screws are used to hold the lawn mower pieces together.

Apply Lawn mowers have wedges. A wedge is a simple machine made of two slanted sides that end in a sharp edge. Where do you think you would find a wedge inside a lawn mower?

Vocabulary Smart Cards

technology
work
wheel and axle
wedge
lever
inclined plane
pulley
screw
design process
research
prototype

Play a Game!

Cut out the Vocabulary Smart Cards.

Cover the words on the front of each card with sticky notes.

Use the list of words above to guess which word goes with each picture. Write the word on the sticky note.

Then remove the sticky note to see if you were correct.

wedge

cuña

technology

tecnología

lever

palanca

work

trabajo

inclined plane

plano inclinado

wheel and axle

eje y rueda

use of science knowledge to invent tools and new ways of doing things

Draw an example.

uso del conocimiento científico para inventar instrumentos y nuevas maneras de hacer las cosas

---

two slanted sides that end in a sharp edge

Draw an example.

dos lados inclinados que terminan con un borde filoso

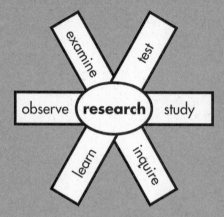

Make a Word Wheel!

Choose a vocabulary word and write it in the center of the Word Wheel graphic organizer. Write synonyms or related words on the wheel spokes.

---

the use of a force to move an object across a distance

Write a nonexample of this word.

uso de una fuerza para mover un objeto, por cierta distancia

---

a simple machine to lift and move things by using a stiff bar that rests on a support

List three examples of this word.

máquina simple que se usa para levantar y mover cosas mediante una barra rígida que tiene un punto de apoyo

---

a round object attached to a post

Draw and label a machine that has a wheel and axle.

objeto redondo unido a una barra

---

a slanting surface that connects a lower level to a higher level

Write a synonym for this word.

superficie inclinada que conecta un nivel bajo con un nivel más alto

 70

research

hacer una
investigación

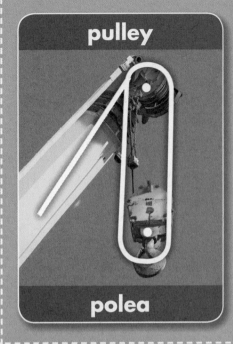

pulley

polea

prototype

prototipo

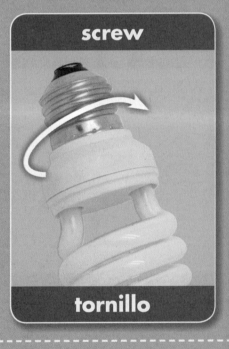

screw

tornillo

design process

The Design Process

Step 1: Identify the Problem

Step 2: Do Research

Step 3: Develop Possible Solutions

Step 4: Choose One Solution

Step 5: Design and Construct a Prototype

Step 6: Test the Prototype

Step 7: Communicate Results

Step 8: Evaluate and Redesign

proceso de
diseño

a machine that can change the direction or amount of force needed to move an object

What is the base word in this word?

....

....

máquina que puede cambiar la dirección o la cantidad de fuerza necesaria para mover un objeto

---

to look for facts about something

Write three examples of research.

....

....

....

buscar datos sobre algo

---

an inclined plane wrapped around a center post

Write a sentence using this word.

....

....

....

plano inclinado enrollado alrededor de un eje central

---

the first working product that uses a design

Write a synonym for this word.

....

....

el primer producto que funciona y que sigue un diseño

---

a step-by-step method used to solve a problem

Write a sentence using this word.

....

....

....

método que sigue pasos y que se usa para resolver un problema

Study Guide

REVIEW THE BIG ?   How can technology affect our lives?

Science, Engineering, and Technology

Lesson 1

What is technology?

- Scientific discoveries can lead to the development of new technology.
- Technology can help people solve problems.

Lesson 2

What is a machine?

- In science, work is done when a force moves an object.
- Simple machines, such as pulleys, make work easier.
- Complex machines are made of two or more simple machines.

Lesson 3

What is the design process?

- The design process is a step-by-step method used to solve a problem.
- People research and develop possible solutions to problems.

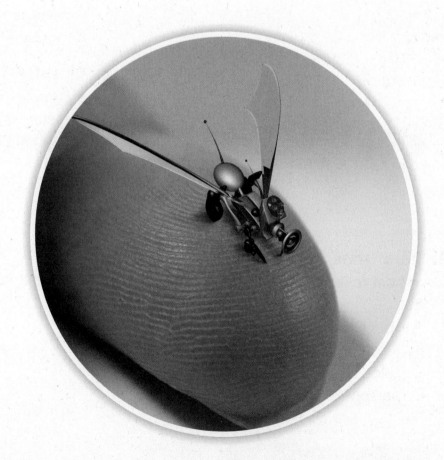

Lesson 1

What is technology?

1. Vocabulary The use of science knowledge to invent new ways of doing things is called _____.
A. scientific methods
B. evidence
C. a tool
D. technology

2. Write about it Explain how solar panels can improve our lives. Use the word technology.

....
....
....
....
....
....
....

3. Determine A Global Positioning System relies on signals sent from a(n) _____.
A. space satellite
B. X ray
C. solar panel
D. person

Lesson 2

What is a machine?

4. Evaluate What kind of simple tool is a nail? What is one way you could use a nail?

....
....
....

5. Vocabulary What machine is an inclined plane wrapped around a center post?
A. lever
B. pulley
C. wedge
D. screw

6. Classify The nail clippers are a complex machine made up of two simple machines. Label each simple machine.

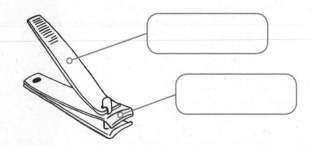

Lesson 3

What is the design process?

7. ◉ **Main Idea and Details**
Read the selection. Then complete the graphic organizer.

> When using the design process, you can do research in many ways. You can read a newspaper. You can watch a film. You can use the Internet. It is important to do different kinds of research.

Main Idea

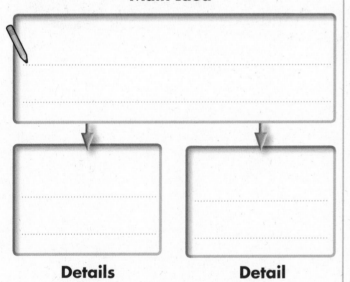

Details   **Detail**

8. Determine After you test a prototype, you communicate information to other people. This information is called _____.

A. a hypothesis

B. results

C. a story

D. an investigation

9. **APPLY THE BIG ?**   **How can technology affect our lives?**

Think about a product you use. How do you think it was made? Use the vocabulary words *technology* and *design process*.

Benchmark Practice

Fill in the bubble next to the answer choice you think is correct for each multiple-choice question.

1 Which technology protects people from diseases?

Ⓐ vaccines
Ⓑ solar panel
Ⓒ Global Positioning System
Ⓓ computer chip

2 What is the first step in the design process?

Ⓐ Choose one solution.
Ⓑ Do research.
Ⓒ Identify the problem.
Ⓓ Test the prototype.

3 Which simple machine is used to raise the flag on a flagpole?

Ⓐ pulley
Ⓑ lever
Ⓒ inclined plane
Ⓓ wedge

4 The first working product that uses a design is called a _____.

Ⓐ method
Ⓑ technology
Ⓒ redesign
Ⓓ prototype

5 Simple machines make doing work easier. Describe how you could use a wheel and axle.

Studying Clouds From Space

My World

Big World

Did you ever lie on your back and look at the clouds? Clouds can form interesting shapes. They also can tell you things about the weather. For example, cirrus clouds are thin, feathery clouds high in the air. Cirrus clouds are a sign of fair weather. Stratus clouds cover the sky like a blanket. They often bring rain or snow.

Some scientists study clouds from space using satellites. They are trying to understand how clouds affect Earth's climate. Some satellite tools measure the sunlight that bounces off clouds. Scientists are finding that low, thick clouds reflect sunlight back into space. These clouds have a cooling effect on Earth.

Cirrus clouds are different. They allow sunlight to pass to Earth. The heat is then trapped. These clouds have a heating effect.

REVIEW THE BIG ? What other examples of technology help people study the weather?

77

What parachute design works best?

A group of people on a small island need supplies dropped off. You cannot land a plane on the island. The supplies are fragile and must be dropped slowly so they do not break when they land. The area the supplies must be dropped off at is very small. You need to design a parachute to drop the supplies for the people that need them.

Identify the problem.

☐ **1.** Identify the problems you need to solve with your **design.**

....

....

....

....

....

....

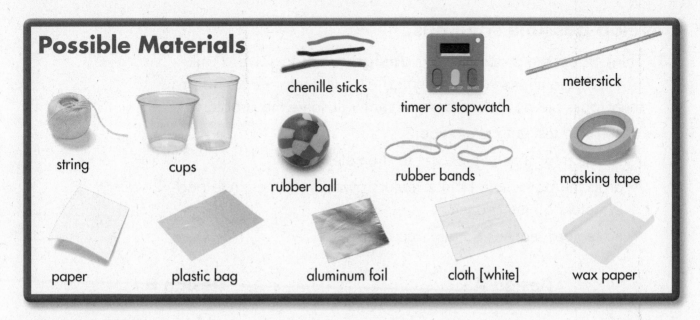

Possible Materials

chenille sticks

timer or stopwatch

meterstick

string

cups

rubber ball

rubber bands

masking tape

paper

plastic bag

aluminum foil

cloth [white]

wax paper

Do research.

☑ **2.** Think about the problems you have identified.
Research **design** solutions others have used.
Brainstorm ideas with others.
List three solutions others have used.

Develop possible solutions.

3. Think about the problems your **design** needs to solve. Think about the solutions you researched. Use this information to draw three possible parachute designs that will solve the problems.

When you test your prototype:

- set up a target circle 50 cm in diameter.
- drop the parachute from 2 meters away from the circle and 2 meters off the ground.
- have your teacher do all three trials.

Design A	Design B

Choose one solution.

4. Choose one design to test. Tell which design you chose. Explain your choice.

Design and construct a prototype.

☑ **5.** Draw the **design** you will use to make a prototype.
Label each part. Say what it is made of.

Show how your
parachute design
will carry the ball.

☑ **6.** List the materials you used in your prototype.

....

....

....

Test the Prototype

☑ **7.** Have your teacher test your **design** three times.

☑ **8.** **Record** the time it takes for your parachute to land.

☑ **9.** **Measure** the distance the payload landed from the center of the circle.

	Prototype Testing Results	
Trial	**Time to Land** (sec)	**Distance from Center of Circle** (cm)
1		
2		
3		
Average		

Communicate Results

☑ **10.** What parts of your **design** worked in your prototype? Use the results of your trials and your **observations** to support your conclusions.

....

....

....

☑ **11.** What parts of your design could be improved? Explain.

....

....

....

Evaluate and Redesign

☑ **12.** Think about what did and did not work.
Use what you learned from testing to **redesign** your prototype.
Write or draw your design changes.

Master Investigator

Create a trading card for a new card game about scientific investigation. Your card will represent a scientific investigator. Describe the investigator's strengths and weaknesses. Include a question the investigator might ask to solve a problem. Compare cards to discover the best scientific investigator!

Make a Model

Use paper, glue, colored markers, and other supplies to build a model of something. You can build a rocket, a car, a bridge, or anything that interests you. Describe the parts of your model and how the parts work together.

- How does your model help explain how the real object works?

- How is your model not exactly the same as the real object?

Make a Poster

Make a poster that teaches about the different kinds of simple machines. Use magazine pictures that show simple machines, or draw your own pictures. Label each simple machine. Write how each simple machine helps people do work.

Using Scientific Methods

1. Ask a question.
2. State your hypothesis.
3. Identify and control variables.
4. Test your hypothesis.
5. Collect and record your data.
6. Interpret your data.
7. State your conclusion.
8. Go further.

Life Science

How can trees
live in Blue Cypress Lake?

Plants

Chapter 3

Blue Cypress Lake is found in southeastern Florida. Cypress trees can live and grow in slow-moving water.

 Predict How can cypress trees live and grow in water?

....

....

....

How do plants grow and change?

How do plants change?

☑ **1.** Put a wet paper towel in a plastic resealable bag. Add three pinto beans between the towel and the bag.

☑ **2.** Seal the bag shut. Tape it to a window.

☑ **3. Collect Data** Draw and **record** your **observations** every other day.

Materials

plastic bag

pinto beans

tape

wet paper towels

Data Table

Day	Observations

☑ **4.** Choose a **variable** to change when the seeds grow roots. For example, change the direction of the bag, the amount of light the bag receives, or the temperature inside the bag.

☑ **5. Predict** how your plants will change.

Inquiry Skill
As you observe the growing plants, you **collect data** to show how they change.

Explain Your Results

6. Communicate Explain how your plants reacted to the change.

◎ Text Features

Text features, such as headings, highlighting, pictures, and captions, give you clues about what you will read.

A **heading** tells what the content that follows is about.

A **picture** shows something you will read about.

A **caption** tells specific information about a picture.

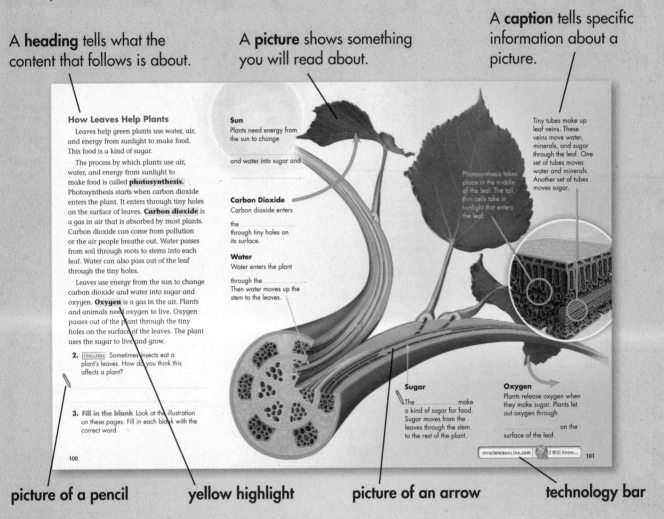

How Leaves Help Plants

Leaves help green plants use water, air, and energy from sunlight to make food. This food is a kind of sugar.

The process by which plants use air, water, and energy from sunlight to make food is called **photosynthesis.** Photosynthesis starts when carbon dioxide enters the plant. It enters through tiny holes on the surface of leaves. **Carbon dioxide** is a gas in air that is absorbed by most plants. Carbon dioxide can come from pollution or the air people breathe out. Water passes from soil through roots to stems into each leaf. Water can also pass out of the leaf through the tiny holes.

Leaves use energy from the sun to change carbon dioxide and water into sugar and oxygen. **Oxygen** is a gas in the air. Plants and animals need oxygen to live. Oxygen passes out of the plant through the tiny holes on the surface of the leaves. The plant uses the sugar to live and grow.

2. CHALLENGE Sometimes insects eat a plant's leaves. How do you think this affects a plant?

3. **Fill in the blank** Look at the illustration on these pages. Fill in each blank with the correct word.

100

Sun
Plants need energy from the sun to change

and water into sugar and

Carbon Dioxide
Carbon dioxide enters the

through tiny holes on its surface.

Water
Water enters the plant through the
Then water moves up the stem to the leaves.

Photosynthesis takes place in the middle of the leaf. The tall, thin cells take in sunlight that enters the leaf.

Tiny tubes make up leaf veins. These veins move water, minerals, and sugar through the leaf. One set of tubes moves water and minerals. Another set of tubes moves sugar.

Sugar
The _____ make a kind of sugar for food. Sugar moves from the leaves through the stem to the rest of the plant.

Oxygen
Plants release oxygen when they make sugar. Plants let out oxygen through _____ on the surface of the leaf.

myscienceonline.com   I Will Know...   101

picture of a pencil   yellow highlight   picture of an arrow   technology bar

Practice It!

Read the text features in the chart below. Find the text features in the textbook pages shown above. Write a clue that each one gives you about the content.

Text feature	Clue
yellow highlight	
picture of a pencil	
technology bar	

How can you classify plants?

Tell which characteristics you think can help you classify each plant.

my planet diary

Science Stats

Statistics are pieces of information that can help us answer questions. Statistics can help us determine the oldest known living plant. In 2004, scientists in Sweden discovered tree roots that are about 9,550 years old. The tree they found is called a Norway spruce. It is only 4 meters tall. The part of the tree we see is not very old. The roots of the tree are old. Each time the tree above ground dies, a new tree starts growing from the roots.

Which trees have lived above ground the longest? The oldest trees above ground are most likely bristlecone pine trees. One bristlecone pine tree in California is almost 5,000 years old.

bristlecone pine tree

What is the oldest part of the oldest tree in the world?

....

Underline the statistic that tells about the age of the Norway spruce.

I will know how to classify plants into major groups based on the physical characteristics of the plants.

Words to Know

flowering plant
spore

Classify Plants

At grocery stores, people sort food into groups. This helps shoppers find the right foods. Scientists classify living things, such as plants, in a similar way. Scientists classify plants by sorting them into groups. This helps us identify plants.

You can classify plants into groups by color, size, and shape. You can classify plants by how they reproduce, or produce offspring. You can also classify plants by their flowers or seeds.

1. ◉ **Text Features** Look at the text features on this page. Identify one text feature and the clue it gives you.

Text feature	Clue
Heading	It tells me I will be learning how plants are classified.

2. **Classify** These water lilies have large leaves that float on water. What is another way you can classify these water lilies?

....

....

....

Flowering Plants

One way to classify plants is by whether a plant produces flowers. An orange tree and a cactus do not look alike, but they are both flowering plants. **Flowering plants** are plants with seeds that grow flowers. Orange trees grow flowers with seeds. These seeds can grow into new plants.

There are different groups of flowering plants. Each group has different kinds of roots, stems, leaves, and flowers. For example, dogwood trees have a stiff, woody stem. This stem helps dogwoods grow tall. Iris plants do not have a woody stem. Iris plants grow closer to the ground.

Leaves fall off dogwood trees in the fall. The leaves grow back in the spring. Trees that lose and grow leaves in this way are called *deciduous* trees.

3. (Circle) the words that tell about flowering plants.

4. ◎ **Text Features** Why does the word *deciduous* look different from other words on this page?

....

....

Dogwood trees can grow taller than 6 meters. Dogwoods produce flowers. These flowers make seeds. The seeds can grow into new dogwoods.

Groups of Flowering Plants

One kind of flowering plant is the magnolia tree. It produces colorful flowers. Some magnolias are deciduous. Others keep their leaves all winter. Magnolia trees have a strong, woody stem. This stem helps magnolias grow tall. They range in height from shorter than 3 meters to taller than 20 meters.

Iris plants grow a long, thin stem and leaves. This stem allows iris plants to bend when winds blow against them. Iris plants lose both stem and leaves in the fall. The roots live through the winter. The stem and leaves grow back from the roots in the spring. During the spring, iris plants produce colorful flowers.

Rosebushes are another kind of flowering plant. They grow as small shrubs or long vines. Rose stems are strong and have sharp prickles. These stems allow rosebushes to grow large. The prickles protect the plant. Most rose flowers are colorful.

5. ◉ **Compare and Contrast** Look at the flowering plants on this page. How are they alike and different?

....

....

6. **Evaluate** What is an advantage of a thin stem?

....

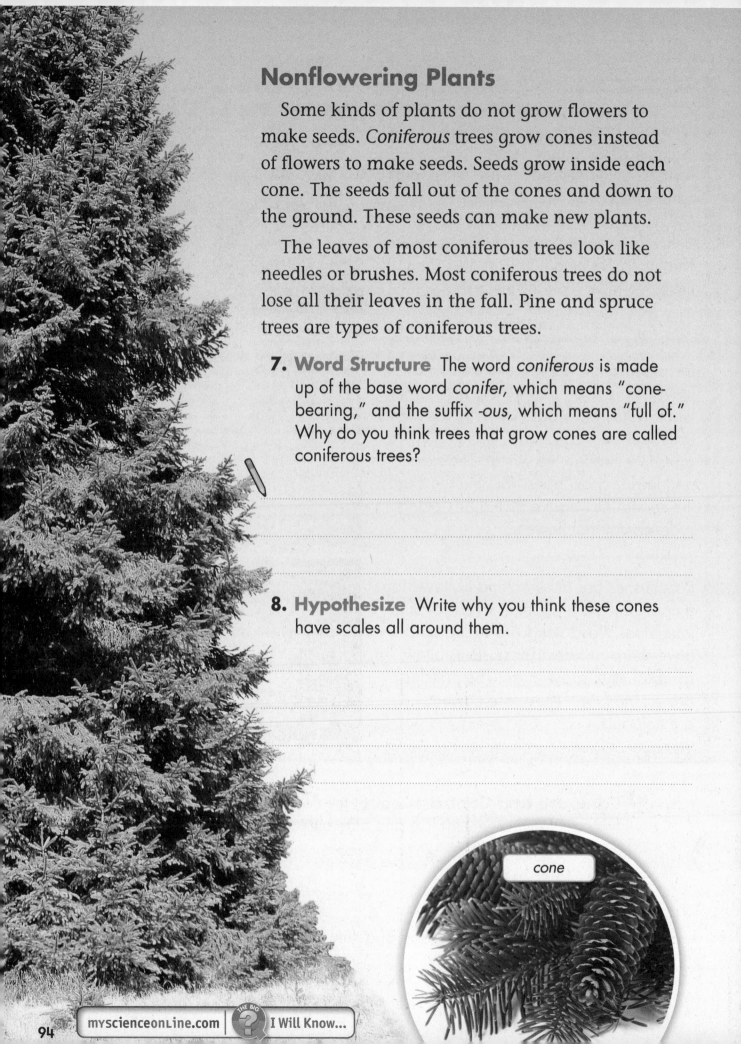

Nonflowering Plants

Some kinds of plants do not grow flowers to make seeds. *Coniferous* trees grow cones instead of flowers to make seeds. Seeds grow inside each cone. The seeds fall out of the cones and down to the ground. These seeds can make new plants.

The leaves of most coniferous trees look like needles or brushes. Most coniferous trees do not lose all their leaves in the fall. Pine and spruce trees are types of coniferous trees.

7. **Word Structure** The word *coniferous* is made up of the base word *conifer*, which means "cone-bearing," and the suffix *-ous*, which means "full of." Why do you think trees that grow cones are called coniferous trees?

....

....

....

8. **Hypothesize** Write why you think these cones have scales all around them.

....

....

....

....

cone

Spores

Ferns and mosses are two kinds of plants that do not make seeds. They reproduce by making spores. A **spore** is a small cell that grows into a new plant. Mosses produce spores at the end of their stalks. Ferns produce spores on the undersides of their leaves.

Mosses and ferns reproduce by making spores.

spore

fern

moss

9. Distinguish How are spores and seeds different from cones?

10. Classify Look at the three plants to the right. How would you classify each plant?

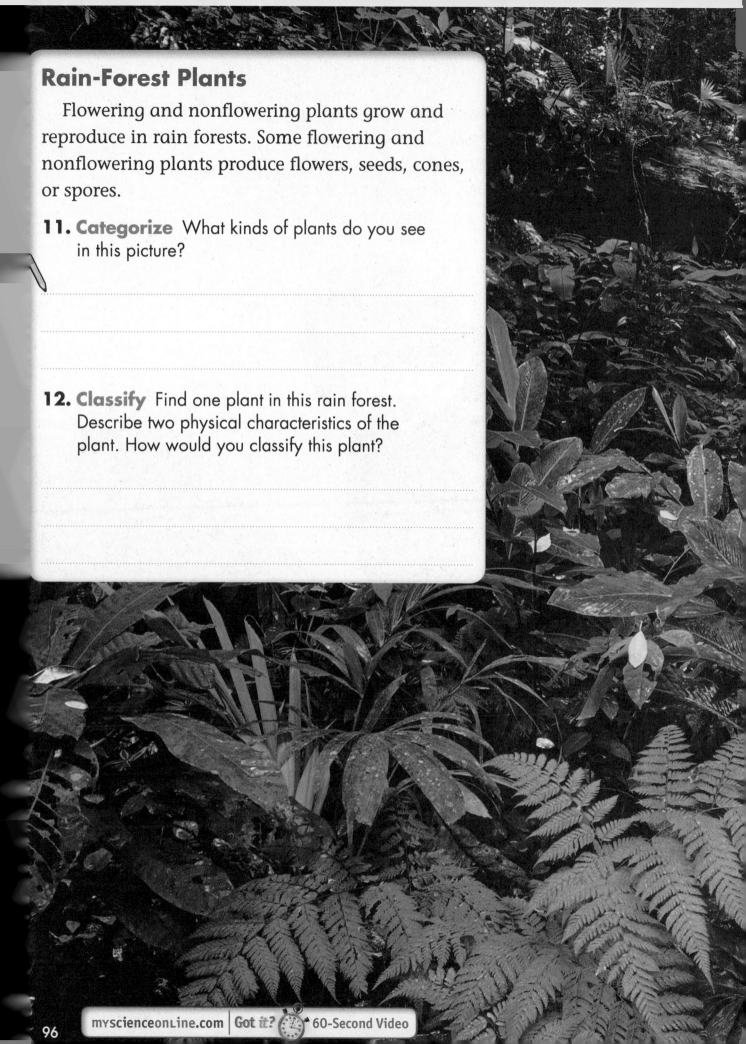

Rain-Forest Plants

Flowering and nonflowering plants grow and reproduce in rain forests. Some flowering and nonflowering plants produce flowers, seeds, cones, or spores.

11. Categorize What kinds of plants do you see in this picture?

....

....

....

12. Classify Find one plant in this rain forest. Describe two physical characteristics of the plant. How would you classify this plant?

....

....

....

myscienceonLine.com | Got it? 60-Second Video

At-Home Lab

Plants You See
Find a plant near where you live. Draw a picture of it. Write down three features of the plant. Bring your picture to class. Post your picture and compare it with other pictures. Then, classify the plant as flowering or nonflowering.

Got it?

13. **Classify** How would you classify an unknown plant that does not have flowers?

....

....

14. **Explain** Think about what you learned about plants in this lesson. How do we classify living things?

....

....

☐ **Stop!** I need help with ....

❙❙ **Wait!** I have a question about ....

▶ **Go!** Now I know ....

Lesson 2

How do plants use leaves to make food?

Tell how you think leaves help plants.

Inquiry **Explore It!**

How does sunlight affect plant survival?

☐ **1. Observe** a green leaf on a plant. Gently fold a piece of foil completely around the whole leaf. Be sure the foil cannot fall off.

☐ **2.** Place the plant near a sunny window. Wait one week.

☐ **3.** Take off the foil. Observe. Compare what you observed before and after the leaf was covered.

Materials

plant

foil

Be careful! Wash your hands when finished.

Explain Your Results

4. Infer What do you think happened to the leaf? Explain.

myscienceonline.com | **Explore It!** Animation

UNLOCK THE BIG ?

I will know that leaves help plants live, grow, and make food.

Words to Know

photosynthesis
carbon dioxide
oxygen

What Plants Need

Plants need food, air, water, and space to live and grow. Many plants live and grow in soil. The four main parts of a flowering plant are leaves, roots, stems, and flowers. In different kinds of plants, these parts may look alike. They may also look different.

Unlike animals, plants make their own food. Plants need energy from the sun to make food. Energy from the sun enters leaves and helps plants make food. This food helps plants grow.

1. ◎ **Text Features** Look at the text features on this page. Identify one text feature and the clue it gives you.

Text feature	Clue
Heading	It tells me that I'll read about what plants need.

Bromeliad plants are like other plants. They use energy from the sun to make food.

How Leaves Help Plants

Leaves help green plants use water, air, and energy from sunlight to make food. This food is a kind of sugar.

The process by which plants use air, water, and energy from sunlight to make food is called **photosynthesis.** Photosynthesis starts when carbon dioxide enters the plant. It enters through tiny holes on the surface of leaves. **Carbon dioxide** is a gas in air that is absorbed by most plants. Carbon dioxide can come from pollution or the air people breathe out. Water passes from soil through roots to stems into each leaf. Water can also pass out of the leaf through the tiny holes.

Leaves use energy from the sun to change carbon dioxide and water into sugar and oxygen. **Oxygen** is a gas in the air. Plants and animals need oxygen to live. Oxygen passes out of the plant through the tiny holes on the surface of the leaves. The plant uses the sugar to live and grow.

2. [CHALLENGE] Sometimes insects eat a plant's leaves. How do you think this affects a plant?

_____

_____

3. **Fill in the blank** Look at the illustration on these pages. Fill in each blank with the correct word.

Sun
Plants need energy from the sun to change

_____

and water into sugar and

_____ .

Carbon Dioxide
Carbon dioxide enters

the _____
through tiny holes on
its surface.

Water
Water enters the plant

through the _____ .
Then water moves up the
stem to the leaves.

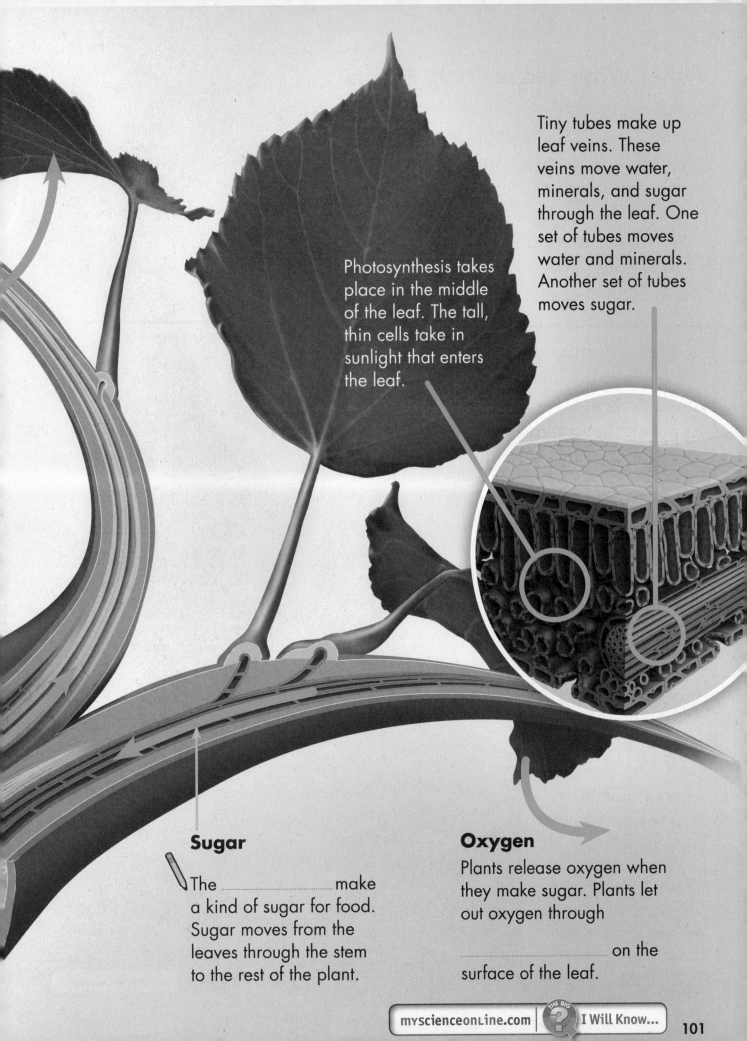

Tiny tubes make up leaf veins. These veins move water, minerals, and sugar through the leaf. One set of tubes moves water and minerals. Another set of tubes moves sugar.

Photosynthesis takes place in the middle of the leaf. The tall, thin cells take in sunlight that enters the leaf.

Sugar

The .... make a kind of sugar for food. Sugar moves from the leaves through the stem to the rest of the plant.

Oxygen

Plants release oxygen when they make sugar. Plants let out oxygen through

.... on the surface of the leaf.

Other Ways Leaves Help Plants

Leaves help plants in other ways. Leaves can help plants control the amount of water in the plant. If plants have too much water, leaves let some water out through the tiny holes on their surface. A plant can also stop water loss by closing these holes. Plants in dry environments may have wax- or fuzz-coated leaves. This coating helps keep in water. The stonecrop succulent has waxy-coated leaves to keep in water.

Plant leaves can also protect the plant from being eaten. Leaves can be poisonous, sharp, or tough to chew. Sharp leaves may have spines. Hungry animals may not eat a cactus plant with sharp leaves.

4. **Identify** List two ways a leaf can help a plant.

....

....

At-Home Lab

Leaves and Air
Place a clear sandwich bag over leaves on a tree branch. Observe the bag for two days. Tell what you see. Explain your observations.

stonecrop succulent

Poison ivy is a woody vine. It is found in forests across North America. Poison ivy causes an itchy rash, blistering, and burning of the skin.

5. **Draw** Think about a plant in your neighborhood. Draw a leaf from this plant. Describe to a partner how you think the leaf helps the plant.

Got it?

6. List five things plants need to make food.

....

....

7. **UNLOCK THE BIG ?** Think about what you learned about plant leaves in this lesson. How do plants grow and change?

....

....

■ **Stop!** I need help with ....

❚❚ **Wait!** I have a question about ....

▶ **Go!** Now I know ....

Lesson 3

How do plants use roots and stems to grow?

Envision It!

Circle, in different colors, the roots, stems, and leaves of these mangrove trees.

Inquiry **Explore It!**

Which way will roots grow?

☐ **1.** Fold and place the towels in the cup. Wet the towels.

☐ **2.** Place the seeds in different directions.

☐ **3. Observe** the seeds every day for one week. Watch the way the roots grow.

Materials

2 paper towels

plastic cup

water

4 bean seeds

Explain Your Results

4. Infer Write what you learned about the way roots grow.

....

....

I will know how roots and stems take in, transport, and store water and nutrients the plant needs to grow.

Word to Know

nutrient

How Roots Help Plants

Look at all the roots of the fir tree in the picture. Plants need roots and stems to take in and move materials a plant needs to live and grow.

The root system of a plant is often below the ground. You usually cannot see it. Roots keep the plant stable in the ground. Roots store food made by the plant's leaves. Roots also take in water and materials called minerals from the soil. The plant gets nutrients from the water and minerals. A **nutrient** is any material needed by living things for energy, growth, and repair. Plants need nutrients to live and grow.

1. **Determine** Look at the picture of the fir tree roots. What would happen if the plant's roots did not store food?

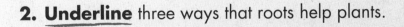

2. **Underline** three ways that roots help plants.

Fir tree roots take in nutrients from the soil.

Types of Roots

Have you ever eaten a carrot? Many plants have one large root called a *taproot*. Carrots and dandelions are examples of taproots. Taproots grow deep into the soil toward Earth's center due to gravity. Taproots take in water and nutrients from the soil. The roots also store food made by the plant.

In some plants, such as grass and pine trees, roots spread out in many directions. This type of root is called a *fibrous root*. Like taproots, fibrous roots store food, take in water and nutrients, and grow toward Earth's center due to gravity. Fibrous roots of the same plant are all about the same size. They grow longer than taproots. Fibrous roots also grow close to the surface to take in water after it rains.

root hair

3. Fill in the blank Look at the illustration of the root. Fill in each blank with the correct word.

_____ enters the root through the root hairs. All roots have root hairs. The more root hairs a plant has, the more water the plant can take in. Roots with many root hairs grow far into the soil to

reach water and _____ .

4. CHALLENGE Which type of roots could help a plant more in a dry area—a fibrous root or a taproot?

pumpkin stem

5. **Analyze** What is the role of the pumpkin's stem?

....

....

....

....

....

....

How Stems Help Plants

Stems support the leaves, flowers, and fruits of plants. Stems often grow up toward the light, their main source of energy. Most plant stems have tiny tubes that move water and minerals from the roots to the leaves. Other tubes move food from the leaves to the stems and roots.

Some stems are thin and grow along the surface of the ground. For example, the stem of a pumpkin can grow roots and a new plant. Other stems, called vines, grow parts that wrap around objects that support the plant. Ivy is a vine that grows on the ground or on buildings.

Lightning Lab

Look at Plant Roots
Work with an adult. Cut a carrot in half. Look at the cross section. List what structures you see. Try this with another root. On the same paper, list the structures of the other root.

Types of Stems

Plant stems come in many different shapes, sizes, and colors. Some stems grow below ground. Other stems such as this cactus stem grow above ground. Notice how thick cactus stems can grow. Cactus stems swell up to store water. As the cactus uses stored water due to heat, the stems shrink. Cactus stems are thick and waxy. This keeps them from losing water. Cactus stems help them survive in a desert.

6. ◎ **Text Features**
Which text features on this page help you understand different types of stems?

....

....

....

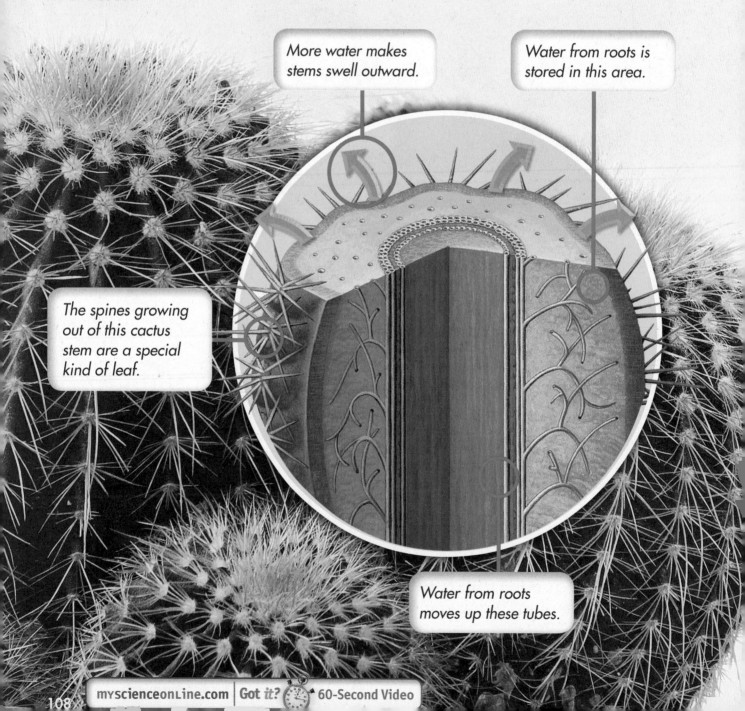

More water makes stems swell outward.

Water from roots is stored in this area.

The spines growing out of this cactus stem are a special kind of leaf.

Water from roots moves up these tubes.

myscienceonline.com | Got it? ⏱ 60-Second Video

Parts of some stems grow below ground. Have you eaten a potato? You eat the part of the stem that stored food below ground. Stems that grow below ground can make new stems from buds, such as the potato's "eyes." These buds grow up out of the ground and become new plants.

7. **Compare** Look at the cactus stem and potato. How do these stems help each plant?

....

....

....

....

Got it?

8. **Hypothesize** How could a plant grow in soil without many minerals?

....

....

9. **UNLOCK THE BIG ?** Why are roots and stems important to the growth of a plant?

....

....

⬛ **Stop!** I need help with ....

⏸ **Wait!** I have a question about ....

▶ **Go!** Now I know ....

Lesson 4

How do plants use flowers or cones to reproduce?

Circle what is helping these plants make new plants.

Inquiry **Explore It!**

What is inside a seed?

☐ **1.** Split your seed in half.

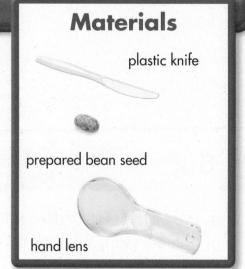

Materials

plastic knife

prepared bean seed

hand lens

☐ **2. Observe** the split seed. Draw what you see.

Be careful! Be careful using the plastic knife. Wash your hands after handling seeds.

Explain Your Results

3. Infer Where do you think a tiny young plant gets the food it needs to grow?

....

....

myscienceonline.com | **Explore It!** Animation

I will know how plants reproduce using seeds and cones.

Words to Know

reproduce
pollinate
germinate

Reproduction

Most plants make seeds that grow into new plants. Some plants grow stems or roots that grow into new plants. Plants can reproduce both ways. When plants **reproduce,** they make more of the same kind. For example, maple trees produce seeds. These seeds can grow into new maple trees.

Each seed carries information from the parent plants. The seed uses this information and food stored from the parent plant in the seed to grow into a new plant. The new plant will be like its parents. After seeds are produced, they may scatter or move away from the parent plant. This gives the new plant more room to grow.

1. **Predict** What may happen if seeds do not scatter?

2. **Determine** Each seed in the picture below has a tiny parachute. How do you think these parachutes help the seeds scatter?

seed with parachute

Parts of a Flower

Flowering plants grow flowers that make seeds. Flowers have different parts. One part makes pollen. Another part, the petals, attracts bees and other animals to the flower. Animals or wind can **pollinate,** or carry pollen to, another flower. Pollination happens when animals or wind move pollen to the part of the flower that makes seeds. After pollination, seeds form near the center of the flower. Another part, fruit, often grows around the seed to protect it. A peach is an example of a fruit.

3. ⊙ **Text Features** Tell what these captions helped you learn about plant reproduction.

4. **Summarize** What is the function of one part of a flower?

....

....

....

....

....

Pollen sticks to the bodies of bees as bees look for food. Bees can carry this pollen to the part of another flower that makes seeds.

A flower's colorful petals attract insects and other animals that pollinate the flower.

The tip of this part of the flower makes pollen.

Pollen from this part of the plant helps form seeds.

myscienceonline.com   THE BIG ?   I Will Know...

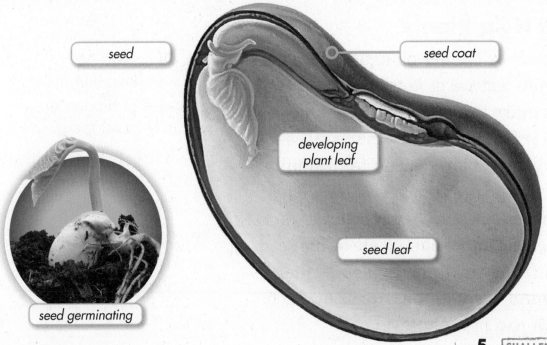

seed

seed coat

developing plant leaf

seed leaf

seed germinating

How Seeds Grow

Seeds have different shapes, sizes, and colors. All seeds have the same parts. Every seed has material inside it that can grow into a new plant. The seed is covered by a seed coat. The seed coat protects this material. Many seeds have one seed leaf or two seed leaves. As the tiny plant grows, it uses food from the seed.

Seeds need air, the right amount of water, and the right temperature to **germinate,** or begin to grow. With the right conditions, the young plant, or seedling, germinates. The seedling uses food stored in the seed to grow.

As the seedling grows, it grows out of the soil. Leaves grow from the stem. The leaves use sunlight to make sugar. The plant uses the sugar for food. The seedling can grow into an adult plant that has flowers. The flowers are pollinated and new seeds form. If these new seeds germinate, they can grow into new plants. Then the cycle begins again.

5. CHALLENGE Look at the illustration of the seed. Why do you think the seed coat is important?

....

....

....

Go Green

Food and Energy
Energy and resources are needed to grow food. The food must be moved from the farm to the store. This also uses energy. Think of ways you can avoid wasting food. Make a list. Share your list with your classmates.

How Cones Help Plants

Cones are made by conifer plants. Conifer plants grow cones instead of flowers to make seeds. Conifers make two types of cones. One cone is a small pollen cone. The other cone is a large seed cone. Wind blows pollen from small pollen cones to large seed cones. When pollen sticks to the large seed cones, seeds begin to grow inside. A seed grows under each scale of the seed cone. When the seeds are fully developed, they float to the ground. If conditions are right, each seed can grow into a new plant.

6. **Describe** What happens after the seed in a cone is fully developed?

....

....

7. **State** Write a caption for the photo below.

....

....

....

....

....

First, wind blows pollen from these small cones to larger cones on other trees.

Next, seeds begin to grow inside the cones.

Do the math!

Elapsed Time

If you plant a green bean seed, when can you eat green beans? You can eat them when fruit ripens. Different plants have different lengths of time from seed to fruit. Use the table and calendars to answer the questions.

1 Solve If you plant cucumber seeds on May 21, when can you eat cucumbers?

2 Solve If you eat ripe tomatoes on July 29, when were the seeds planted?

Days from Seed to Fruit	
green bean seeds	58 days
cucumber seeds	55 days
tomato seeds	59 days

Got it?

8. **Analyze** What role do flowers play in plant reproduction?

9. **UNLOCK THE BIG ?** Think about what you learned in this lesson. How do plants grow and change?

⬜ **Stop!** I need help with

⏸ **Wait!** I have a question about

▶ **Go!** Now I know

What are the life cycles of some plants?

Write the numbers 1, 2, 3, or 4 to show the sequence in the life of this tomato plant.

my planet diary

FunFact

The titan arum grows on the island of Sumatra, in Indonesia. Here, the flower has opened.

The titan arum is a plant that produces a very large flower. The titan arum begins life as a seed. Each year the plant develops a single large leaf. The leaf produces food for the plant. After the leaf dies, the plant remains inactive for a few months. Then a new leaf forms.

When the titan arum is mature, or fully grown, it produces a flower. The flower is typically 1.5 meters tall. That's probably taller than you are! The biggest flowers can grow over 3 meters tall. The flower gives off a foul smell. This smell attracts insects.

Why do you think the titan arum needs to attract insects?

myscienceonline.com | my planet diary

Words to Know

life cycle

Plant Life Cycles

Living things change during their lives. Most living things begin their lives small and then grow larger. They may develop certain features as they change into adults. They reproduce to make more living things of the same kind. Eventually, living things die. The stages through which a living thing passes during its life are called a **life cycle.**

Most plants go through similar stages during their life cycles. But plant life cycles can differ in important ways. For example, plants reproduce in different ways. Most plants make seeds that can grow into new plants. Some plants reproduce by making spores instead of seeds. Plants that reproduce in different ways have different life cycles.

1. ◉ **Text Features** (Circle) three text features on this page.

Every acorn contains a seed. The seed can grow into a new oak tree. Most oak trees grow for at least 20 years before making seeds.

Life Cycle of a Flowering Plant

A pumpkin plant is a kind of flowering plant. The life cycle of a pumpkin plant has several stages, as shown in the diagram.

 1 Germinating Seed

A pumpkin seed germinates when water, oxygen, and warm temperatures are present. A stem grows up and roots grow down.

2 Growth

The young plant grows leaves and starts to make sugar for food. It grows into an adult plant with flowers.

4 Adult Plant with Seeds

The pumpkin is a fruit made by the pumpkin plant. It contains seeds formed after pollination. The seeds can become new plants.

 **3 Pollination**

Some pumpkin flowers make pollen. Other flowers use that pollen to make seeds. Pollination happens when pollen moves from one pumpkin flower to another.

2. Infer In stage 3, what likely moves pollen from one flower to another?

....

....

Life Cycle of a Conifer Plant

Pine trees are conifers. Conifer plants grow cones instead of flowers to make seeds.

1 **Germinating Seed**

To germinate, a pine tree seed needs water, oxygen, and warm temperatures. A seedling grows from the germinated seed.

4 **Adult Plant with Seeds**

Seeds develop in the seed cones. The seeds fall to the ground when the cones open. The seeds can become new plants.

2 *Over many years, the pine seedling grows into a tall adult tree. The tree makes small pollen cones and larger seed cones.*

3 *Small pollen cones make pollen. Wind carries the pollen to the large cones, where seeds are made.*

3. ⦿ **Text Features** Compare the two life cycles shown on these pages. Then, in the blank spaces, write titles for stage 2 and stage 3 in the life cycle of the pine tree.

4. **Draw** In the box, draw a simple life cycle for a Kalanchoe plant.

Other Plant Life Cycles

Some plants have two kinds of life cycles. They make seeds that can grow into new plants. But they can also reproduce another way. The stem of a strawberry plant can bend over and touch the soil. New roots form on the stem. They grow into the soil and a new strawberry plant forms. Dandelion plants use their roots to reproduce. Their roots send stems up out of the soil. The stems grow into new dandelion plants.

Some plants use leaves to reproduce. The Kalanchoe plant shown below reproduces this way. Tiny new plants grow from the edges of the adult's leaves. The tiny plants fall off and send roots into the soil.

Ferns and mosses make spores instead of seeds. A spore can start to grow when it falls to the ground. This forms a new fern or moss plant.

This Kalanchoe plant is forming tiny new plants along its leaf edges.

Life Cycle Length

Some plants live for only a short time. For example, many desert plants grow, flower, and make seeds over a period of a few weeks. Their seeds germinate only when rain falls. Other plants have a one-year or two-year life cycle. For example, farmers have to plant new green bean seeds every spring.

Many trees can live longer than humans do. The chart to the right shows the average length of the life cycles of some of these trees.

Type of Tree	Average Length of Life Cycle
American elm	175 to 200 years
Bristlecone pine	3,000 years
Douglas fir	300 years
Redwood	500 years

5. ⊙ **Sequence** Look at the chart. List the tree names in order from the shortest life cycle to the longest.

....

....

Got it?

6. **Compare** How are the life cycles of flowering plants and conifer plants alike?

....

....

7. **UNLOCK THE BIG ?** Think about what you learned about plant life cycles in this lesson. How do plants grow and change?

....

....

⬛ **Stop!** I need help with ....

⏸ **Wait!** I have a question about ....

▶ **Go!** Now I know ....

How does water move through celery?

Follow a Procedure

☑ **1.** Cut a thin slice from the end of a celery stalk. **Observe** it with a hand lens or microscope. In the chart, draw what you see.

☑ **2.** Put the stalk into the water with blue food coloring. Wait 24 hours.

☑ **3.** Cut 2 cm off the stalk's end. Then cut a thin slice from the new end. Observe it with a hand lens or microscope. Draw what you see.

☑ **4.** Observe the whole stalk. Draw what you see.

Materials

stalk of celery

scissors

hand lens

water with blue food coloring

microscope (optional)

metric ruler

Be careful! Be careful with scissors.

Inquiry Skill
You use one or more of your senses when you make **observations.**

Observations of Celery		
Slice Before Dye	**Slice After Dye**	**Whole Stalk After Dye**

Analyze and Conclude

5. Compare the slices. How are they different?

....

....

6. Infer During this **investigation,** what happened to the celery stalk in the blue water?

....

....

7. UNLOCK THE BIG ? Which parts of plants move water to the leaves?

....

....

....

Botanical Illustrator

Do you like to draw? If so, perhaps you would like to be a botanical illustrator. A botanical illustrator draws or paints plants to show what they look like. To draw plants well, you have to be a good observer of nature. This way you can show the details that make plants different. When you draw, you must show the right size and shape of each plant part.

To be a botanical illustrator, you need a degree from a college or art school. Most of your classes would be in art. Some of your classes might also be in biology. You could work for a museum or botanical garden. You might draw illustrations to be used in science books or nature–reserve brochures.

Heeyoung Kim is a botanical illustrator who paints wildflowers. She researches each flower before painting it. Heeyoung Kim wants people to see the beauty of flowers.

REVIEW THE BIG ?

Illustrate What did you learn in this chapter that can help you draw detailed images of how a plant grows and changes?

Vocabulary Smart Cards

flowering plant
spore
photosynthesis
carbon dioxide
oxygen
nutrient
reproduce
pollinate
germinate
life cycle

Play a Game!

Cut out the Vocabulary Smart Cards.

Work with a partner. Spread out the Vocabulary Smart Cards on a table. Use the word in a sentence. Refer to the definition if you are not familiar with the word.

Have your partner repeat with another Vocabulary Smart Card.

carbon dioxide

dióxido de carbono

flowering plant

angiosperma

oxygen

oxígeno

spore

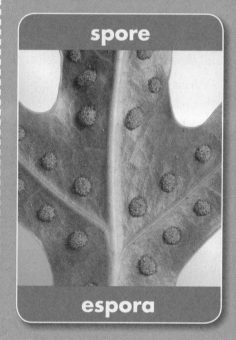

espora

nutrient

nutriente

photosynthesis

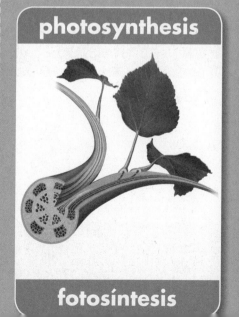

fotosíntesis

a plant with seeds that grows flowers

Draw an example.

planta con semillas que produce flores

a gas in air that is absorbed by most plants

Write a sentence using this term.

....

....

....

gas en el aire que la mayoría de las plantas absorben

Make a Word Frame!

Choose a vocabulary word and write it in the center of the frame. Write or draw details about the vocabulary word in the spaces around it.

a small cell that grows into a new plant

Write a sentence using this word.

....

....

....

célula pequeña que se convierte en una planta nueva

a gas in the air that plants and animals need

Write a sentence using this word.

....

....

....

gas en el aire que las plantas y los animales necesitan para vivir

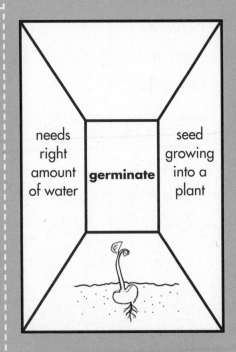

needs right amount of water — **germinate** — seed growing into a plant

the process by which plants use air, water, and energy from sunlight to make food.

Draw a picture.

proceso por el cual las plantas usan el aire, el agua y la energía del sol para producir alimento

any material needed by living things for energy, growth, and repair

Write two words related to this word.

....

....

cualquier sustancia que los seres vivos necesitan para obtener energía, crecer y reponerse

life cycle

ciclo de vida

reproduce

reproducir

pollinate

polinizar

germinate

germinar

to make more of the same kind

Write the noun form of the word.

....

....

....

hacer más de una misma cosa

---

the stages through which a living thing passes during its life

Write a sentence using this word.

....

....

....

estados por los que pasa un ser vivo durante su vida

---

to carry pollen to

Draw an example.

llevar polen de un lugar a otro

---

to begin to grow

Draw an example.

empezar a crecer

Lesson 1

How can you classify plants?

- Plants can be classified according to their characteristics, such as flowering and nonflowering.
- Some plants make seeds and some plants make spores.

Lesson 2

How do plants use leaves to make food?

- Leaves use air, water, and energy from the sun to make food for plants. This process is called photosynthesis.
- Leaves can help control the amount of water in a plant.

Lesson 3

How do plants use roots and stems to grow?

- Roots hold the plant in the ground and store food.
- Stems support and protect plants.

Lesson 4

How do plants use flowers or cones to reproduce?

- Many plants make seeds using flowers or cones.
- A seed has material inside it that can grow into a new plant.
- If conditions are right, a seed can germinate into a seedling.

Lesson 5

What are the life cycles of some plants?

- The stages through which a living thing passes during its life are called a life cycle.
- Plants that reproduce in different ways have different life cycles.

Chapter Review

How do plants grow and change?

Lesson 1

How can you classify plants?

1. **Compare and Contrast** What do cones and flowers have in common?

2. **Suggest** Name one kind of plant that grows very tall and does not produce flowers.

Lesson 2

How do plants use leaves to make food?

3. **Text Features** What do captions for pictures in a lesson tell you?

4. **Decide** What is one thing a plant must do before it can make sugar and oxygen?

Lesson 3

How do plants use roots and stems to grow?

5. **Explain** How does the stem of a plant respond to light?

6. **Analyze** Describe one way stems help a plant.

7. **Compare and Contrast** How are roots and stems alike and different?

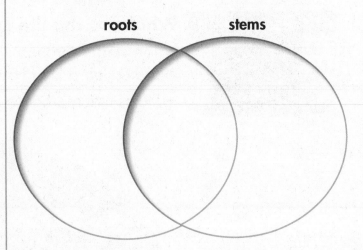

roots   stems

Lesson 4

How do plants use flowers or cones to reproduce?

8. **Vocabulary** When a plant _____, roots grow and a seedling begins to grow.
   A. reproduces
   B. scatters
   C. germinates
   D. blows

9. **Infer** Bees help pollinate apple trees. How might a disease that kills bees affect the number of apples on the trees? Explain.

....

....

....

....

....

....

Lesson 5

What are the life cycles of some plants?

10. **Identify** In the life cycle of a conifer, what stage must happen before the plant can make seeds?

....

11. **Determine** Do all plants begin their life cycle as a seed? Explain.

....

....

....

12. **APPLY THE BIG ?** **How do plants grow and change?**

··

Use the terms *carbon dioxide*, *oxygen*, and *nutrient* to describe how plants grow and change.

....

....

....

....

....

....

Fill in the bubble next to the answer choice you think is correct for each multiple-choice question.

1 How would you classify a pine tree?

Ⓐ spore
Ⓑ flowering plant
Ⓒ nonflowering plant
Ⓓ fern

2 A new plant that has just grown out of the soil is a _____.

Ⓐ germinate
Ⓑ system
Ⓒ seedling
Ⓓ seed leaf

3 What might happen to a plant if the tiny holes on the surfaces of the leaves were covered?

Ⓐ More roots would grow.
Ⓑ Leaves would use more carbon dioxide.
Ⓒ Leaves would produce more oxygen.
Ⓓ Leaves would not produce much oxygen and sugar.

4 A cactus stores the most water in its _____.

Ⓐ roots
Ⓑ leaves
Ⓒ stem
Ⓓ flowers

5 Leaves turn carbon dioxide and water into what two things?

Ⓐ sugar and oxygen
Ⓑ seedlings and sugar
Ⓒ oxygen and stems
Ⓓ nutrients and sugar

6 How are roots and leaves important to a plant?

....

....

....

....

....

Living Things

Chapter
4

When a kangaroo is born, it is blind and has no fur. It is about the size of a peanut. It climbs into its mother's pouch to finish developing. The young kangaroo stays there for months to eat, sleep, and grow.

Predict What might happen if a baby kangaroo left its mother's pouch too soon?

....

....

 How do living things grow and change?

How can shells be classified?

☑ **1. Observe** how the shells are alike and different.

☑ **2. Classify** Sort the shells into groups and label each group.

☑ **3. Record** the labels you used.

....

....

....

☑ **4.** Observe how other groups classified their shells. What labels were used?

....

....

....

Materials

shells

labels

Inquiry Skill
You **classify** objects when you sort them according to properties you observe.

Explain Your Results

5. **UNLOCK THE BIG ?** Explain how you approached the task of **classifying** the shells.

....

....

....

◉ Sequence

- **Sequence** is the order in which events take place.
- Clue words such as *first*, *next*, *then*, and *finally* can help you figure out the sequence of events.

Classify Animals

Scientists can classify animals according to their behaviors, such as how they act, and their physical characteristics, such as hair. Scientists may classify a slug such as the one below. Scientists may first identify whether or not the slug has a backbone. Next, they can find out what the slug eats. Finally, scientists can compare and contrast the slug to other animals.

Practice It!

Complete the graphic organizer to show the sequence of classifying animals.

First

Next

Finally

sea slug

Lesson 1

How can you classify animals?

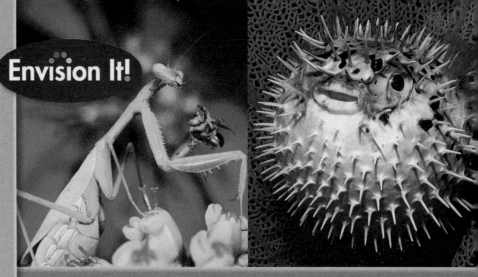

Tell which characteristics you think can help you classify each animal.

Inquiry **Explore It!**

Materials

pipe cleaner

10 pasta wheel pieces

9 jelly rings

How does a backbone move?

☑ **1. Make a model** of a backbone. Knot one end of a pipe cleaner.

☑ **2.** String a pasta wheel and then a jelly ring.

☑ **3.** Keep going. Use all the wheels and rings.

☑ **4.** Knot the other end of the pipe cleaner.

Explain Your Results

5. Observe how the **model** moves. Discuss and explain how a backbone moves.

....

....

....

....

....

myscienceonLine.com | **Explore It!** Animation

I will know how to classify animals into major groups based on characteristics and behaviors.

Words to Know

trait   invertebrate
vertebrate   arthropod

Classify Animals

Animals are classified into groups. Animals can be classified by what we want to learn about them. Animals can also be classified by how they look. Scientists identify body features, such as long ears or short fur, to classify animals. A feature passed on to a living thing from its parents is called a **trait.** Traits can include an animal's behavior or its physical characteristics. Animals can also be classified by where they live or how they act.

One animal can be placed into different groups. For example, a group of animals that eat mice can include snakes, hawks, and owls. A group of animals that fly can include hawks and owls but not snakes.

1. (Circle) some ways animals are classified.

2. **Suggest** What is another reason you might not classify a snake with hawks and owls?

....

....

....

Animals with Backbones

One main characteristic scientists use to classify animals is whether or not they have a backbone. An animal with a backbone is called a **vertebrate.** For example, cats, birds, and fish are vertebrates. Vertebrates may look different, but they all have a backbone and other bones. Bones grow as the animals grow. Bones support the body. This allows some vertebrates to grow very big.

3. Infer What allows a giraffe to grow so tall?

Read the next page. Then answer these questions.

4. Differentiate What is one way reptiles and amphibians are different?

5. Circle two traits an animal can have to be classified as a mammal.

Fish

Fish are vertebrates that live in water. Most fish have slippery scales, breathe through gills, and lay eggs. Fish are cold-blooded vertebrates.

6. Illustrate Draw a fish.

Amphibians

Amphibians are cold-blooded vertebrates. They have smooth, moist skin. They hatch from eggs. Frogs, toads, and salamanders are amphibians. Most young amphibians live in water. They get oxygen through their gills and skin. Most amphibians develop lungs to breathe air out of the water.

Reptiles

Snakes, lizards, turtles, and crocodiles are reptiles. Reptiles are cold-blooded vertebrates. They have dry, scaly skin. They breathe air through lungs. Most reptiles lay eggs.

7. Illustrate Draw a reptile.

Birds

Birds are warm-blooded vertebrates with feathers and bills. Feathers help birds stay warm. Wings and light bones help most birds fly. They breathe air through lungs. All birds hatch from eggs.

Mammals

The vertebrates you probably know best are mammals. Mammals are warm-blooded vertebrates. They usually have hair that keeps them warm. Mammals breathe air through lungs and feed milk to their young. Most mammals are born alive instead of hatching from eggs.

Animals Without Backbones

Most animals do not have bones or skeletons inside their bodies. Animals without backbones are called **invertebrates.** Sea stars, butterflies, and spiders are invertebrates.

Invertebrates have structures other than bones to give them their shape. A soft sac filled with liquid supports worms and sea jellies. A hard shell supports clams and lobsters. Insects have a hard covering on the outside of their bodies. These kinds of structures cannot support very big animals. Most invertebrates are smaller than most vertebrates.

You may not notice some invertebrates because many are very small. Yet invertebrates live all over Earth. In fact, there are many more invertebrates than vertebrates. For example, several million tiny roundworms may live in one square meter of soil.

8. [CHALLENGE] How do you think Earth can support more invertebrates than vertebrates?

....

....

....

....

....

Lightning Lab

Classify Different Animals

Draw an animal. Describe two features such as how the animal moves and what it eats. Draw another animal. Compare the features. Write how the animals are alike and different. Then classify them.

slug

orangutan

Groups of Invertebrates

Sea Jellies

Sea jellies have soft bodies and long, stinging body parts. The body of a sea jelly is made mostly of water. A sea jelly stuns its prey before pulling it into its stomach. Most sea jellies live in the ocean.

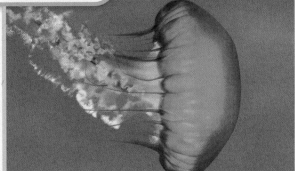

Worms

Worms are animals with long, soft bodies and no legs. Have you ever seen an earthworm in the soil? These invertebrates help keep soil healthy.

Mollusks

Mollusks are animals with soft bodies. Some mollusks include octopuses, squids, clams, and snails. Many mollusks have hard shells and eyes.

9. Illustrate Draw a mollusk.

Arthropods

Arthropods are the largest group of invertebrates. An **arthropod** is an animal that has a hard covering outside its body. The bodies of arthropods have more than one main part, and their legs have joints. Insects, spiders, and crabs are all arthropods.

10. Classify Look at the pictures to the left. How would you classify each animal?

....

....

Animal Birth

Another trait that helps scientists classify animals is the way they give birth. Most animals begin in small eggs. The eggs grow to different sizes. The young animals are then born in different ways.

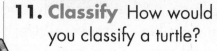

Eggs

Many animals hatch from eggs. For example, all birds hatch from eggs. Most fish, amphibians, and reptiles also hatch from eggs. Crocodiles lay eggs, as most other reptiles do. After growing in the eggs for two or three months, young crocodiles hatch from the eggs.

Live Birth

Most mammals have live births. This means that the young animal is born instead of hatching from an egg. You may have seen images of a lion with her young cubs. She gave live birth to the cubs after being pregnant for about four months.

11. Classify How would you classify a turtle?

....

....

12. ⊙ Sequence What two things happen before a crocodile hatches from an egg?

....

....

....

....

myscienceonline.com | Got it? 🕐 60-Second Video

Do the math!

Analyze a Bar Graph

Different fish swim at different speeds. Usually, larger fish swim faster than smaller fish. Use the bar graph about the speeds of fish to answer these questions.

1 Solve What is the speed of the fastest fish?

2 Order Using the data in the graph, list the fish in order from slowest to fastest.

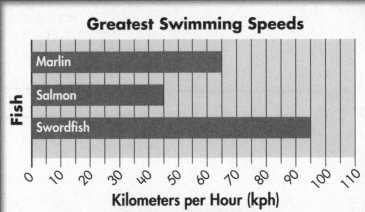

Greatest Swimming Speeds

Fish: Marlin, Salmon, Swordfish

Kilometers per Hour (kph)
0 10 20 30 40 50 60 70 80 90 100 110

Got it?

13. Categorize A rattlesnake and a black widow spider both make poison. Why might they be classified in different groups?

....

....

14. Explain Think about what you learned in this lesson. How do we classify animals?

....

☐ **Stop!** I need help with ....

❚❚ **Wait!** I have a question about ....

▶ **Go!** Now I know ....

Lesson 2

How are offspring like their parents?

Circle the two pictures that show behaviors an animal must learn.

my planet diary

DISCOVERY

Karl von Frisch

A honey bee scout flies out of the hive to look for food. It finds flowers full of sweet nectar. How can the scout communicate to the other bees where the food is? Beginning in the 1920s, Karl von Frisch studied bee behavior. He discovered that the scout bee performs a dance. The dance tells other bees where to find the food. The bees in the hive are born knowing what the dance means.

What do you think the bees will do after they see the scout's dance?

....

....

....

I will know that some characteristics and behaviors are inherited and some are learned or acquired.

Draw an ✗ on the pictures that show behaviors an animal is born knowing how to do.

Words to Know

inherit

instinct

Both Alike and Different

Why do kittens look like cats and not like dogs? Why does a corn seed grow into a corn plant and not a tomato plant? Most young plants and animals grow to look like their parents. Some plants and animals look like their parents even when they are very young.

The young antelope in the picture shares many characteristics with its parent. For example, the young antelope has the same body shape as its parent. Its fur is about the same length too.

The young antelope is also different in some ways. For example, its horns are much smaller than its parent's horns. The young antelope's horns will grow larger as it gets older. But even then, its horns may not have the exact shape or size of its parent's horns.

1. ◉ **Compare and Contrast** Describe other ways in which the young antelope and its parent are alike and different.

....

....

....

....

Inherited Characteristics

Young plants and animals are called offspring. Why do offspring often look like their parents?

Many characteristics of plants and animals are inherited. **Inherit** means to receive from a parent. An inherited characteristic is one that is passed on from parents to their offspring. An inherited characteristic is also called a trait. Animals inherit traits such as color and the shape of their body parts. Plants inherit traits such as leaf shape and flower color. The traits of an animal or plant often help it to survive in its environment.

Humans also inherit traits. You may have inherited traits such as hair color and eye color from your parents.

2. **Underline** the words that tell what *inherit* means.

3. **Analyze** This frog's skin color is inherited. How does it help the frog survive?

....

....

Young pine trees inherit green, needlelike leaves from adult pine trees.

Acquired Characteristics

Not all characteristics are inherited from parents. Suppose a woman has her ears pierced. Her offspring will not be born with pierced ears. Pierced ears are an acquired characteristic. You acquire, or get, them during your lifetime. Only characteristics that you are born with can be passed to your offspring.

Plants and animals develop acquired characteristics through interactions with their environment. For example, a plant's leaves may turn brown if it gets too much sun. Brown leaves are an acquired characteristic. The plant's offspring will not have brown leaves.

4. **List** Look at the tree in the picture. Write one inherited characteristic and one acquired characteristic of the tree.

....

....

The scars on this elephant seal's body are from fighting other seals. The scars are an acquired characteristic.

Massive winds have helped cause this tree's slanted shape.

149

Inherited Behavior

Behaviors are things that animals do. A behavior that an animal is born able to do is an **instinct.** Instincts are inherited behaviors. One instinct is an animal's response to hunger. For example, baby birds open their mouths when a parent brings food. Puppies are born knowing how to suck milk.

Some animals have an instinct to move, or migrate, when the seasons change. Some butterflies migrate thousands of miles. They fly to warm places to survive the winter. Other animals, such as bats, have an instinct to hibernate during winter. When animals hibernate, their body systems slow down. This saves energy. The animals don't need as much food to survive.

Baby birds are born knowing how to open their mouths for food.

5. **Explain** Explain in your own words what *migrate* means.

....

....

6. **Apply** Dogs have many instincts. Describe a behavior of dogs that you think is an instinct. Explain why you think the behavior is inherited.

....

....

....

Most types of spiders have an instinct to build webs.

Learned Behaviors

Animals learn some behaviors from their parents or other adults. For example, chimpanzees learn how to use a stick as a tool. They use the stick to catch and eat insects. Chimpanzees are not born knowing how to use tools. They learn how to do this by watching other chimpanzees. Young chimpanzees also must learn which foods are safe to eat. Their mothers and other adults teach them.

Humans learn many behaviors from their parents or other adults. You learned how to read and do math in school. A parent may have taught you how to tie your shoelaces or eat with a spoon. You were not born knowing how to do these things.

A chimpanzee pokes a stick into an insect nest. It pulls out the stick. Then it eats the insects that are on the stick.

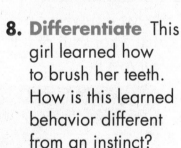

7. ◉ **Main Idea and Details** What is the main idea of this page?

8. **Differentiate** This girl learned how to brush her teeth. How is this learned behavior different from an instinct?

151

Small Differences in Traits

Offspring often look like their parents. Offspring can also look like each other. But they may not look exactly alike. Different animals of the same kind can look and act different. For example, two brown rabbits can have brown offspring. They may also have white or gray offspring.

Differences That Can Help an Animal

Some differences in the way an animal looks or acts can help it survive and reproduce. For example, rock pocket mice live in rocky habitats in desert areas. Some habitats have light brown rocks. Others have black rocks. The mice have either light brown or black fur. Scientists have found that a mouse's color often matches the rocks in its habitat. Why would this be? Owls hunt and eat mice. However, owls cannot see light brown mice on light brown rocks or black mice on black rocks.

9. **Describe** Write a caption for the picture above.

....

....

....

10. **Circle** the mouse with the fur color that helps it survive on light-colored sand. Tell what kind of habitat it may not survive in.

Differences That Can Harm an Animal

Small differences in traits can harm an animal. Some traits can make it harder for an animal to survive and reproduce.

Suppose two light brown mice have offspring. Most are light brown, but some are black. Which offspring are more likely to survive in a habitat of light brown rocks? The light brown offspring will be hard for owls to see. But black mice are easier to see on light brown rocks. The black offspring are more likely to be eaten by owls. They are less likely to survive and have offspring of their own.

11. **Apply** Tell why you think there may be few owls with poor eyesight in a habitat.

Owls are most likely to hunt and eat mice they can see easily.

Got it?

12. **Name** What are two ways an animal is able to acquire a behavior?

....

....

13. **Apply** How do webbed feet help a duck survive?

....

....

⬛ **Stop!** I need help with ....

⏸ **Wait!** I have a question about ....

▶ **Go!** Now I know ....

Lesson 3

What are the life cycles of some animals?

Label the pictures 1 through 3 to show the correct sequence in the life cycle of a bald eagle.

Inquiry **Explore It!**

What is the life cycle of a grain beetle?

☐ **1. Observe** several mealworms. **Record** a stage you see.

☐ **2.** Observe the mealworms for about 3 weeks.

☐ **3.** Draw each new stage you see.

Materials

mealworms in habitat cup

hand lens

crayons or markers

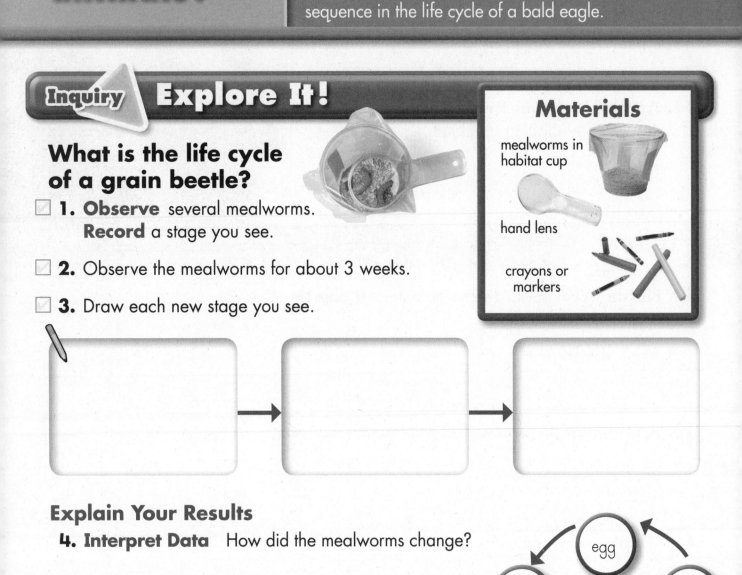

Explain Your Results

4. Interpret Data How did the mealworms change?

....

....

....

myscienceonline.com | **Explore It!** Animation

I will know how different animals grow and change during their life cycles.

Words to Know

larva

pupa

metamorphosis

Life Cycles

An animal's life starts out as an egg. Sometimes the egg develops into a young animal inside the mother's body. Then the mother gives birth to a live young. For other animals, the mother lays an egg outside of her body. Eagles have their young in this way. First, the mother eagle lays an egg. Next, the eaglet, a young eagle, develops inside the egg. Finally, the eaglet hatches when it is ready.

After birth, an animal begins to grow. It develops into an adult and then it can reproduce. Eventually, it dies. Its life cycle is complete.

1. ◉ **Sequence** Complete the graphic organizer to sequence the steps in an eagle's birth.

After they are born, bear cubs grow bigger and develop into adults.

First

Next

Finally

Life Cycle of a Butterfly

The life cycle of a butterfly has four stages, as shown in the diagram. A butterfly looks very different at each stage of its life. It also behaves in different ways.

For example, compare the larva and adult stages in the diagram. A **larva** is the second stage in the life cycle of some insects. A butterfly larva is called a caterpillar. It has a worm-like body. It eats plants. It must eat a lot to grow and store energy.

A **pupa** is the stage in an insect's life cycle between larva and adult. A butterfly pupa is protected inside a hard covering called a chrysalis. It does not eat, and it hardly moves.

The adult butterfly that comes out of the chrysalis looks nothing like the larva that went in. It has wings, long legs, and antennae. Some adult butterflies feed on the nectar of flowers. Some do not feed at all. After laying eggs, the adult butterfly will die.

2. **Apply** In the blank spaces, write titles for stage 2 and stage 3 in the life cycle of the butterfly.

3. **Infer** Why is it important that the butterfly larva store energy by eating a lot?

....

....

....

1 Egg

A butterfly begins life in a tiny egg. The egg in this picture has been magnified, or made to look bigger.

4 Adult Butterfly

The adult butterfly breaks out of the chrysalis. It flies away to find a mate. It will lay eggs if it is a female. Eventually, the butterfly will die.

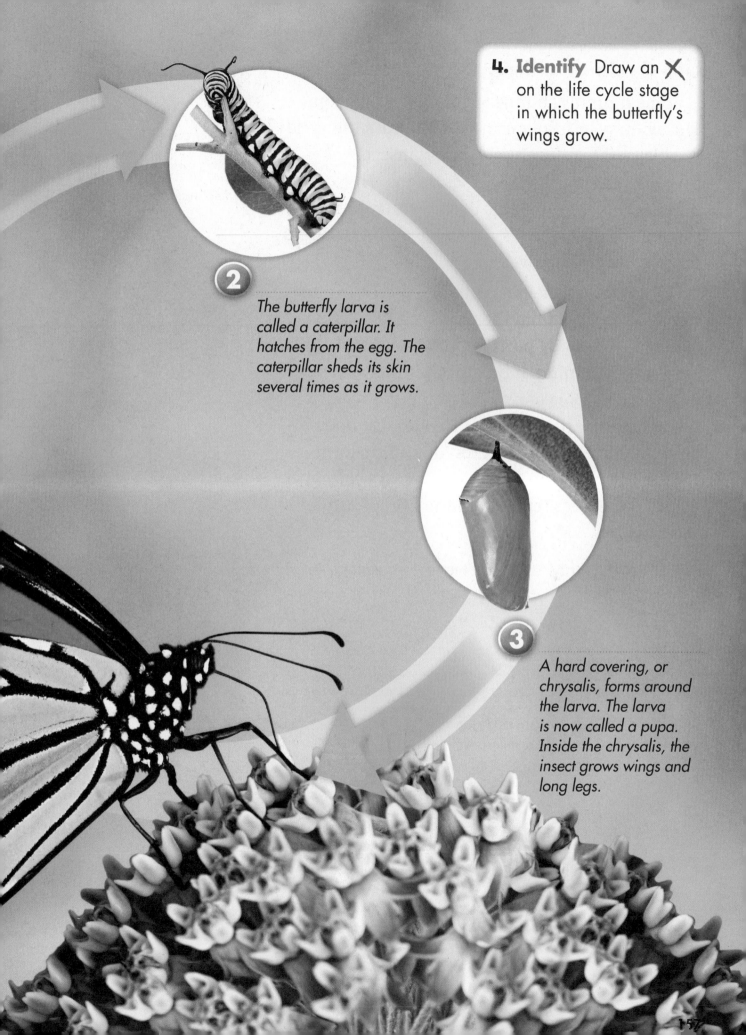

4. Identify Draw an ✗ on the life cycle stage in which the butterfly's wings grow.

2

The butterfly larva is called a caterpillar. It hatches from the egg. The caterpillar sheds its skin several times as it grows.

3

A hard covering, or chrysalis, forms around the larva. The larva is now called a pupa. Inside the chrysalis, the insect grows wings and long legs.

Life Cycle of a Frog

Some animals change form as they develop. This change in form during an animal's life cycle is called **metamorphosis.** Many insects go through metamorphosis. Frogs do too. Frogs are amphibians. Amphibians live in water during some parts of their lives. They live on land during other parts of their lives.

A frog life cycle begins with an egg. The young frog that hatches from the egg is called a tadpole. A tadpole has body parts for living in water. It has a tail for swimming. It breathes with gills like fish do. As the tadpole grows, it develops body parts for living on land. It grows legs. The tail disappears. Lungs replace gills. Finally, an adult frog forms. It uses its legs to hop. An adult frog lays eggs in water. Some frogs reproduce many times before they die.

5. **Identify** Draw an X on the life cycle stage in which the frog lives on land.

 Eggs

Mother frogs often lay hundreds or thousands of eggs in the water. The eggs are surrounded by a jelly-like material.

4 **Adult Frog**

The adult frog lives on land and in water. It returns to the water to lay its eggs.

6. Determine the Factors List body parts and other materials from the diagram that help keep frogs alive and healthy.

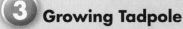

....

....

....

2 **Tadpole**

A tadpole hatches from each frog egg. Tadpoles live underwater and breathe with gills.

3 **Growing Tadpole**

The tadpole changes as it grows. Its tail becomes shorter, and its legs begin to grow. It develops lungs for breathing, and its gills disappear.

Go Green

Frog Habitats
A habitat is the place where a plant or animal lives. Find out where frogs live. Make a list of things that a frog habitat must have so the frog can complete its life cycle. Then explain how you can help protect frog habitats.

Life Cycle of a Mammal

Unlike amphibians and insects, young mammals do not change very much as they become adults. Many mammals look like their parents when they are born. Like you, they grow as they get older.

7. Compare How is a young bobcat similar to an adult bobcat?

8. Contrast In what way is an adult bobcat different from a young bobcat?

....

....

1 Egg
Young bobcats develop from eggs inside the mother's body. They are born when they are ready to live outside the mother's body.

2 Kitten
Young bobcats are called kittens. The mother bobcat's body makes milk. The kittens drink the milk.

3 Growth
The young bobcats grow bigger. The mother bobcat takes care of them.

4 Adult
When the young bobcats grow to be adults, they can reproduce.

Some animals go through their entire life cycle quickly. For example, most insects live for less than one year. Other animals live much longer. The length of an animal's life is called its life span. The graph below shows the life spans of some animals.

9. Analyze What pattern do you see in the graph?
....
....
....
....

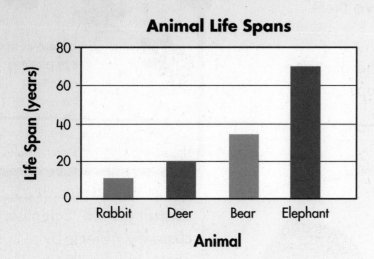

Animal Life Spans

Got it?

10. **UNLOCK THE BIG ?** How is a mammal's life cycle different from a frog or butterfly life cycle?

....
....
....

11. **Describe** How must a frog's body change before it can live on land?

....
....

⬜ **Stop!** I need help with ....

⏸ **Wait!** I have a question about ....

▶ **Go!** Now I know ....

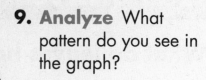

What do leaves have in common?

Follow a Procedure

☐ **1.** Spread out the leaves. **Observe** them. Which have similar shapes?

☐ **2.** Make a yarn circle for each kind of shape. You may have from 3 to 5 groups.

☐ **3. Classify** Place leaves with similar shapes in the same circle.

Materials

10 leaves or leaf pictures

5 yarn circles

Inquiry Skill Scientists **classify** objects by observing their traits.

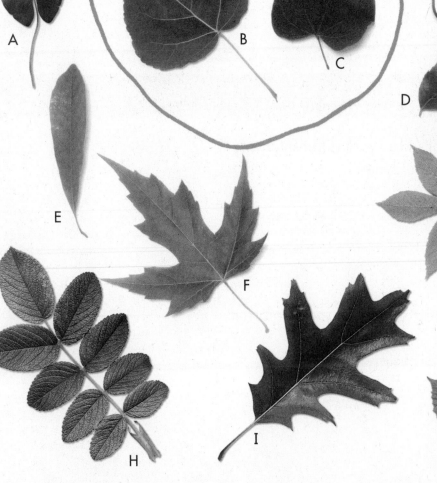

☐ **4. Record** Draw each leaf in its group. Explain how the shapes of each group are alike.

Leaf Observations

Leaf Drawings or Letters of Leaves	How Are the Leaf Shapes Alike?
Group A	
Group B	
Group C	
Group D	
Group E	

Analyze and Conclude

5. Describe another way to **classify** the leaves.

....

6. UNLOCK THE BIG **?** Why might it be helpful to classify leaves?

....

....

STEM Shark Tracking

Scientists track sharks with devices to learn where, when, and why sharks travel the ocean. How does a tracking device work? First, scientists attach the tracking device to the shark's dorsal, or back, fin. Then, when the dorsal fin breaks the surface of the ocean, a radio signal is transmitted to a satellite. Next, the satellite receives the signal and locates the shark. Last, the satellite transmits the shark's position to a central computer. Each time the tag transmits a signal, the computer plots, or marks, its position. These positions are shown on a map. They show the shark's movements over time. Engineering and technology are helping scientists study sharks.

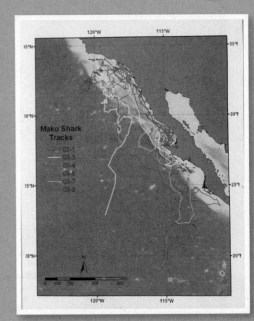

This mako shark was tracked around the Baja Peninsula for several months.

Illustrate Draw an illustration of how the signal from the tracking device goes from the shark to the central computer.

Vocabulary Smart Cards

trait
vertebrate
invertebrate
arthropod
inherit
instinct
larva
pupa
metamorphosis

Play a Game!

Cut out the Vocabulary Smart Cards.

Work with a partner. Spread out two sets of Vocabulary Smart Cards on a table. One set should show the definition, and the other should show the word.

Have your partner pick a card and find the definition that matches the word.

Have your partner repeat with another word.

arthropod

artrópodo

trait

rasgo

inherit

heredar

vertebrate

vertebrado

instinct

instinto

invertebrate

invertebrado

a feature passed on to a living thing from its parents	an animal that has a hard covering outside its body
Use a dictionary. Find as many synonyms for this word as you can.	Write a sentence using this word.
característica que pasa de padres a hijos entre los seres vivos	animal que tiene el cuerpo envuelto por una cubierta dura

Interactive Vocabulary

Make a Word Frame!

Choose a vocabulary word and write it in the center of the frame. Write the definition in the box above. Write examples in the box on the left. Write some things that are not examples in the box on the right. Write something to help you remember this word in the box below.

an animal with a backbone	to receive from a parent
Write three examples.	Write an example of an inherited characteristic.
animal que tiene columna vertebral	recibir de un progenitor

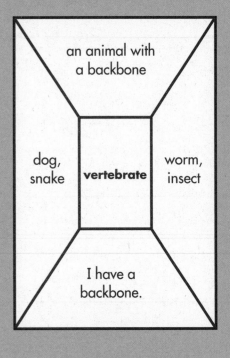

an animal without a backbone	a behavior an animal is born able to do
What is the prefix of this word? What does this prefix mean?	Write a sentence using this word.
animal que no tiene columna vertebral	conducta que tiene un animal desde que nace

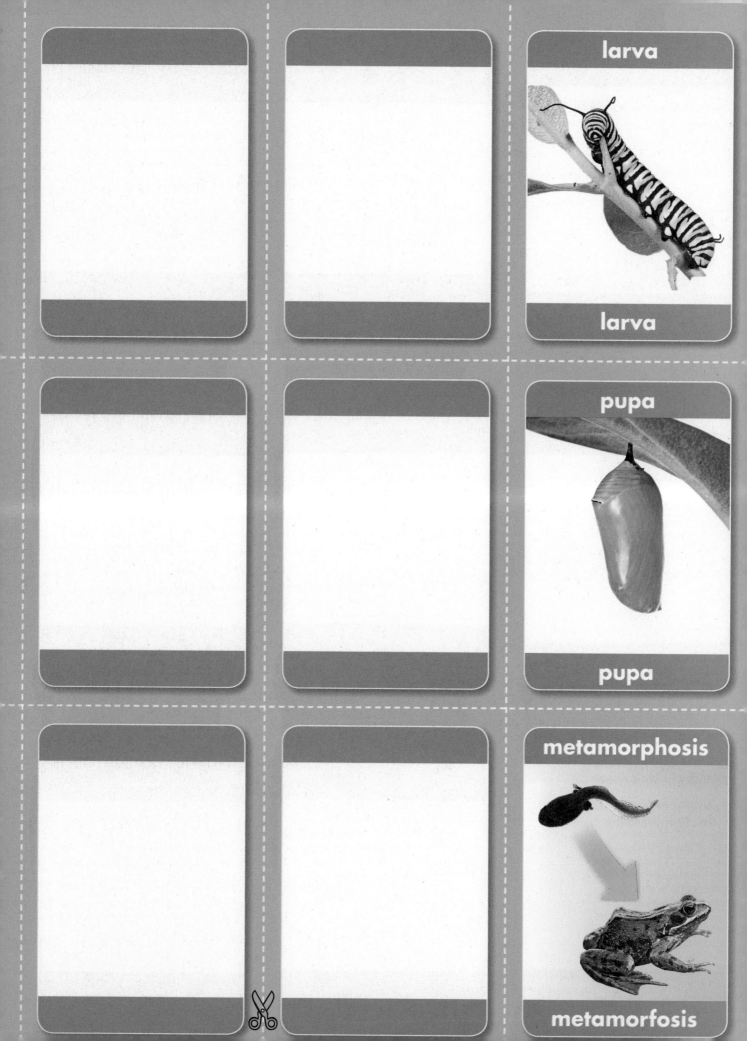

larva

larva

pupa

pupa

metamorphosis

metamorfosis

second stage of the life cycle of some insects

Write a sentence using this word.

....

....

....

segunda etapa del ciclo de vida de algunos insectos

stage of an insect's life cycle between larva and adult

Draw an example.

etapa de la vida de un insecto entre larva y adulto

....

....

....

a change in form during an animal's life cycle

Name two animals that go through metamorphosis.

....

....

....

cambio de la forma de un animal durante su ciclo de vida

....

....

....

Lesson 1

How can you classify animals?

- Animals can be classified according to their characteristics, such as whether or not they have a backbone.
- Some animals hatch from eggs and others have live births.

Lesson 2

How are offspring like their parents?

- Animals and plants inherit certain characteristics from their parents. Other characteristics are acquired.
- Animal behaviors can be inherited or learned.

Lesson 3

What are the life cycles of some animals?

- Some insects and amphibians change form as they develop into adults. This process is called metamorphosis.
- Mammals do not change very much as they become adults.

Chapter Review

REVIEW THE BIG **?**

How do living things grow and change?

Lesson 1

How can you classify animals?

1. **Vocabulary** A(n) _____ is an animal without a backbone.
   A. vertebrate
   B. whale
   C. invertebrate
   D. mammal

2. **Categorize** Why can different animals be grouped in more than one way?

Do the math!

3. What is the difference in speed between a barracuda and the southern bluefin tuna?

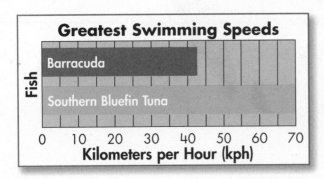

Greatest Swimming Speeds

Fish: Barracuda, Southern Bluefin Tuna

Kilometers per Hour (kph): 0 10 20 30 40 50 60 70

Lesson 2

How are offspring like their parents?

4. **Compare and Contrast** How are young bobcats and their parents alike and different?

5. **Identify** Which of the following is an acquired characteristic?
   A. sunburn
   B. eye color
   C. hair color
   D. height

6. **Suggest** Name one learned behavior and one inherited behavior of a chimpanzee.

Lesson 3

What are the life cycles of some animals?

7. **⊙ Sequence** A monarch butterfly's life cycle has four stages. What is the correct order?
   A. egg, pupa, adult, larva
   B. egg, pupa, larva, adult
   C. egg, larva, pupa, adult
   D. egg, adult, pupa, larva

8. **Vocabulary** A frog's change in form during its life cycle is called a(n) _____.
   A. amphibian
   B. metamorphosis
   C. tadpole
   D. life span

9. **Contrast** How is the birth of a baby chicken different from the birth of a baby cat?

....
....
....
....
....

10. **Write About It** Describe what happens during the pupa stage of a butterfly's life cycle.

....
....
....
....
....
....
....
....
....

11. **APPLY THE BIG ?** **How do living things grow and change?**

Describe the stages in the life cycle of a dog.

....
....
....
....
....
....

Fill in the bubble next to the answer choice you think is correct for each multiple-choice question.

1 Which animal goes through metamorphosis during its life cycle?

Ⓐ duck

Ⓑ cat

Ⓒ butterfly

Ⓓ turtle

2 Which is an example of an instinct?

Ⓐ rowing a boat

Ⓑ reading

Ⓒ hibernating

Ⓓ having curly hair

3 Animals can be divided into two groups based on whether they have _____ or not.

Ⓐ backbones

Ⓑ tails

Ⓒ fur

Ⓓ lungs

4 When a tadpole becomes an adult frog, it _____.

Ⓐ grows a longer tail

Ⓑ breathes with lungs

Ⓒ lives underwater

Ⓓ breathes with gills

5 An inherited trait is one that _____.

Ⓐ you are not born with

Ⓑ is passed on from parents to their offspring

Ⓒ you learn how to do

Ⓓ is passed on from offspring to their parents

6 Name the invertebrate group all of the following animals belong to: mosquito, spider, beetle, and crab.

....

....

Classify Local Animals

Take a look around. You might be surprised at all the animals you can find in your neighborhood. You can find tiny ants living in a crack in the sidewalk. You can see birds flying. You might even see a deer passing through your backyard.

You might look for butterflies in your yard. There are many different kinds of butterflies. Like all insects, butterflies have six legs and three body parts. However, what you are most likely to notice are their colorful wings.

You can classify animals you find. Look for animals with your parent or guardian. Find out if there are more vertebrates or invertebrates in your neighborhood. Write down your descriptions of each animal. Take or draw a picture. Then, use your school library to research these animals.

APPLY THE BIG ? What kinds of animals are in your neighborhood? Were there more vertebrates or invertebrates? How do they change and grow?

....

....

....

Why does the grass need the bison?

Ecosystems

 Try It!   **How can you recycle some materials?**

Lesson 1 **What is an ecosystem?**

Lesson 2 **How do living things get energy?**

Lesson 3 **How do ecosystems change?**

Investigate It! **What can you find in your local ecosystem?**

American bison live on grasslands in the United States. Like many other grassland animals, they depend on grass for food.

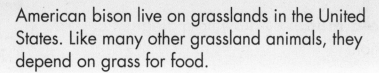

Predict How do you think bison help grassland plants to grow and stay healthy?

....

....

....

 How do living things interact?

How can you recycle some materials?

Recycle, reuse, and reduce to save resources.

☐ **1. Observe** the materials.

☐ **2.** Brainstorm inventions you could make from the materials.

....

....

....

☐ **3.** Select one invention to make from the materials.

☐ **4. Make a model** by drawing a diagram of your invention.

Materials

tape

milk carton scissors

black pen

glue

plastic bottles

☐ **5. Communicate** Share what your invention does.

Explain Your Results

6. **UNLOCK THE BIG ?** **Communicate** Describe how your invention uses recycled materials to save resources.

....

....

....

Cause and Effect

- A **cause** is why something happens. An **effect** is what happens.
- When you read, sometimes clue words such as *because* and *since* signal a cause-and-effect relationship.

The Big Fire

The forest fire started when lightning struck a tree. Because the fire grew quickly, firefighters had trouble putting it out. The fire destroyed hundreds of acres of woodland. It killed trees, grasses, and other plants. Because animals could not find food and shelter, they moved to other places.

Apply It!

Use the graphic organizer below to write a cause and effect found in the example paragraph.

Cause

Effect

What is an ecosystem?

Circle two living things in the picture.
Draw an **X** on two nonliving things.

my planet Diary — Connections

Wetlands once covered about 392 million acres (159 million hectares) in what is now the United States. Today, Alaska, Florida, Louisiana, Minnesota, and Texas have the most acres of wetlands. Alaska has lost little of its wetlands. But wetlands in many other states are disappearing. Consider Louisiana. The state loses areas of wetlands the size of a football field every 30 minutes!

You can use geography skills to understand how Louisiana's wetlands are changing. Look at the maps. The first map shows Louisiana's coast in 1839. The second map shows the same coast more than 150 years later. The green areas are areas of wetland. Notice the changes.

Draw on the 1993 map. Use a red pencil to show how you think the map would change if wetland loss continues.

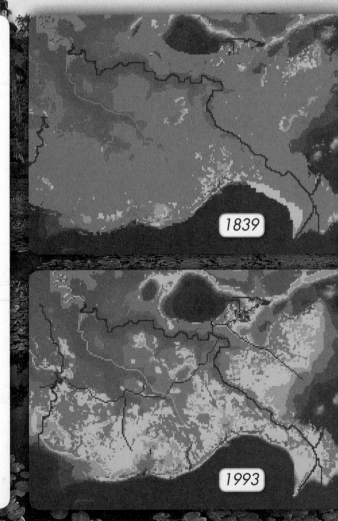

1839

1993

myscienceonline.com | my planet Diary

UNLOCK THE BIG ?

I will know how living and nonliving things interact in an ecosystem.

Words to Know

ecosystem population
habitat community

Places for Living Things

How is the place where a bear lives different from the place where an earthworm lives? Each kind of living thing needs a certain environment. A living thing's environment is everything around it. An environment has living and nonliving parts. The living parts include plants, animals, and other living things.

Sunlight is a nonliving part of an environment. The sun's rays warm other nonliving parts, such as air, water, and soil. Because of the sun's heat, Earth's air, water, and soil are warm enough for living things.

1. **Apply** What parts of an environment are affected by the sun's heat?

2. **Describe** Explain how bears interact with living and nonliving things.

Parts of an Ecosystem

The living and nonliving parts of an environment interact. *Interact* means to act together. These interacting parts make up an **ecosystem.** The pictures on these pages show a marsh. A marsh is a type of wetland ecosystem.

The living parts of an ecosystem depend on nonliving parts. For example, plants need sunlight, soil, air, and water to grow. The living parts also depend on one another. For example, animals eat other living things. Some animals use plants for shelter.

3. Identify Draw another living thing you might find in this wetland. Tell how it interacts in the ecosystem.

Box turtles live on land near wetlands. Marsh and pond turtles live in the water.

4. Predict Tell what might happen to a marsh turtle if the water in the ecosystem dried up.

Water is a nonliving part of wetlands. Plants and animals need water to live and grow.

Grasses grow in marsh wetlands. They need sunlight, soil, air, and lots of water.

Great egrets eat fish, frogs, and other small animals that live in the marsh.

5. **Predict** How do you think turtles interact with insects in the ecosystem?

....

....

6. **Describe** How might this raccoon interact with living and nonliving things in this marsh?

....

....

....

....

....

Raccoons eat plants, fish, and small animals that live in the marsh. They often sleep in nearby trees.

This monkey's habitat is the trees in a rain forest.

Habitats

The place where a living thing makes its home is its **habitat.** A habitat has everything that a plant or animal needs to live. A habitat can be the water in a wetland. It can be the soil beneath a rock or even a crack in a sidewalk.

7. Describe What is the habitat of the bluespot butterflyfish in the picture below?

Groups Within Ecosystems

All the living things of the same kind that live in the same place make up a **population.** The coral reef ecosystem shown below includes many different populations. For example, all of the bluespot butterflyfish living around the reef make up one population. A coral reef also may have populations of crabs, clams, sharks, and other animals.

All the populations that live in the same place make up a **community.** Populations in a community depend on each other.

8. Apply Circle a living thing that is not part of the bluespot butterflyfish population in this coral reef community.

Three bluespot butterflyfish swim over a coral reef.

myscienceonline.com | Got it? 60-Second Video

Ecosystems Change

Ecosystems may change over time. When one part of an ecosystem changes, other parts are affected too. For example, a hurricane may damage the fruit trees in a forest where monkeys live. The monkeys may not be able to find enough fruit to eat. The monkey population may become smaller. Then there would be less food for animals that feed on monkeys. Their populations might become smaller too.

9. ◉ **Cause and Effect** (Circle) one cause in the text. **Underline** one effect.

10. **Suggest** What is another way an ecosystem could be destroyed?

....

At-Home Lab

Local Ecosystem
Observe a terrarium ecosystem or an ecosystem in a park or your backyard. In a science notebook, list the living and nonliving parts. How do the living things get what they need from the ecosystem?

Got it?

11. **UNLOCK THE BIG ?** Think about what you learned in this lesson. How do living things interact?

....

....

12. **Describe** How do living and nonliving things interact in a wetland ecosystem such as a marsh?

....

....

☐ **Stop!** I need help with ....

❚❚ **Wait!** I have a question about ....

▶ **Go!** Now I know ....

How do living things get energy?

Envision It!

Circle a living thing that can make its own food.

Inquiry **Explore It!**

What do yeast use for energy?

☑ **1.** Shake $\frac{1}{2}$ spoonful of yeast on a watermelon slice.

☑ **2.** Put the watermelon slice in the bag. Seal it. Set it in a warm place. **Observe** with a hand lens.

☑ **3.** After 1, 2, and 3 hours, observe the yeast. **Record** any changes.

Materials

watermelon slice

yeast

plastic bag

spoon

hand lens

Yeast Observations	
Time	Appearance of Yeast on Watermelon Slice
After 1 hour	
After 2 hours	
After 3 hours	

Explain Your Results

4. Infer Where did the yeast get the energy to grow?

....

....

myscienceonline.com | **Explore It!** Animation

Draw an ✗ on a living thing that must eat food to get energy.

UNLOCK THE BIG ?

I will know how energy flows through ecosystems in a food chain. I will know how a food web is organized.

Words to Know

producer   decomposer
consumer   food chain

Energy Roles in Ecosystems

Every living thing needs energy to stay alive and grow. Living things get energy in different ways. Green plants use sunlight along with air and water to make sugar. The sugar is the plants' food. It gives plants the energy they need. A living thing is called a **producer** if it makes, or produces, its own food.

Many living things cannot make food. They get energy from food that they eat, or consume. A living thing that eats other organisms is called a **consumer.**

When plants or animals die, their stored-up energy is unused. Decomposers use this energy. A **decomposer** is a living thing that breaks down waste and dead plant and animal matter.

1. **Label** Write whether the living thing in each picture is a producer, consumer, or decomposer.

Puffins eat fish to get energy.

....

Mushrooms break down a dead tree for energy.

....

A fern plant takes in sunlight to make food.

....

Food Chains

Most ecosystems get energy from sunlight. Plants and other producers transform the sun's energy into food energy. This food energy from producers can be passed along a food chain. A **food chain** is the transfer of energy from one living thing to another.

In a food chain diagram, arrows show the flow of energy. The first link in the food chain on these pages is the sun. A producer, such as grass, is the next link. The producer uses the sun's energy to make food. Next, a consumer, such as a prairie dog, eats the producer. The producer passes energy to the consumer. That consumer may then be eaten by another consumer, such as an eagle. In this way, energy from a producer can be passed from one consumer to another.

The consumers in a food chain can be classified by what they eat. Some consumers eat only plants. They are called *herbivores*. Some consumers eat only other animals. They are called *carnivores*. Other consumers eat both plants and animals. They are called *omnivores*.

2. **Explain** Complete the captions in the diagram to explain how energy is transferred in this food chain.

3. **Identify** Draw an ✗ on the consumer that is an herbivore. (Circle) the consumer that is a carnivore.

4. **Infer** Decomposers are not shown in the diagram. Tell what role you think they play in this food chain.

Grassland Ecosystem

A food chain begins with energy from the ....

Golden eagles eat prairie dogs. Energy passes from the .... to the ....

Grasses use air, water, and energy from the .... to make food.

Prairie dogs eat grass. Energy passes from the .... to the ....

Food Webs

Do you eat the same food at every meal? Some animals do not always eat the same things either. Ecosystems have many food chains. Food chains combine to form a food web. A food web is a system of overlapping food chains in an ecosystem. Food webs show that energy flows in many different ways in an ecosystem. Energy can flow from one producer to many consumers. One consumer can be eaten by many other consumers.

5. **Draw** an ✗ on the consumer in this food web that is an omnivore.

6. **Identify** List the consumers in this food web that eat prairie dogs.

....

....

....

This diagram shows an example of a food web from the Great Plains.

myscienceonline.com | Got it? 🕐 60-Second Video

Changes in Food Webs

All of the living things in a food web are connected. If one part of a food web is removed or changed, other parts change. For example, prairie dogs build colonies on the grassy plains. But people also settle on these plains. This reduces the habitat for prairie dogs. Their numbers may decrease. With fewer prairie dogs to eat, black-footed ferrets may not have the food they need. The ferrets may die out. This change can affect the badgers who eat ferrets. Badgers may have to look for other food.

7. ◎ **Cause and Effect** <u>Underline</u> two effects in the text that may result if the number of prairie dogs is reduced.

Lightning Lab

Draw a Food Web
Choose an ecosystem such as a forest or ocean. Draw a food web that shows how energy is transferred from one living thing to another. Tell what might happen if part of the food web disappeared.

Got it?

8. ◎ **Compare and Contrast** How are food chains and food webs alike and different?

....

....

9. **UNLOCK THE BIG ?** Think about what you learned about food chains and food webs. How do living things interact?

....

....

....

▢ **Stop!** I need help with ....

Ⅱ **Wait!** I have a question about ....

▶ **Go!** Now I know ....

How do ecosystems change?

Tell how this forest fire will affect the living things in this ecosystem.

Inquiry Explore It!

How can pollution affect an organism?

☐ **1. Measure** Add 30 mL of water to Cup A. Add 30 mL of vinegar to Cup B.

☐ **2.** Add 1 spoonful of sugar and $\frac{1}{2}$ spoonful of yeast to both cups. Stir gently.

30 mL water
$\frac{1}{2}$ spoonful yeast
1 spoonful sugar

30 mL vinegar
$\frac{1}{2}$ spoonful yeast
1 spoonful sugar

☐ **3.** Put the cups in a warm place.

☐ **4. Observe** the yeast after 5, 10, and 15 minutes.

Explain Your Results

5. Infer Which cup is a **model** of a polluted habitat for yeast? Explain.

Materials

safety goggles

2 plastic cups

vinegar

graduated cylinder

spoon

water

yeast

sugar

clock

mysienceonline.com | **Explore It!** Animation

UNLOCK THE BIG ?

I will know how ecosystems change. I will know that some changes can help and other changes can harm the living things in an ecosystem.

Word to Know

adaptation

Tell another way that a forest ecosystem could change.

Ecosystem Change

Ecosystems are always changing. These changes can be rapid and widespread, such as when a fire burns through a forest. But even smaller changes can have many effects.

Think about what happens when a 200-year-old tree falls in a storm. Throughout its life, the tree shaded the forest floor. Now the forest floor will receive much more sunlight. Seedlings that require a lot of sunlight will have a chance to grow. Other plants that grow best in shade might not survive.

The change may affect animals too. Birds that nested in the tree may need to find a new home. But the fallen tree may provide habitat for salamanders and other animals.

A fallen tree provides shelter for a salamander.

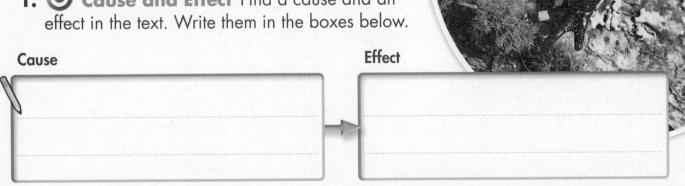

1. ◎ **Cause and Effect** Find a cause and an effect in the text. Write them in the boxes below.

Cause

Effect

Living Things Cause Change

All living things need resources like water and food. Living things get what they need from their environments. As they do this, they cause changes in their environments. For example, people cut down trees to build homes. They clear land in order to grow food in open fields. But people are not the only living things that cause change.

Look at the groundhogs in the pictures. Groundhogs live underground in tunnels, or burrows. As they dig their burrows, they change the environment. These changes can be harmful. Groundhogs can damage crops, lawns, and the roots of trees. But some living things benefit from changes that groundhogs cause. Foxes, rabbits, and other animals often live in burrows made by groundhogs. Groundhogs also improve soil by mixing it as they dig. This benefits plants that grow in the soil.

2. **Evaluate** What is one positive effect of the changes groundhogs cause? What is one negative effect?

....

....

....

....

....

A groundhog burrow can have many rooms and entrances.

myscienceonline.com | THE BIG ? | I Will Know...

Read a Graph

Mexican gray wolves used to live in parts of the southwest United States. But as more people settled in this area, the wolves' ecosystem changed. Wolves had less space in which to live. Eventually, wolves disappeared from the region. In 1998, scientists began a project to raise more wolves and release them into the wild. This graph shows changes in the wolf population during the first ten years of the project.

Changes in Wolf Population

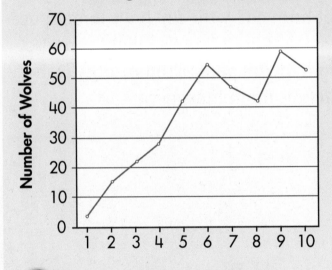

3 **Summarize** How did the size of the wolf population change during the first ten years of the project?

....

....

....

1 **Determine** During which years did the population of wolves increase each year?
A. Year 1 to Year 6
B. Year 6 to Year 8
C. Year 6 to Year 9
D. Year 1 to Year 9

4 **Predict** What is one factor that could stop the wolf population from growing? Explain.

....

....

....

....

2 **Identify** In which year was the wolf population the largest?

3. **Underline** four things in the text that can change ecosystems.

4. **Infer** In some areas, forest rangers start forest fires on purpose. Why do you think they might do this?

Natural Events Cause Change

Natural events can also change ecosystems. Fires can burn forests. Hurricanes can wash away beaches and knock down trees. They can also cause floods. Floods change ecosystems too. They kill plants and can destroy animal habitats.

Droughts can also change ecosystems. During a drought, very little rain falls. Plants die from lack of water. If animals cannot find enough water, then they may die or move to other places.

Not all living things are harmed by changes to ecosystems. A forest fire may destroy many trees and animals' homes. But the fire also clears dead plants and wood from the forest floor. Then trees that were not harmed by the fire have more space to grow. Plants that need more sunlight can also grow. Ash from the fire makes soil healthy. Ash contains minerals that plants need.

Go Green

Conserve Water
All living things need water. Droughts affect people, plants, and animals. Think about how you use water each day. Create a list of ways that you can save water. Share your list with a partner.

Plants grow in an area cleared by fire.

Seasonal Change

In some ecosystems, the cycle of the seasons brings major changes. For example, summers may be warm, but winters may be very cold and snowy. Some plants die in winter. Food may be hard to find for some animals.

Many plants and animals have adaptations that help them survive these changes. An **adaptation** is a trait that helps a living thing survive in its environment. For example, some trees shed their leaves before winter. This reduces the amount of water they need to take in during winter. Some animals, such as bats and ground squirrels, hibernate, or sleep, through the winter.

Some trees shed their leaves in winter. When spring comes, new leaves will grow.

5. **Word Structure** You can change some verbs to nouns by adding the suffix *–ion*. For example, the word *adaptation* comes from the verb *adapt*. Write the verbs that the nouns below are based on. Say a sentence using each word.

hibernation ....

migration ....

6. [CHALLENGE] Do you think the tree in the pictures makes food during the winter? Explain.

....

....

Some birds migrate, or move, to warmer places during winter. This golden plover will travel more than a thousand miles when it migrates.

Living Things Return

On May 18, 1980, the volcano Mount St. Helens erupted in the state of Washington. This eruption was huge. The blast changed the ecosystem. It knocked over trees. It burned whole forests and killed many animals. Rivers of mud covered large areas. The volcano released a cloud of ash into the air. Winds carried the ash around the world.

There were few signs of life after the eruption. Over time, however, wind carried the seeds of grasses, flowers, and trees to the mountain. New plants began to grow. Soon spiders and beetles arrived. Birds returned to live in the standing dead trees. Small and large mammals also returned. Each new change allowed more kinds of plants and animals to live there again. The ecosystem is not the same as it was before the eruption. But it is recovering.

Ash poured from Mount St. Helens for nine hours after the eruption.

7. **Generalize** What generalization can you make about ecosystems based on Mount St. Helens?

....

....

....

....

Few plants and animals remained alive on Mount St. Helens after the eruption. Some animals that lived underground survived.

8. **Infer** Look at the pictures. Why do you think plants returned to Mount St. Helens before insects and other animals did?

Got it?

9. **UNLOCK THE BIG ?** Give an example of how an animal can cause a change in an ecosystem that harms other living things.

10. **Explain** Describe two ways a forest fire can be helpful to plants.

⬜ **Stop!** I need help with ....

⏸ **Wait!** I have a question about ....

▶ **Go!** Now I know ....

What can you find in your local ecosystem?

Follow a Procedure

☐ **1.** Use 2 strings to divide a square meter of land into 4 squares. **Measure** the length of each side to make sure the sections are squares. Use index cards to label the squares A, B, C, and D.

☐ **2.** Use a hand lens to look for living things in Square A. **Record** the living things you **observe.**

☐ **3.** Observe the nonliving things. Record the things you find.

☐ **4.** Repeat for each square.

Materials

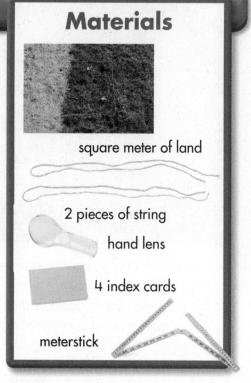

square meter of land

2 pieces of string

hand lens

4 index cards

meterstick

Be careful! **Wash your hands when finished.**

Inquiry Skill
When you record information you have **observed,** you are collecting data.

Observations		
Square	Living Things	Nonliving Things
A		
B		
C		
D		

Analyze and Conclude

5. What living things were present in the most squares?

....

....

....

6. **ANSWER THE BIG ?** What nonliving things did you **observe** in your investigation?

....

....

....

....

....

Minnesota Valley National Wildlife Refuge, Minnesota

THE NATIONAL WILDLIFE REFUGE SYSTEM

The National Wildlife Refuge System was started more than 100 years ago. Its purpose was to set aside land to save plant and animal species. Today, the system includes more than 550 refuges. There is at least one refuge in every state. In fact, there is probably a refuge close enough for you to visit.

A refuge does more than protect individual plants and animals. It also protects habitats. Different refuges protect different types of habitats. For example, Minnesota Valley National Wildlife Refuge provides wetland habitat for migrating ducks. It is one of the few urban refuges in the country. More than three million people live in the area surrounding the refuge.

blue-winged teal

white-tailed antelope squirrel

Stillwater National Wildlife Refuge, Nevada

REVIEW THE BIG ? Why is protecting habitats important to saving plant and animal species?

Parker River National Wildlife Refuge, Massachusetts

common snapping turtle

Vocabulary Smart Cards

ecosystem
habitat
population
community
producer
consumer
decomposer
food chain
adaptation

Play a Game!

Cut out the Vocabulary Smart Cards.

Work with a partner. Choose a Vocabulary Smart Card.

Write two or three sentences using the vocabulary word.

Have your partner repeat with another Vocabulary Smart Card.

community

comunidad

ecosystem

ecosistema

producer

productor

habitat

hábitat

consumer

consumidor

population

población

the living and nonliving
things that interact in an
environment

Write an example of this
word.

....

....

todos los seres vivos y
las cosas sin vida que
interactúan en un área
determinada

---

all the populations that live
in the same place

Write a sentence using this
word.

....

....

....

....

todas las poblaciones que
conviven en el mismo lugar

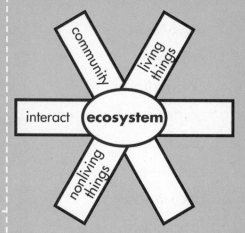

Make a Word Wheel!

Choose a vocabulary word
and write it in the center of
the Word Wheel graphic.
Write synonyms or related
words on the wheel spokes.

---

the place where a living
thing makes its home

Draw an example.

el lugar donde un ser vivo
establece su hogar

---

a living thing that makes, or
produces, its own food

Write a sentence using this
word.

....

....

....

ser vivo que genera,
o produce, su propio
alimento

---

all the living things of the
same kind that live in the
same place

What is the suffix of this
word?

....

....

....

todos los seres vivos de la
misma especie que viven en
el mismo lugar

---

a living thing that eats other
organisms

Write the verb form of this
word.

....

....

....

ser vivo que se alimenta de
otros organismos

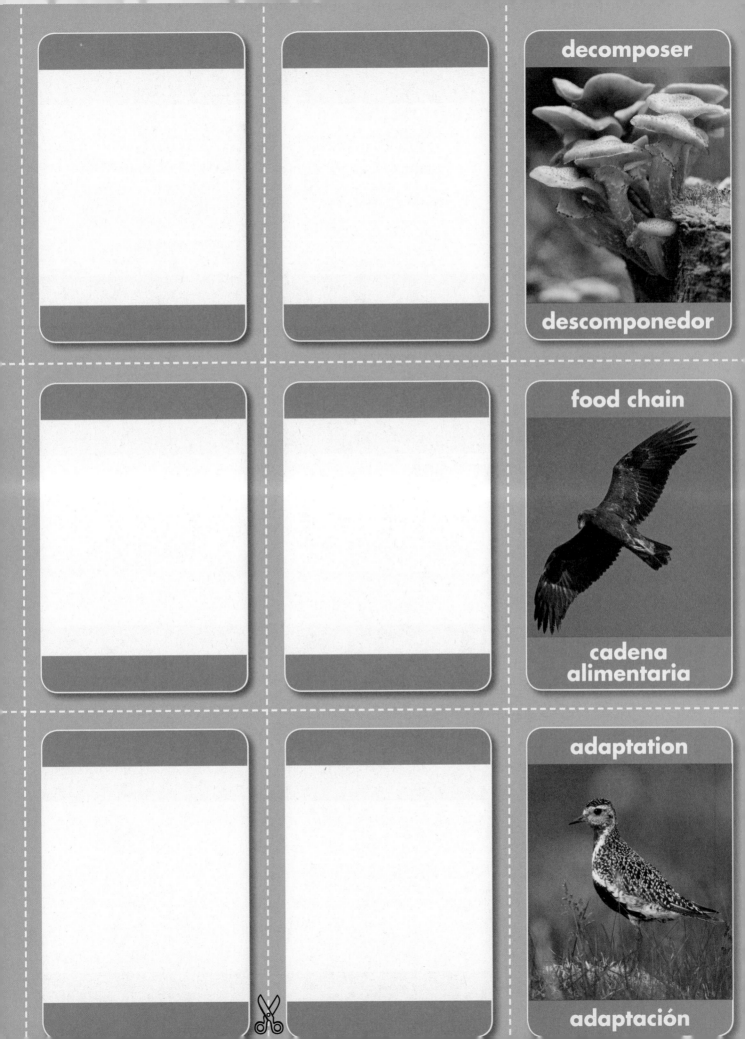

decomposer

descomponedor

food chain

cadena alimentaria

adaptation

adaptación

a living thing that breaks down waste and dead plant and animal matter

Write an example of this word.

....

....

....

ser vivo que destruye residuos y materia de animales y vegetales muertos

---

the transfer of energy from one living thing to another

Draw an example.

transmisión de energía de un ser vivo a otro

---

a trait that helps a living thing survive in its environment

Write an example of this word.

....

....

....

rasgo de los seres vivos que los ayuda a sobrevivir en su medio ambiente

Lesson 1

What is an ecosystem?

- An ecosystem is all the living and nonliving things that interact in an environment.
- Populations and communities are groups within ecosystems.

Lesson 2

How do living things get energy?

- The sun's energy flows to living things through a food chain.
- A food web is a system of overlapping food chains in an ecosystem.

Lesson 3

How do ecosystems change?

- Living things can cause changes in their environment.
- Changes can help some living things and harm others.
- Natural events, such as droughts, can change ecosystems.

Chapter Review

REVIEW THE BIG ?

How do living things interact?

Lesson 1

What is an ecosystem?

1. **Vocabulary** All the populations living in the same place form a(n)_____.
   A. community
   B. resource
   C. ecosystem
   D. habitat

2. **Predict** Desert snakes eat kangaroo rats. What do you think would happen to the population of rats if the population of snakes grew larger? Why?

3. **Write About It** Describe how a raccoon in a marsh interacts with a living part and a nonliving part of the ecosystem.

Lesson 2

How do living things get energy?

4. **Vocabulary** A living thing that breaks down waste and dead plant and animal matter is called a ___.
   A. carnivore
   B. producer
   C. consumer
   D. decomposer

5. **Identify** Which of the following is an example of an herbivore?
   A. coyote
   B. golden eagle
   C. grasshopper
   D. snake

6. **Suggest** List three living things that might be part of a prairie food chain. Explain how they get energy.

Lesson 3

How do ecosystems change?

7. Look at the graph below. Describe the overall change in the wolf population from Year 5 to Year 10.

....

....

....

Changes in Wolf Population

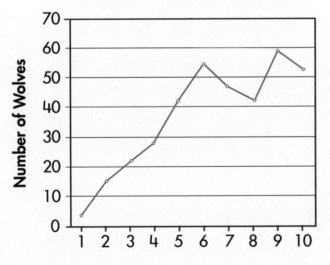

8. Give an Example Describe an adaptation that helps an animal survive seasonal changes in its ecosystem.

....

....

9. ◉ **Cause and Effect** Forest fires can change ecosystems. Describe a negative effect and a positive effect of a forest fire.

....

....

....

....

....

....

....

....

10. **APPLY THE BIG ？** **How do living things interact?**

....

Think about an ecosystem that may be affected by humans. Describe one example of how humans interact with the living things in the ecosystem.

....

....

....

....

....

Fill in the bubble next to the answer choice you think is correct for each multiple-choice question.

1 Which of the following is an example of a decomposer?

Ⓐ the sun
Ⓑ a grasshopper
Ⓒ a mushroom
Ⓓ a bear

2 What do sunlight, soil, air, and water all have in common?

Ⓐ They are nonliving parts of an ecosystem.
Ⓑ They are a community.
Ⓒ They are living parts of an ecosystem.
Ⓓ They are part of a population.

3 Which statement is true about how changes in the environment affect the living things in an ecosystem?

Ⓐ Changes harm all living things.
Ⓑ Changes benefit all living things.
Ⓒ Changes harm some living things and benefit others.
Ⓓ Changes are not harmful.

4 Some trees shed their leaves before winter. What is this an example of?

Ⓐ an adaptation
Ⓑ a competition
Ⓒ an ecosystem
Ⓓ a population

5 Which of the following is an example of an interaction between a living part of an ecosystem and a nonliving part?

Ⓐ bird nesting in a tree
Ⓑ snake eating an insect
Ⓒ frog hiding under a lily pad
Ⓓ fish finding shelter in water

6 Think about what humans eat. What type of consumer are most humans?

....

....

myscienceonline.com | Benchmark Practice

Zoo Designer

Have you ever wondered who designs zoos? A zoo designer plans new zoos or improves older ones. Zoo designers build safe environments that meet the animals' needs. Animals in a zoo come from many different places. Each kind of animal is adapted to a specific environment. Some animals have special adaptations to help meet their needs. A zoo designer has to understand each animal's adaptations.

For example, a polar bear has thick fur that keeps it warm in an arctic environment. A zoo designer needs to make a cold-weather environment that meets the polar bear's adaptation. Some zoo designers design a space based on an animal's adaptation to seasons. For example, penguins are from Antarctica. The lighting of penguin exhibits mimics the amount of light in Antarctica in different seasons.

Name an animal. How do you think a zoo designer would build a habitat to meet the needs of this animal?

Materials

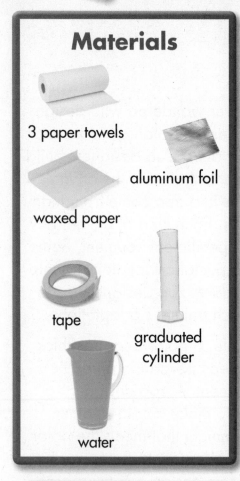

3 paper towels

aluminum foil

waxed paper

tape

graduated cylinder

water

Inquiry Skill
Every experiment must have a **hypothesis,** a testable statement.

How can plants survive in the desert?

Some plants have flat leaves. Many cactus plants have leaves shaped like needles. Some leaves have a waxy coating. The shape of the leaf helps the plant survive.

Ask a question.

How can a leaf's structure help a plant hold water?

State a hypothesis.

1. Write a **hypothesis.** Circle one choice and finish the sentence. If a leaf is narrow and thin and has a waxy coating, it will lose water
   (a) *more slowly*
   (b) *more quickly*
   than flat leaves or leaves without a waxy coating because

   ....

   ....

   ....

Identify and control variables.

2. In an **experiment** you change only one **variable.** Everything else must remain the same. What must stay the same? Give one example.

   ....

   ....

3. Tell the one change you will make.

   ....

   ....

Design your test.

☑ **4.** Draw how you will set up your test.

☑ **5.** List your steps in the order you will do them.

Do your test.

☐ **6.** Follow the steps you wrote.

☐ **7. Record** your results in the table.

Work Like a Scientist
It is important to make careful observations. Record all of your observations. Use charts or graphs to help you record.

Collect and record your data.

☐ **8.** After one day, describe your towels in the chart below.

Interpret your data.

☑ **9.** Compare how damp the towels were after one day.

....

....

....

....

☑ **10.** How does the shape and size of a leaf affect how fast a leaf loses water? Why?

....

....

....

....

☐ **11.** How does a waxy coating help a plant?

....

....

State your conclusion.

12. You conducted an **experiment** to test your **hypothesis.** Compare your hypothesis with your results. **Communicate** your conclusions.

....

....

....

13. Infer What are 2 adaptations cactuses have that help them survive in the desert?

....

....

Germinating Seeds

Seeds need the right conditions to germinate and grow. Use plastic cups, potting soil, and bean seeds to find out how well seeds germinate and grow with different amounts of water.

• What happened when you watered the seeds too much?

• What happened when you watered the seeds too little?

Animals and Seasons

Different animals respond to seasons and temperatures in different ways. Think about three animals in your area. Draw pictures of how they look and where they live during summer. Then draw pictures of how they look and where they live during winter. Write a description of the ways that the animals in your area respond to changing seasons.

• Why do you think animals respond to changing seasons?

Using Scientific Methods

1. Ask a question.
2. State your hypothesis.
3. Identify and control variables.
4. Test your hypothesis.
5. Collect and record your data.
6. Interpret your data.
7. State your conclusion.
8. Go further.

Life Cycle Poster

Choose an animal that lives in your state. Make a poster that shows the stages in the animal's life cycle. The poster should include:

• pictures of what the animal looks like at each stage of development

• captions describing how the animal changes at each stage

• arrows connecting the stages in the correct sequence

Earth Science

How can a tree break apart a mountain?

Earth and Weather

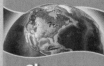

Try It! How does water temperature affect evaporation?

Lesson 1 What is the water cycle?

Lesson 2 What are weather and climate?

Lesson 3 What are minerals and rocks?

Lesson 4 What is soil?

Lesson 5 How do we describe features of Earth's surface?

Lesson 6 What are weathering and erosion?

Investigate It! What can cause rock to crack?

Rocks and mountains never seem to change. However, features of Earth's surface are always changing. Plants and other living things play a role in changing Earth's surface.

Predict How could a tree break apart rock?

....

....

....

THE BIG ? How do forces cause changes on Earth's surface?

How does water temperature affect evaporation?

When water changes from a liquid to a gas, it evaporates.

☑ 1. **Predict** how water temperature affects evaporation.

....

....

☑ 2. Choose a water and fill the plastic cup halfway. Write the temperature on the cup.

☑ 3. Put the lid on the cup.

☑ 4. Put an ice cube on the lid.

☑ 5. **Observe** Describe what you see in your cup. Compare your results with other groups.

....

....

....

....

Explain Your Results

6. **Draw a Conclusion** How did water temperature affect evaporation?

....

....

....

Materials

plastic cup

ice cube

lid

water (cold, room temperature, warm)

Inquiry Skill
You use what you observe to help **draw a conclusion.**

● Sequence

The order in which events happen is the **sequence** of those events. Sequence can also mean the steps you follow to do something.

Tornado!

The air was humid on that day, and the sky looked dark and greenish. First, the tornado sirens began to wail. People took cover underground. Next, hailstones started to fall. The wind began knocking down trees and poles. Finally, the tornado arrived. It sounded like a freight train as it ripped off roofs, pulled up trees, and overturned cars.

Practice It!

Use the graphic organizer to list the sequence of events in the paragraph above.

First

_____

_____

↓

Next

_____

_____

↓

Finally

_____

_____

What is the water cycle?

Envision It!

Circle the places where you think there is water.

my planet diary

Connections

Baton Rouge   Biloxi   Mobile
Houston   Pensacola   Tallahassee
            New Orleans
                                                    Tampa
                                            Fort Myers
Corpus Christi

Gulf of Mexico

You can use a map and your geography skills to help you understand why some places have a lot of storms. Did you know that New Orleans, Louisiana, is the third wettest city in the United States? This city gets about 162 cm (64 in.) of rain each year. Why does New Orleans get so much rain? Blame it on the Gulf of Mexico. Storms from the Atlantic Ocean pick up moisture from the warm waters of the Gulf. These storms then drop heavy rainfall as they move over land.

Look at the map. What other places might get a lot of rain? Explain why.

....

....

....

UNLOCK THE BIG ?

I will know the processes of the water cycle.

Words to Know
....
condensation
evaporation
water cycle
precipitation

Water on Earth

You could call Earth "the blue planet." That is because nearly three-fourths of Earth's surface is covered by water. Most water is in the ocean.

Earth's water is found in different forms. It can move from one place to another. Suppose you follow a particle of water for a year. First, you might find the water particle crashing on a beach in an ocean wave. Next, you might find it drifting in the sky as part of a cloud. Finally, you might find it floating down as snow.

Most of Earth's water is salty ocean water.

1. ◎ **Sequence** Read the second paragraph again. Complete the graphic organizer to show the cycle of a water particle.

First

> ....

Next

> Drifting in the sky as part of a cloud

Finally

> ....

Reduce Water Use

There is only a certain amount of fresh water on Earth. It must be used again and again. Think about how you use water. Describe three ways that you could use less water.

Condensation

The water vapor rises into the air and cools. As it cools, the vapor changes into tiny water droplets. This change from a gas into a liquid is called **condensation.** The water droplets collect and form clouds.

2. **Underline** the words in the caption that tell what *condensation* means.

Evaporation

The sun's warmth causes water on Earth's surface to evaporate. **Evaporation** is the change from liquid water to water vapor, a gas.

Water Cycle

The movement of water from Earth's surface into the air and back again is the **water cycle.** The water cycle is important because it gives Earth a constant supply of fresh water. Most of Earth's water is salty ocean water that you cannot drink.

Water changes form, or state, as it moves through the water cycle. After water moves through the stages of the water cycle, the cycle begins again. Read the captions and follow the arrows to find out more.

Precipitation

Water particles in the clouds join together. When they become heavy, they fall to Earth as rain, snow, sleet, or hail. Water that falls to Earth is called **precipitation.**

Storage

Some precipitation seeps into the ground. Other precipitation, called runoff, flows over the land and collects in streams, lakes, and the ocean.

Got it?

3. **Identify** List the steps of the water cycle.

....

....

4. **Conclude** Why is the sun important to the water cycle?

....

....

....

☐ **Stop!** I need help with ....

❚❚ **Wait!** I have a question about ....

▶ **Go!** Now I know ....

Lesson 2

What are weather and climate?

Envision It!

Describe the weather in the picture.

Inquiry **Explore It!**

How does an anemometer work?

☐ **1.** Make an anemometer like the one in the picture.

Mark the bottom of one cup with an X.

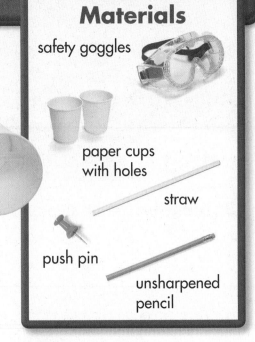

☐ **2.** Use your anemometer to **measure** the wind in different places. **Observe.**

Materials

safety goggles

paper cups with holes

straw

push pin

unsharpened pencil

 **Be careful!** **Wear safety goggles.**

Explain Your Results

3. Communicate Tell how your anemometer works.

....

....

....

....

myscienceonline.com | **Explore It!** Animation

UNLOCK THE BIG ?

I will know the difference between weather and climate. I will know how tools are used to measure weather conditions.

Words to Know

weather   atmosphere
climate   humidity

Why We Measure Weather

How would you describe the weather today? **Weather** is what the air is like outside. You might say it is too hot or too cold. Someone else might not agree. Words like *hot* and *cold* mean different things to different people.

You could also describe the weather by saying that the temperature is 34° Celsius, or 93° Fahrenheit. Celsius and Fahrenheit are scales used to measure temperature. Scientists measure weather so that they can describe its characteristics exactly. If a scientist reports that the temperature is 34° Celsius, people everywhere can understand what that means.

1. **Underline** the sentence that tells why scientists measure weather.

2. **Measure** Look at the thermometer. Would the red line go up or down if the temperature got colder?

....

A thermometer is a tool used to measure the temperature of the air. Do you think this thermometer shows the temperature in the picture?

3. Apply Suppose someone asked you what summers are like where you live. Are they asking about weather or climate? How do you know?

Weather and Climate

Weather includes the kinds of clouds in the sky and the amount of water in the air. It also includes the air temperature and how the wind is blowing.

You can describe your local weather. Can you describe the climate? Weather and climate are not the same thing. Weather is what the air is like in a place at a single moment. **Climate** is the pattern of weather in a place over many years. Climate includes an area's average temperatures. It also includes the average amount of precipitation. The climate of a place can change, but it takes many years. Weather can change every day.

Moist winds blow from the ocean causing rain or snow on the west side of this mountain range.

Factors That Affect Climate

Different places have different climates. The amount of sunlight a place receives affects climate. Sunlight hits Earth most directly at the equator. The equator is an imaginary line that circles Earth halfway between the North Pole and the South Pole. Places near the equator usually have warmer climates than places farther from it.

The ocean also affects climate. Places near the ocean often have milder temperatures than places inland. They also may receive more precipitation.

Mountains and other landforms may affect climate too. Look at the picture. The west side of the mountain has mild, wet winters. The other side of the mountain has cold, dry winters.

Altitude also affects climate. Altitude is the height above sea level. Temperatures at the top of a mountain would be colder than temperatures at the bottom.

4. **Explain** Look at the diagram below. Write why you think the climate is dry on the east side of the mountain range.

The air over the east side becomes drier after the rain or snow has fallen.

Factors That Affect Local Weather

Have you ever wondered how the weather reporter on Tuesday can predict the weather on Saturday? Scientists study temperature, speed, and direction of wind to predict weather. They measure air pressure and the amount of moisture in the air too. They also look at wind and ocean currents.

Wind Currents

The **atmosphere** is the blanket of air that surrounds Earth. This blanket of air is constantly moving. The atmosphere is made up of gases that have no color, taste, or odor. These gases have weight. The weight of the atmosphere presses down on Earth. This pressing down is called air pressure.

Moving air is called wind. Heat from the sun, air pressure, and Earth's rotation work together to cause wind. The sun heats up the air in some areas more than other areas. Warm air has less pressure than cold air. Cool air sinks because it has more pressure. This makes warm air rise. Winds form as air flows from areas of high pressure to areas of low pressure. Earth's rotation influences the direction of the flow.

Jet streams are fast winds high above Earth's surface. Jet streams can affect local weather by changing temperatures, surface winds, and precipitation.

5. Describe What causes wind?

....

....

Ocean currents are like rivers of warm and cold water. The red arrows show warm currents. The blue arrows show cold currents.

Ocean Currents

The ocean affects the water cycle and climate. The ocean affects weather too. The ocean can absorb, store, and release vast amounts of heat. Changes in ocean temperatures help produce hurricanes, floods, droughts, and other severe weather events.

Ocean currents are bodies of water that move in a certain direction. Winds blowing across the ocean's surface help produce waves. Waves, in turn, cause currents. Currents affect weather and climate by carrying the ocean's heat from place to place.

6. **Sequence** How does wind affect the ocean's heat?

....

....

....

Lightning Lab

Measure and Record Temperatures

Place a thermometer outside. Wait 10 minutes. Read the thermometer. Record the temperature in degrees Celsius and Fahrenheit. Repeat every morning, at the same time, for a week. Graph the temperatures. Describe what you observed to a partner.

Tools for Measuring Weather

Scientists use a number of tools to help them measure and describe weather. These tools also help them predict what the weather will be like.

An anemometer measures wind speed. A wind vane shows the direction from which the wind is blowing. Both wind speed and direction affect the weather.

Scientists use a hygrometer to measure how much water vapor is in the air. The amount of water vapor in the air is called **humidity.** The humidity is low when air is dry. The humidity is high when air has more water vapor in it.

A rain gauge measures water too. A rain gauge measures how much rain has fallen.

7. **Circle** the two tools used to measure wind.

8. **Draw** an ✗ on the two tools used to measure water.

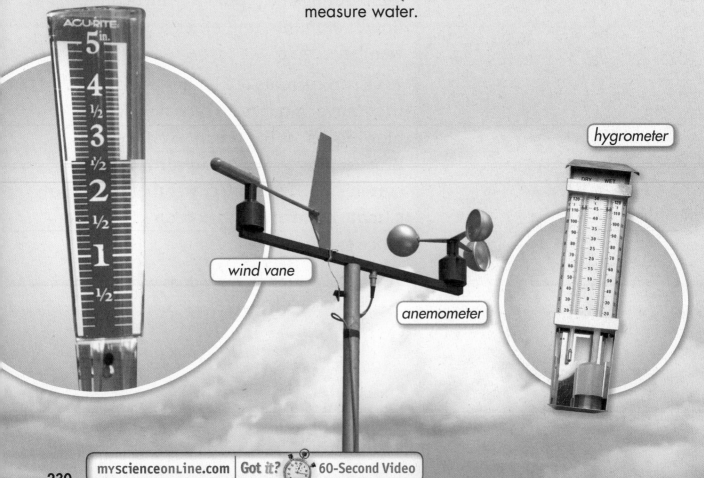

wind vane

anemometer

hygrometer

Scientists can measure air pressure with a tool called a barometer. Changes in air pressure are clues to the kind of weather that is on the way. Low air pressure often means the weather will be cloudy or rainy. High air pressure often means fair weather with sunny, clear skies.

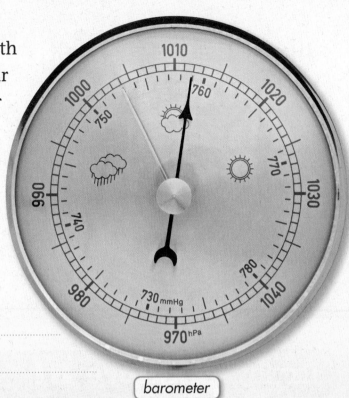

barometer

9. **Predict** Look at the barometer. If the air pressure becomes lower, how might the weather change?

....

....

Got it?

10. **Describe** How are weather and climate different?

....

....

11. **Infer** A hygrometer shows that the humidity has changed from high to low. How has the air changed?

....

....

⬛ **Stop!** I need help with ....

⏸ **Wait!** I have a question about ....

▶ **Go!** Now I know ....

What are minerals and rocks?

Envision It!

Circle the two rocks that you think are the same. Explain.

Inquiry Explore It!

How can you sort rocks?

- ☐ **1.** Pour the soil sample through a sieve over a paper towel. Gently shake.

- ☐ **2.** Remove the rocks from the sieve. Sort them.

- ☐ **3.** Pour the sand and silt in a jar with water.

- ☐ **4.** Put the lid on the jar and shake for 15 seconds. Set this aside for 5 minutes. **Observe.**

Be careful! Wash your hands after handling the rocks.

Explain Your Results

5. What did you **observe** in the jar?

....

....

....

6. Classify What property did you use to sort the rocks?

....

....

Materials

mixture of small rocks, pebbles, sand, and silt

sieve

paper towels

jar with lid and water

clock with second hand

myscienceonline.com | **Explore It! Animation**

I will know what rocks are made from. I will know how rocks are grouped.

Words to Know

rock   sedimentary
mineral   rock
igneous rock   metamorphic
       rock

Minerals and Rocks

Rocks are everywhere on Earth. **Rock** is natural, solid, nonliving material made of one or more minerals. A **mineral** is a natural, nonliving material that makes up rock.

Each mineral has its own properties that can be used to identify it. Rocks get their properties partly from the minerals they contain. The properties of rocks include color and texture. In some rocks the bits of minerals, called grains, are big enough to see. The size and pattern of a rock's grains is called texture.

1. ◎ **Compare and Contrast** Complete the graphic organizer to show how rocks and minerals are alike and different.

granite

quartz

Quartz is one mineral in granite rock.

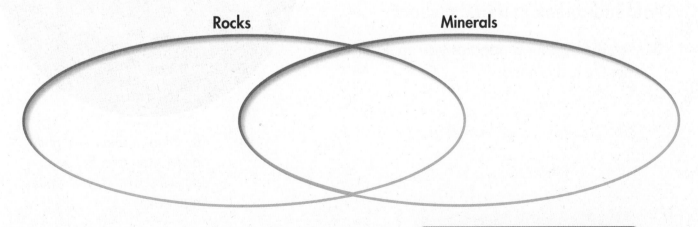

Rocks   Minerals

Identifying Minerals

You can identify minerals by their properties. Color is a property of a mineral that is easy to see. But some minerals can be found in different colors. For example, the mineral quartz can be pink, purple, yellow, brown, white, or black.

Another way to identify a mineral is by the color in its powder form. When you rub a mineral across a rough surface, it may leave a streak mark or powder. A mineral's streak is always the same color, even if pieces of the mineral are different colors.

You can also use luster to identify minerals. Luster is a property that describes how a mineral reflects light. Minerals can be pearly, silky, greasy, glassy, dull, or metallic.

A mineral can be identified by testing its hardness too. Talc is a mineral that is so soft you can scratch it with your fingernail. The hardest mineral is diamond.

You can also identify minerals by how they break apart along weak, flat areas when force is used. This is called cleavage. Some minerals break in one direction. Other minerals break in two or more directions. Mica breaks in one direction. Diamonds break in four directions.

3. **Apply** List four properties you could use to identify a diamond.

....

....

The mineral magnetite has the property of magnetism. Objects that contain iron are pulled to the magnetite.

2. **Underline** the text that explains why you cannot identify a mineral by its color alone.

The mineral sulfur is slightly harder than talc. But you can still scratch it with your fingernail.

Some Properties of Minerals

Mineral		Streak	Luster	Hardness	Cleavage
Halite		white	glassy	can be scratched with a penny	three directions
Copper		reddish brown	metallic	can be scratched with a knife blade	none
Fluorite		white	glassy	can be scratched with a knife blade	four directions

Rock Groups

Rocks can be placed into three main groups. Rocks in each group formed in a certain way. Each group contains many kinds of rocks.

Igneous Rock

Melted rock sometimes forms beneath Earth's surface. **Igneous rock** forms when melted rock cools and hardens. Sometimes the melted rock cools slowly below ground. Then the mineral grains in the igneous rock may be large. Other times the melted rock comes to the surface and cools quickly. Then the grains may be too small to see.

4. Infer This igneous rock is called obsidian. Did it form above ground or below? How do you know?

....

....

Igneous rock can come from volcanoes.

This canyon wall is made of sandstone, a sedimentary rock.

Sedimentary Rock

Rock that forms from sediments is called **sedimentary rock.** Sediments are tiny bits of rock, shells, and other materials. Sediments settle to the bottom of rivers, lakes, and oceans. Over millions of years, the sediments are pressed together and cemented to form new rocks. Sedimentary rocks form in layers—one layer at a time.

5. Distinguish (Circle) the oldest layer of the canyon wall you can see.

Metamorphic Rock

Rock that has been changed by heat and pressure is called **metamorphic rock.** Shale is a sedimentary rock. Heat and pressure underground change the minerals in the shale. The shale becomes slate, a metamorphic rock. Granite is an igneous rock. It can be changed into gneiss, a metamorphic rock.

6. Recall What two forces cause shale to change into slate?

7. [CHALLENGE] A metamorphic rock can be changed into sedimentary rock. Explain how this might happen.

Lightning Lab

Rock Detective
Gather ten rocks. Observe their colors, textures, and shapes. Which rock group do you think each belongs to—igneous, sedimentary, or metamorphic? Record your observations in a chart.

myscienceonline.com | Got *it?* 60-Second Video

Look at the chart below. It shows how rocks can change from one type to another.

Igneous	Sedimentary
Granite Granite is igneous rock that has large grains. Granite is often used in building materials. 	**Shale** Shale is a sedimentary rock with thin layers. 

Changed into

Metamorphic

Gneiss This gneiss was once granite. The grains in gneiss are arranged in layers. 	**Slate** This slate was once shale. Slate also has thin layers. 

Got it?

8. **Describe** What are rocks made up of?

....

....

9. UNLOCK THE BIG **?** The three main groups of rocks are igneous, sedimentary, and metamorphic. Can a rock from one group ever change so that it is placed in a different group? Explain.

....

....

⬜ **Stop!** I need help with ....

⏸ **Wait!** I have a question about ....

▶ **Go!** Now I know ....

Lesson 4

What is soil?

Circle the soil that you would use to grow a bean plant. Explain why you chose that soil.

Inquiry **Explore It!**

What makes up soil?

☑ **1. Observe** each soil. Use the microscope. Feel the soil.

☑ **2. Record** your observations.

Observations of Soils

Soil	How It Looks	How It Feels
Sandy soil		
Clay soil		
Loam soil		

Materials

sandy soil

clay soil

loam soil

pocket microscope

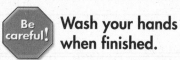

Be careful! **Wash your hands when finished.**

Explain Your Results

3. Interpret Data What was in the soil you **observed**?

....

....

myscienceonline.com | **Explore It!** Animation

I will know what soil is made of. I will know why some soil is better for growing plants.

Words to Know

soil
loam

Parts of Soil

Many living things depend on soil. **Soil** is the layer of loose material that covers most of Earth's land. Soil has the materials plants need to grow. People need healthy soil to grow food.

All soil has the same four substances. Tiny pieces of rock make up most of the soil. These tiny pieces, called particles, come from larger rocks that have broken up. Air and water are also found in soil.

The last ingredient in soil is humus. Humus is made of the remains of plants and animals that were once alive. Humus is an important part of soil. As plant and animal remains in humus decay, or break down or rot, nutrients are released. A nutrient is a substance needed by living things for energy and growth. Water and nutrients help plants live, grow, and survive.

1. **Predict** Name two things these girls might observe in soil.

....

....

....

Soil Layers

Soil is organized into layers. Different places have soil layers of different thicknesses and color.

Topsoil

Topsoil is the top layer. Topsoil is usually the darkest layer because it contains the most humus. Most plants grow in topsoil. Animals such as worms, spiders, and insects also make their homes in topsoil. Humus contains much of what plants need to grow.

Earthworms mix soil as they dig through it. That improves the soil.

Subsoil

Subsoil is under topsoil. It is often lighter in color than topsoil. It does not have as much humus as topsoil. Subsoil includes pieces of broken rocks. Tree roots grow into the subsoil. Water from precipitation may be in this layer.

2. **Infer** Why is subsoil lighter in color than topsoil?

....

....

....

Bedrock

Bedrock is below subsoil. As this rock breaks down, it provides resources for making new soil.

3. ◉**Text Features** How do the headings in the text help you understand the picture?

....

....

Go Green

Compost

Find out how compost helps enrich soil and keeps plants healthy. Research how to build a compost pile. Write and draw a recipe for compost. Start your own compost pile at home or school.

4. **CHALLENGE** What could you use to make a model for the layers of soil?

....

....

....

....

Kinds of Soil

People grow plants in loam.

Soil is not the same everywhere. Soil near your home may be different from soil at your school. Part of what makes soils different is the types of rock particles each soil contains. Sand, silt, and clay are the three main types of particles found in soil.

Most soils are a mix of sand, silt, and clay. Soil with this mixture is called **loam.** Loam also contains air, water, and humus.

5. **Infer** Two samples of topsoil are different colors. What is one possible reason for the difference?

....

....

Do the math!

Read a Graph

Loam is good soil for growing most plants. Loam holds water loosely enough for plant roots to soak it up. The graph shows the amount of different substances in loam.

1 Solve If the values in the graph add up to 100%, what percentage of loam is made of air?

2 Determine What material makes up the greatest percentage of loam?

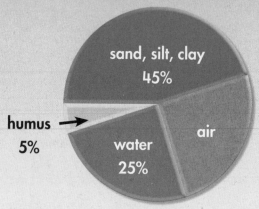

Substances in Loam

- sand, silt, clay 45%
- humus 5%
- water 25%
- air

3 Suppose humus and water each made up 15% of loam. How would the graph look different?

Sand

Sand has large rock particles. Sandy soil feels rough and gritty. Water passes quickly through it. Plant roots may not be able to soak up water fast enough in sandy soil.

Silt

Silt has medium-sized particles that are more closely packed together. Wet silt feels slippery and smooth. Although water passes through it, silty soil holds water better than sand.

Clay

Clay particles are the smallest. Wet clay feels smooth and sticky. Clay holds water so well that plants growing in it may "drown" if roots cannot get the air they need.

6. **Summarize** Some soils hold too much water. Others do not hold enough. How might this affect the growth of plants?

....

....

Got it?

7. **Conclude** Why are water and humus important parts of healthy soil?

....

....

8. **Identify and Compare** Identify two types of rock particles found in soil. Tell how they are alike.

....

....

⬜ **Stop!** I need help with ....

⏸ **Wait!** I have a question about ....

▶ **Go!** Now I know ....

Lesson 5

How do we describe features of Earth's surface?

Name three features of Earth's surface shown in this picture.

my planet diary

Not all volcanoes are easy to see. Some are hidden under the ocean's surface. They are called submarine volcanoes. Submarine volcanoes are common in certain areas of the ocean floor. When one erupts, it can blast steam and rock pieces high above the ocean's surface.

Melted rock that flows from a submarine volcano cools quickly in water. Each time the volcano erupts, more material is released. In this way, a submarine volcano can grow over time and form an island.

How do you think scientists find the location of submarine volcanoes?

....

....

an explosion of steam, ash, and rock from a submarine volcano

Surtsey Island, off the coast of Iceland, formed when a submarine volcano erupted.

UNLOCK
THE BIG
?

I will know about Earth's landforms and the processes that form them.

Words to Know

landform
lava

Landforms

The outer surface of Earth is a layer of rock called the crust. The crust covers all of Earth. The crust can have different shapes, such as mountains, hills, and valleys. Each shape is an example of a landform. A **landform** is a solid feature of Earth's crust.

Landforms are constantly changing. Some changes happen quickly. For example, during landslides, rocks and earth move rapidly down a slope. Other changes happen slowly. Mountains can take millions of years to form.

1. **Underline** the names of three landforms in the text.

2. **Infer** Do you think the landform in the picture below formed slowly or quickly? Explain.

....

....

....

This landform is called a butte.

Features on Earth's Surface

Landforms can be different shapes and sizes. Bodies of water are another type of feature found on Earth's surface. Moving water is one of many forces that can shape landforms. Rivers can act like saws, cutting through rock. Flooding rivers deposit sediments on their banks. Ocean waves break apart rocks and move sand. These processes are constantly changing Earth's crust.

3. Identify (Circle) two landforms in the diagram that are shaped by moving water.

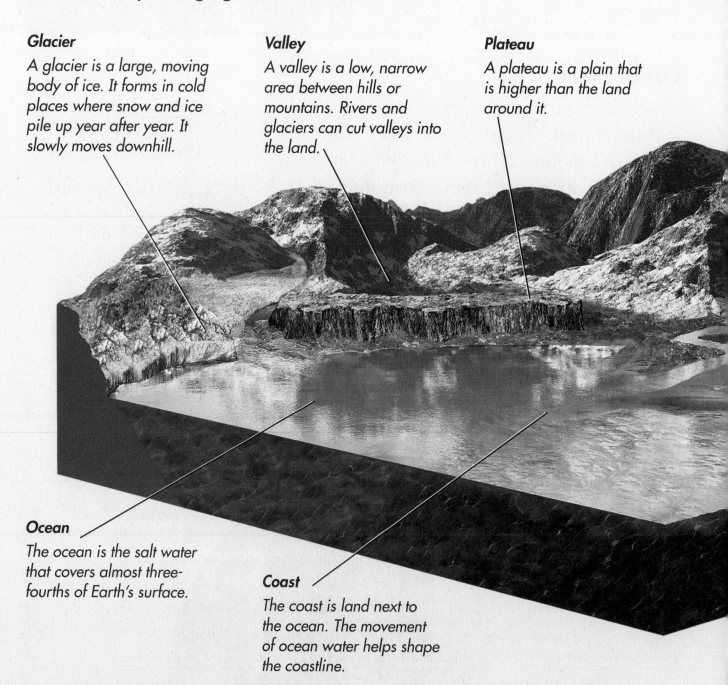

Glacier

A glacier is a large, moving body of ice. It forms in cold places where snow and ice pile up year after year. It slowly moves downhill.

Valley

A valley is a low, narrow area between hills or mountains. Rivers and glaciers can cut valleys into the land.

Plateau

A plateau is a plain that is higher than the land around it.

Ocean

The ocean is the salt water that covers almost three-fourths of Earth's surface.

Coast

The coast is land next to the ocean. The movement of ocean water helps shape the coastline.

myscienceonline.com | THE BIG ? | I Will Know...

4. Conclude How might a glacier form a valley?

....

....

....

....

Volcano

A volcano is an opening in Earth's crust. Pressure inside Earth can force hot, melted rock up through the volcano.

Mountain

A mountain is a landform high above the land around it. Some mountains form when blocks of rock are pushed up or drop down along cracks in Earth's crust.

Lake

A lake forms when the flow of water slows enough to fill an area.

Hill

A hill is a high place on Earth's surface, but not as high as a mountain. Hills often have rounded tops.

Plain

A plain is a large, mostly flat area.

River

A river is a large natural stream of water.

5. Classify Look at the diagram. Draw an ✗ on features that are NOT landforms. Tell why they are not landforms.

At-Home Lab

Landforms and Water
Make a list of landforms and bodies of water in your area. Draw pictures of two of them. Explain how they might have formed.

247

Rapid Changes to Earth's Surface

Volcanoes and earthquakes cause rapid—and sometimes dangerous—changes to Earth's surface.

Volcanoes

Volcanoes begin in the layer below Earth's crust called the mantle. Here, melted rock called magma forms. First, magma collects in a pocket called a magma chamber. Next, magma pushes up through weak spots in the crust. Then, magma erupts through a bowl-shaped crater. Magma that flows onto Earth's surface is called **lava**. Finally, the lava cools and hardens, forming igneous rock. If a volcano erupts many times, layer after layer of rock can form.

6. ◉ **Sequence**
Number the events on the diagram to show the sequence of a volcano erupting.

Flowing lava can burn everything in its path.

crater

.... *When magma flows onto Earth's surface, it is called lava.*

.... *The lava cools and hardens, forming rock.*

.... *Magma pushes upward through weak spots in Earth's crust.*

.... *Magma collects in a magma chamber.*

magma chamber

myscienceonline.com | Got it? ⏱ 60-Second Video

Earthquakes

Earth's crust is broken into large sections or parts. These parts move. Most of the time they move very slowly. But sometimes parts of the crust can shift suddenly. The sudden shift can send vibrations through Earth. These vibrations may shake the ground in all directions. This shaking is an earthquake. Most earthquakes happen along faults, or large cracks in the crust. An earthquake's shaking can make new cracks appear in Earth's surface. It can also cause landslides.

7. **⦿ Cause and Effect** What causes an earthquake's vibrations?

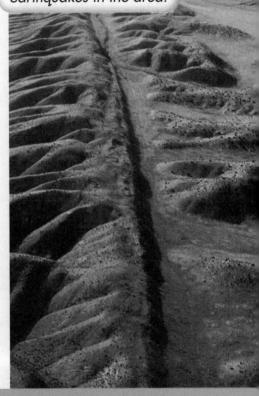

Movements along the San Andreas Fault in California have caused earthquakes in the area.

Got it?

8. **⦿ Compare and Contrast** Select two landforms. What is alike and different about them?

9. **UNLOCK THE BIG ?** How can forces beneath Earth's crust cause changes on Earth's surface?

⬜ **Stop!** I need help with ....

⏸ **Wait!** I have a question about ....

▶ **Go!** Now I know ....

Lesson 6

What are weathering and erosion?

Tell what forces you think could have shaped these rocks.

Inquiry **Explore It!**

How can water wear down a mountain?

☐ **1.** Put soil in the pan.
Make a model of a mountain.

☐ **2.** Hold the cup with the holes over the soil.

☐ **3.** Pour water into the cup.
Observe what happens.
Record.

Materials

pan

soil

cup with 3 small holes

plastic cup
of water

Be careful! **Wash your hands when finished.**

Explain Your Results

4. Infer Think about what you **observed.** Explain why it occurred.

....

....

....

I will know how weathering and erosion change Earth's features.

Words to Know

weathering

erosion

Weathering by Plants

Landforms are the solid features found on Earth's surface, such as mountains and valleys. Landforms change constantly. For this to happen, rocks in landforms must first break apart. **Weathering** is any process that breaks rocks into smaller pieces.

Weathering changes can be very slow. Some might take centuries. Others may take less than a year. Weathering goes on all the time.

Plants sometimes cause weathering. Their roots can grow into cracks in rocks. As the roots get bigger, they can split and break up the rocks.

1. **Describe** What does weathering do to rocks?

....

....

....

....

2. **Predict** What might happen as these tree roots continue to grow?

....

....

....

....

3. Describe What might have caused this rock to break apart? Write a caption.

....

....

....

Lightning Lab

Always Changing
Identify places in your neighborhood or town that are affected by weathering or erosion. They may be rivers, farm fields, beaches, or other landforms. In your science notebook, describe the Earth processes that helped change these landforms.

Weathering by Water

Water can cause weathering too. Water changes the minerals in some rocks. The rocks become weakened and may begin to break apart.

Water can also cause weathering when it freezes and thaws. Water can get into cracks in rocks. When water freezes, it expands, or grows larger. The ice pushes against the sides of the cracks. Over the years, the rocks may break apart.

Erosion by Water

Sometimes weathered material stays in place. Sometimes it is picked up and slowly or quickly carried to other places. The movement of weathered material is called **erosion.**

Water is one of the causes of erosion. Rainwater can carry away soil from farm fields. Waves cause erosion along shorelines. Rivers carry bits of rock from one place to another. Sand and mud flow over a river's banks during a flood.

Glaciers can also cause erosion. Glaciers are huge bodies of ice and snow that move slowly over Earth's crust. As a glacier moves, it wears away bits of rock and soil and carries them off.

4. Analyze Draw arrows to show which way you think the ocean waves moved sand to form this shoreline.

myscienceonline.com | THE BIG ? I Will Know...

Erosion by Wind

Erosion by wind is common in dry regions, such as deserts. Wind can carry dry sand and soil to other places. Few tall plants grow in deserts. This means there is little to stop the particles of sand and soil from blowing around.

Sand and soil particles can also cause weathering when blown by the wind. The particles bump into rocks and break off tiny grains. Over time, more grains are broken off. The rocks slowly change.

Other Causes of Erosion

Gravity also causes erosion. Gravity pulls rocks and soil downhill. The material moves slowly if the slope is gentle. It can move quickly on steep slopes. A mudflow is the quick movement of very wet soil. A rockslide is the quick movement of rocks down a slope.

Living things can cause erosion too. For example, ground squirrels tunnel through soil. The tunneling allows water and air to move into the ground. This continues the process of erosion.

Gravity pulls loose rock and soil downhill in a rockslide.

5. **Describe** Tell how wind erosion might have caused the shapes in this rock.

....
....
....
....

6. CHALLENGE Are mudflows and rockslides due to weathering, erosion, or both? Explain.

....
....
....
....
....
....

Deposition

The rock and soil that erosion carries away must go someplace. The placing of pieces of Earth's surface in a new place is called *deposition*.

New islands can form as a result of deposition. This happens when rivers carry rock and bits of soil to the ocean. These particles build up over time and can form islands just off the coast.

Wind can also cause deposition. Wind can blow sand into mounds. These mounds are called *sand dunes*. Look at the picture below. Desert winds have formed many sand dunes. The wind continues to change the size and shape of the dunes.

7. Infer Look at the picture below. What most likely caused the ripples in the sand dunes?

8. ◉ **Sequence** Explain why weathering and erosion must happen before deposition can occur.

Weathering, Erosion, and Soil

Soil is made up of tiny pieces of rock, air, water, and humus. The tiny pieces of rock come from larger rocks that have broken up. Rocks are broken up and moved about through weathering and erosion. Small plants sprout in the rock and eventually die. The remains of these plants break down and form humus. Soil develops from different kinds of rocks and plants. This is part of the reason why soils are not alike everywhere in the world.

 9. Explain How do plants help to form soil?

....

....

Got it?

10. Contrast How are weathering and erosion different?

....

....

11. Think about what you learned in this lesson. How do weathering and erosion change Earth's features?

....

....

◻ **Stop!** I need help with ....

❚❚ **Wait!** I have a question about ....

▶ **Go!** Now I know ....

What can cause rock to crack?

Follow a Procedure

☑ **1.** Push the foil end of the sponge into the plaster. Keep the other end out. Wait 1 day.

☑ **2.** On Day 2 pull the sponge out. **Observe** how the plaster has changed. **Record.**

Materials

plastic cup with plaster

sponge with foil

plastic cup with water

Be careful!
Do not put plaster in your mouth. If plaster gets on your hands, wash it off immediately.

Inquiry Skill
Scientists **observe** carefully and record their observations.

3. Fill the foil with water. Put the cup in a freezer. Wait 1 day.

4. On Day 3 observe how the plaster has changed. Record.

Plaster Observations	
Day 2	
Day 3	

Analyze and Conclude

5. Infer What caused the changes you **observed** on Day 3?

....

....

6. How can weathering caused by freezing and thawing change Earth's surface?

....

....

....

Dr. Elissa R. Levine

Dr. Levine is a Soil Scientist for NASA's Goddard Space Flight Center. She has been interested in soil for a long time. She once said, "When I was little, my mother sat me in the soil and showed me all kinds of interesting things to look at and play with. I've been interested in the soil ever since."

Dr. Levine gathers information from pictures taken by satellites that travel high over Earth. The pictures tell about our environment. She also studies the ways that soil changes all around the world. She is trying to find the causes of these changes.

Dr. Levine also teaches about soil to students all over the world. The students gather data about soil. Dr. Levine uses the information to make computer models of the soils. She has found that soil connects all the other parts of our environment together.

List four things that Dr. Levine might have found in soil when she was a child.

....

....

....

....

Dr. Levine uses satellite images to study soil all around the world.

Dr. Levine loved digging in soil as a child. "I was fascinated by its color," she said.

satellite image of the Mississippi River delta

Vocabulary Smart Cards

condensation
evaporation
water cycle
precipitation
weather
climate
atmosphere
humidity
rock
mineral
igneous rock
sedimentary rock
metamorphic rock
soil
loam
landform
lava
weathering
erosion

Play a Game!

Choose a Vocabulary Smart Card.

Work with a partner. Write several sentences using the vocabulary word.

Have your partner repeat with another word.

precipitation

precipitación

condensation

condensación

weather

tiempo atmosférico

evaporation

evaporación

climate

clima

water cycle

ciclo del agua

the change from a gas into a liquid

Write the verb form of the word.

....
....
....

cambio de un gas a líquido

---

water that falls to Earth

Write the verb form of the word.

....
....
....
....

agua que cae a la Tierra

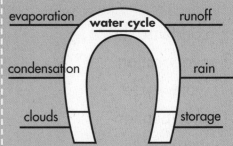

evaporation   water cycle   runoff

condensation   rain

clouds   storage

Make a Word Magnet!

Choose a vocabulary word and write it in the Word Magnet. Write words that are related to it on the lines.

---

the change from liquid water to water vapor

Give an example of this word.

....
....
....

cambio del agua en estado líquida a vapor de agua

---

what the air is like outside

Write a sentence using this word.

....
....
....
....

las condiciones al aire libre

---

the movement of water from Earth's surface into the air and back again

Draw one part of the water cycle. Label it.

movimiento de ida y vuelta que realiza el agua entre el aire y la superficie de la Tierra

---

the pattern of weather in a place over many years

Write a sentence using this word.

....
....
....

patrón que sigue el tiempo atmosférico de un lugar a lo largo de muchos años

metamorphic rock

roca metamórfica

mineral

mineral

atmosphere

atmósfera

soil

suelo

igneous rock

roca ígnea

humidity

humedad

loam

marga

sedimentary rock

roca sedimentaria

rock

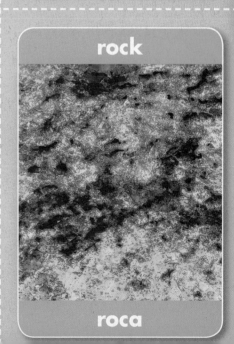

roca

the blanket of air that surrounds Earth

What suffix does this word have?

....

....

....

capa de aire que rodea la Tierra

---

natural, nonliving material that makes up rocks

Write a sentence using this word.

....

....

....

material natural y sin vida del que se componen las rocas

---

rock that forms when existing rock is changed by heat and pressure

What is the suffix of the first word?

....

roca que se forma cuando las rocas existentes cambian debido al calor y la presión

---

the amount of water vapor in the air

Write the adjective form of this word.

....

....

....

....

cantidad de vapor de agua que hay en el aire

---

rock that forms when melted rock cools and hardens

What is the suffix of the first word?

....

....

....

roca que se forma cuando las rocas derretidas se enfrían y endurecen

---

the layer of loose material that covers Earth's land

Write as many synonyms for this word as you can.

....

....

....

capa de material suelto que cubre la superficie de la Tierra

---

natural, solid, nonliving material made from one or more minerals

What is another meaning of this word?

....

....

....

material natural, sólido sin vida, compuesto por uno o más minerales

---

rock that forms when sediments are pressed together and cemented

Write a sentence using this word.

....

....

....

roca que se forma por la acumulación de sedimentos unidos a gran presión

---

soil that contains a mixture of humus and mineral materials of sand, silt, and clay

Write something that is not an example of this word.

....

....

....

suelo que contiene una mezcla de humus y minerales de la arena, cieno y arcilla

erosion

erosión

landform

accidente
geográfico

lava

lava

weathering

meteorización

a solid feature of Earth's crust

Draw an example.

formación sólida de la corteza terrestre

the movement of weathered materials

Write the verb form of this word.

....

....

....

el movimiento de materiales que han sufrido meteorización

....

....

....

....

magma that flows onto Earth's surface

Write a sentence using this word.

....

....

....

....

magma que fluye a la superficie terrestre

....

....

....

....

....

....

....

....

any process that breaks rock into smaller pieces

What is the suffix of this word?

....

....

....

todo proceso que rompe la roca en trozos más pequeños

....

....

....

....

....

....

....

....

Chapter 6
Study Guide

REVIEW THE BIG ? How do forces cause changes on Earth's surface?

Earth Science

Lesson 1

What is the water cycle?

- The movement of water from Earth's surface into the air and back again is called the water cycle.
- Evaporation and condensation are some parts of the cycle.

Lesson 2

What are weather and climate?

- You can use weather tools to measure and describe weather.
- A hygrometer is a weather tool that measures humidity, or the amount of water vapor in the air.

Lesson 3

What are minerals and rocks?

- All rocks are made from one or more minerals.
- Color, streak, and hardness are properties of minerals.
- Igneous, sedimentary, and metamorphic are types of rocks.

Lesson 4

What is soil?

- Soil is made of rock particles, water, air, and humus.
- Sand, silt, and clay are the three main kinds of rock particles found in soil.

Lesson 5

How do we describe features of Earth's surface?

- Landforms are solid features of Earth's crust.
- Landforms are always changing.
- Volcanoes and earthquakes rapidly change Earth's surface.

Lesson 6

What are weathering and erosion?

- Weathering breaks rocks into smaller pieces.
- The movement of weathered materials by forces such as water and wind is called erosion.

Chapter Review

REVIEW THE BIG ?

How do forces cause changes on Earth's surface?

Lesson 1

What is the water cycle?

1. **Vocabulary** Water that falls to the earth is called _____.
   A. evaporation
   B. runoff
   C. precipitation
   D. condensation

2. **Explain** Describe what causes water on Earth's surface to evaporate.

_____

_____

Lesson 2

What are weather and climate?

3. **Predict** The air pressure in your area is rising. How do you think the weather will change?

_____

_____

4. **Determine** What tool would you use to measure the speed of the wind?

_____

Lesson 3

What are minerals and rocks?

5. **Vocabulary** All rocks are made of _____.
   A. clay
   B. minerals
   C. igneous rock
   D. granite

6. **Conclude** A mineral can be scratched with a coin. What can you conclude about the hardness of the mineral compared to the hardness of the coin?

_____

_____

7. **Write About It** What is different about the way igneous and sedimentary rocks form?

_____

_____

_____

_____

Lesson 4

What is soil?

8. ⊙ **Sequence** List the three layers of soil in the correct order from the top layer to the bottom layer.

_____

_____

9. **Compare** How are sandy soil and clay soil alike?

_____

_____

_____

Lesson 5

How do we describe features of Earth's surface?

10. **Classify** Give one example of a slow change in Earth's surface. Give one example of a rapid change in Earth's surface.

_____

_____

_____

11. **Analyze** How does lava change the surface of Earth?

_____

Lesson 6

What are weathering and erosion?

12. Ocean waves are causing erosion at a beach. Each year, 2 meters of beach erode. How long will it take for 24 meters of beach to erode?

_____

13. **APPLY THE BIG ?** **How do forces cause changes on Earth's surface?**

Describe how the rocks that make up a mountain can change over time. Use the terms *weathering* and *erosion* in your answer.

_____

_____

_____

_____

_____

267

Fill in the bubble next to the answer choice you think is correct for each multiple-choice question.

1 Look closely at the rock.

Which characteristic of this rock helps you know that it is sedimentary rock?

- Ⓐ color
- Ⓑ texture
- Ⓒ layers
- Ⓓ grains

2 The size and pattern of minerals in a rock is called _____.

- Ⓐ igneous
- Ⓑ texture
- Ⓒ metamorphic
- Ⓓ granite

3 Which of the following would you use to measure precipitation?

- Ⓐ hygrometer
- Ⓑ rain gauge
- Ⓒ barometer
- Ⓓ anemometer

4 The soil in a bucket feels rough. Water poured into the soil drains quickly to the bottom. What type of rock particle does this soil most likely contain?

- Ⓐ sand
- Ⓑ silt
- Ⓒ clay
- Ⓓ loam

5 Which of the following describes what the air is like outside?

- Ⓐ climate
- Ⓑ altitude
- Ⓒ runoff
- Ⓓ weather

6 Explain how a natural event can cause a rapid change to Earth's surface.

....

....

....

....

Soil Studies

You can find soil almost everywhere. Have an adult help you observe a soil sample from your backyard, the schoolyard, or a nearby park. Pour about a cup of soil onto a sheet of paper so you can get a closer look.

What do you notice about the soil? Is anything growing in it? Does it contain any bugs or worms? How big are the rock particles? Write down your observations.

Discuss with your classmates what they found in their soil. How is your soil different from theirs? How is it the same?

REVIEW THE BIG ? Why might soils from different places contain different parts? What is one question you might ask to help you compare soil samples?

Where are the stars during the day?

Earth and Our Universe

Try It! How can you estimate the number of stars?

Lesson 1 What is a star?

Lesson 2 What do you know about our solar system?

Lesson 3 What are Earth's patterns?

Lesson 4 What is known about the moon?

Investigate It! Why do you see phases of the moon?

Look up at the clear night sky. What do you see? You can see the universe, and it is HUGE! The universe is made up of many stars, planets, and other objects.

Predict What do you think other stars in the universe look like?

....

....

THE BIG ? How do objects in space affect one another?

How can you estimate the number of stars?

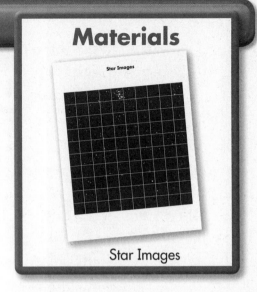

Materials

Star Images

☑ **1. Observe** Describe the star images.

....

....

☑ **2.** How can you **estimate** the number of stars without counting each one?

....

....

Inquiry Skill
Scientists sometimes make **estimates** when exact measurements are not needed.

☑ **3.** Estimate the number of stars that are dim, medium, or bright.

.... Dim   .... Medium   .... Bright

Explain Your Results

4. Communicate Make a graph to show your **estimates** of dim, medium, and bright stars.

Number and Brightness of Stars																			
Dim																			
Medium																			
Bright																			

Brightness of Stars

0 10 20 30 40 50 60 70 80 90 100 110 120 130 140 150 160 170 180 190 200

Number of Stars

5. UNLOCK THE BIG ? Why do you think scientists might want to study the stars?

....

◉ Main Idea and Details

- The **main idea** is the most important idea in a reading selection.
- Supporting **details** tell more about the main idea.

Sky Report

Andromeda is a huge group of stars in the shape of a disk. Andromeda is normally not visible close to city lights. Last night I was at my uncle's house in the country, and I could see Andromeda with just my eyes. It appeared to be just a point of light. When I used a telescope to view Andromeda, it looked bigger and appeared to be a fuzzy star.

Practice it!

Complete the graphic organizer below. Use it to help you list the main idea and details from the sky report you read above.

Andromeda

Main Idea

Detail   **Detail**   **Detail**

What is a star?

Envision It!

Look at the Little Dipper above. Use the bright stars on the right page to finish the drawing of the Big Dipper.

Inquiry **Explore It!**

What tool can help you observe the sun safely?

☑ **1.** Tape foil over the hole on the box end.

☑ **2.** Tape white paper on the inside of the other end.

☑ **3.** Stand with your back to the sun.
Hold the box with the foil facing the sun.
Observe the white paper through the side hole.

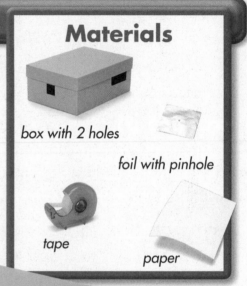

Materials

box with 2 holes

foil with pinhole

tape

paper

foil with pinhole

 Be careful! **Never look directly at the sun.**

Explain Your Results

4. Infer Identify the image you **observed.**

....

....

myscienceonLine.com | **Explore It!** Animation

UNLOCK
THE BIG
?

I will know how stars are different. I will know about star patterns.

Words to Know

star
light-year

Stars and Light

Have you sat outside on a clear night and looked at the sky? Did you see any stars? A **star** is a giant ball of hot, glowing gases that releases energy.

Light from stars takes time to reach Earth. Light travels 300,000 kilometers per second. That is fast! Light from the sun, a star, takes about eight and a half minutes to reach Earth. Light from other stars takes longer. The distance light travels from stars is measured in light-years. A **light-year** is the distance light travels in one year.

1. ◎ **Main Idea and Details** Complete the graphic organizer below. Fill in the main idea about stars.

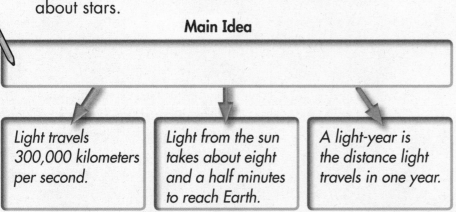

Main Idea

Light travels 300,000 kilometers per second.	Light from the sun takes about eight and a half minutes to reach Earth.	A light-year is the distance light travels in one year.
Detail	**Detail**	**Detail**

Alpha Centauri

Alpha Centauri is the next nearest star to Earth. It is four light-years away from Earth.

Types of Stars

You may see thousands of stars on a clear night. All stars except the sun look like points of light because they are very far away. Some stars appear brighter than others.

Scientists use physical characteristics such as brightness, size, color, and temperature to describe stars. Stars can produce different amounts of light. The sun is a very bright star. It is the closest star to Earth. It may seem that bright stars in the night sky are closer to Earth than dim stars. Actually, some stars that appear dim may be closer to Earth than bright stars. A star's distance from Earth is not the only reason it appears bright. Other features affect the brightness of stars besides its closeness to Earth.

Our sun and most stars in the universe are similar. However, stars can be different sizes. For example, the size of our sun is average. Some stars are larger than our sun. Other stars are smaller. Over time, the size of a star can also change.

Stars can also have different temperatures and colors. Stars can be red, orange, yellow, blue, and white. A star's color is a result of its temperature. For example, blue stars such as Spica are hotter than orange stars such as Bessel's Star.

2. ⊙ **Main Idea and Details** What is the main idea of this page?

....

....

....

....

....

....

3. **Tell** three details about Bessel's Star.

Bessel's Star

Bessel's Star is smaller than our sun. It is about 11 light-years away from Earth. Bessel's Star is really two stars that are very close together. They both glow orange.

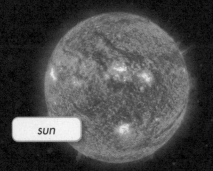

sun

The sun is an average-sized star.

4. ⊙ **Compare and Contrast** Look at the captions about the sun and Spica. How are our sun and Spica alike and different?

....

....

....

....

Spica

The star Spica is larger than our sun, but it looks like a point of light in the sky. Why? Because Spica is about 260 light-years away from Earth. Spica is two blue stars that are very close together.

Patterns of Stars

Groups of stars can be found in distinct areas of the sky. Some groups of stars seem to make patterns or shapes. You can imagine lines drawn between stars to make each pattern. Find the lines drawn in the picture shown.

The stars that make up these patterns look like they are close together in space. They really are very far apart. Some stars are farther from Earth than others. If you look at the same stars from far away in space, they would not make the same pattern.

The patterns of stars you can see change with the seasons. As Earth moves around the sun, these patterns are in different parts of the sky.

5. Trace Look at the image of Ursa Major below. Use your finger to trace the outline of the Big Dipper.

Ursa Major, or the Big Bear, is one of many patterns in the sky. Ursa Major is visible throughout the year. Within Ursa Major, you can see the Big Dipper. The Big Dipper looks like a cup with a handle.

Ursa Major

The star Caph is one star that makes up the star pattern Cassiopeia. Caph is the second brightest star in Cassiopeia. It is 54 light-years from Earth and more than 25 times brighter than our sun. Because of its distance from Earth, it looks like a point of light.

Cassiopeia

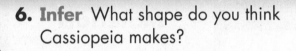

6. Infer What shape do you think Cassiopeia makes?

....

Got it?

7. Explain How are stars different?

....

....

....

8. ◉ **Main Idea and Details** Why do stars often look like points of light?

....

....

⬜ **Stop!** I need help with ....

⏸ **Wait!** I have a question about ....

▷ **Go!** Now I know ....

Lesson 2

What do you know about our solar system?

Draw an ✗ on Earth. **Tell** a partner how you think Earth is different from its neighboring planets.

Inquiry **Explore It!**

What can you learn from a distance model of the solar system?

☐ **1.** Choose a planet. Find your planet's distance in the chart. **Measure** and cut paper to that length. Write your planet's name on the paper. Roll it up.

Materials

metric ruler

meterstick

adding machine paper

scissors

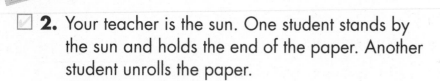

☐ **2.** Your teacher is the sun. One student stands by the sun and holds the end of the paper. Another student unrolls the paper.

Explain Your Results

3. Use your **model** to compare the distances.

....

....

....

Distance Model of Planets from the Sun

Planet	Length of Tape	
	(cm)	(m)
Mercury	30	0.30
Venus	56	0.56
Earth	77	0.77
Mars	120	1.20
Jupiter	400	4.00
Saturn	740	7.40
Uranus	1500	15.00
Neptune	2300	23.00

myscienceonLine.com | **Explore It!** Animation

Words to Know

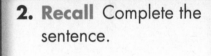

planet
solar system

A Path Around the Sun

You live on the planet Earth. A **planet** is a large, ball-shaped body that revolves, or travels around, the sun. Earth is one of eight planets that revolve around the sun.

The path an object takes as it revolves around the sun is its orbit. Planets travel in an orbit that is a slight oval shape. The strong pull of the sun's gravity holds the planets in their orbits. If it were not for the sun's gravity, Earth would move off through space in a straight line.

2. Recall Complete the sentence.

Earth .... around the sun in its ....

1. Restate What effect does gravity have on the planets?

....

....

....

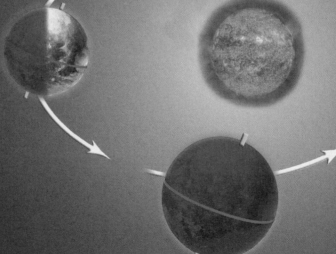

In the diagrams in this lesson, sizes and distances are not true to scale.

Parts of Our Solar System

This diagram shows the eight planets that revolve around the sun. Many of these planets have moons. The sun, the eight planets and their moons, and other objects that revolve around the sun make up the **solar system.** The sun is the center of the solar system.

3. (Circle) the objects in the text that make up the solar system.

Mercury

Venus

Earth

Mars

Jupiter

Distance from the Sun

The solar system is a huge place. Venus is the planet closest to Earth. But it is about 42 million kilometers from Earth. The chart shows the distance of each planet from the sun.

4. **Identify** Draw an ✗ on the planet that is 778 million km from the sun.

5. **Calculate** How much farther from the sun is Venus compared to Mercury?

Distance of Planets from Sun	
Planet	**Distance from Sun**
Mercury	58 million km
Venus	108 million km
Earth	150 million km
Mars	228 million km
Jupiter	778 million km
Saturn	1 billion, 400 million km
Uranus	2 billion, 900 million km
Neptune	4 billion, 500 million km

Saturn

Uranus

Neptune

The sizes and distances in this diagram are not true to scale. Also, the planets rarely line up as shown.

The Inner Planets

The eight known planets are divided into inner and outer planets based on their distances from the sun. The four inner planets are Mercury, Venus, Earth, and Mars. The inner planets have some things in common. They are the planets closest to the sun, and they all have rocky surfaces. But they have many differences too.

6. **Compare** Read the descriptions of the planets. What is one way Mercury and Venus are alike?

....

....

Mercury

Mercury is the closest planet to the sun. Because of this, the surface of Mercury is dry and very hot. Mercury is also the smallest planet. It is less than half the size of Earth. Mercury has no moons.

Venus

Venus is the second planet from the sun. Like Mercury, Venus is a very hot, rocky planet. It has craters, mountains, and valleys. Thick clouds cover the planet and trap the sun's energy, making it very hot. Venus has no moons.

Earth

Earth is the third planet from the sun. Water covers almost three-fourths of Earth's surface. Earth is the only planet in our solar system that supports life. It has the conditions living things need, including mild temperatures, liquid water, and an atmosphere.

Mars

Mars, the fourth planet from the sun, is about half the size of Earth. Mars is called the "red planet" because its surface is reddish-orange. Temperatures on Mars are too cold for liquid water. Mars has volcanoes and deep canyons. It has two moons.

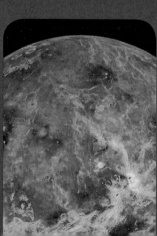

The Outer Planets

The outer planets are Jupiter, Saturn, Uranus, and Neptune. The outer planets are very different from the inner planets. Unlike the rocky inner planets, the outer planets are huge and made mostly of gas. They are called gas giants. Their surfaces are not solid. These planets have thick layers of clouds and strong winds. They also have rings around them. Jupiter's rings are hard to see.

7. ◉ **Main Idea and Details**
What is the main idea of the paragraph?

Jupiter
Jupiter is the fifth planet from the sun and the largest planet. It is over 11 times the size of Earth. Jupiter is covered with thick clouds. It has more than 60 moons. Jupiter's Great Red Spot, shown below, is actually a huge storm.

Saturn
Saturn is the sixth planet from the sun and the second largest planet. Saturn's most famous feature is its rings. The rings, shown below, are made of chunks of ice and rock that circle the planet. Saturn has more than 60 moons.

Uranus
Uranus is the seventh planet from the sun. It is smaller than Saturn or Jupiter but about four times the size of Earth. Uranus is unlike other planets because it rotates on its side. It has 27 moons.

Neptune
Neptune is the farthest planet from the sun. It is so far away that its orbit around the sun takes 165 Earth years. Neptune is slightly smaller than Uranus. It has 13 moons. Neptune's blue color is caused by gases in its atmosphere.

Lightning Lab

Planet Model

Design a model of the eight planets of the solar system using everyday objects such as fruits or balls used in sports. Draw your plan. Show the order of the items. Label each item and the planet it represents.

Pluto, a Dwarf Planet

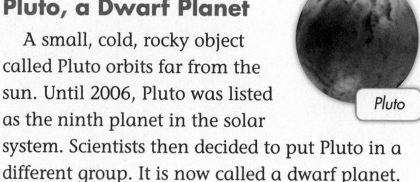

Pluto

A small, cold, rocky object called Pluto orbits far from the sun. Until 2006, Pluto was listed as the ninth planet in the solar system. Scientists then decided to put Pluto in a different group. It is now called a dwarf planet. Pluto is smaller than Earth's moon.

8. **Analyze** Should Pluto still be considered part of the solar system? Explain why or why not. Look back at the definition of *solar system* if you need a clue.

....

....

Do the math!

Use a Chart

The chart below shows how long it takes each outer planet to complete one revolution around the sun. Use the chart to answer the questions.

The Outer Planets	
Planet	**Revolution Time**
Jupiter	12 Earth years
Saturn	29 Earth years
Uranus	84 Earth years
Neptune	165 Earth years

1 **Identify** Which of the outer planets takes the shortest time to revolve around the sun?

....

2 **Calculate** How much longer is the revolution time of Neptune than that of Saturn?

....

3 **Determine** Planets close to the sun take the longest time to revolve around the sun. True or false?

....

Asteroids and Comets

An asteroid is a chunk of rock that orbits the sun. Most asteroids are found in the asteroid belt between Mars and Jupiter. The smallest asteroids are pebble-sized, but some are as wide as the state of Texas.

A comet is a frozen object that orbits the sun. Comets are made of ice, dust, and bits of rock. Comets are much smaller than planets. Only the largest comets can be seen without a telescope.

9. ⊙ **Compare and Contrast** How are asteroids and comets alike? How are they different?

asteroid

comet

....

....

Got it?

10. Identify List the planets in order from the sun.

....

....

11. Summarize What did you learn about our solar system that you did not know before?

....

....

....

⬜ **Stop!** I need help with ....

⏸ **Wait!** I have a question about ....

▶ **Go!** Now I know ....

Lesson 3

What are Earth's patterns?

Envision It!

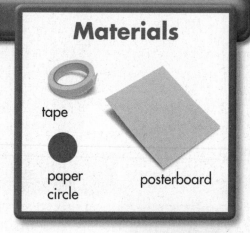

Circle the position of the sun at noon.

Inquiry Explore It!

How can shadows change over time?

Materials

tape

paper circle

posterboard

☑ **1.** Tape a circle on a window.

☑ **2. Observe** the shadow of the circle.
Think of a way to **record** the shadow.

☑ **3.** Record the shadow every
15 minutes for 2 hours.

Explain Your Results

4. What caused the changes you **observed**?

....

....

....

Tape the posterboard to the floor.

5. Predict the position of the shadow in 1 hour.

....

....

....

myscienceonline.com | **Explore It!** Animation

I will know what causes daytime, nighttime, and the seasons. I will know what causes shadows to change.

Words to Know

axis   revolution
rotation

How Earth Moves

As you read this, you may not feel like you are moving. But you are. Earth is always moving. One way Earth moves is that it spins around its axis. Earth's **axis** is an imaginary line that runs between the North Pole and the South Pole. Find Earth's axis in the diagram. Notice that the axis is not straight up and down. It is tilted.

If you could look down at the North Pole, you would see that Earth turns in a counterclockwise direction. This direction is opposite to the direction in which the hands of a clock move. You could also say that Earth turns from west to east.

1. ◉ **Main Idea and Details** The main idea of the first paragraph is *Earth spins around its axis.* List two details that support the main idea.

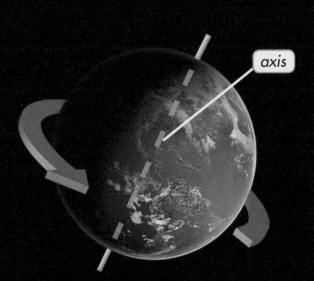

axis

Day and Night

Earth's spinning causes day and night. Earth makes one complete spin on its axis, or **rotation**, every 24 hours. During this time, half of Earth faces the sun. That half of Earth has day. The half of Earth that is not facing the sun has night. As Earth spins, or rotates, a different part of Earth turns to face the sun.

Earth's spinning also causes changes in the sun's position in the sky. These changes follow a pattern. In the morning, the sun appears to rise in the east. During the day, the sun seems to move across the sky and then set in the west. You might think the sun moves around Earth. But the sun only appears to move across the sky. Actually Earth is moving.

Honolulu 3:00 A.M.

2. Describe Write how the sun seems to change position in the sky during a day.

Seattle 6:00 A.M.

Look at the diagram of Earth's rotation and the pictures on these pages. When it is still nighttime in Honolulu, Hawaii, the sun is rising in Seattle. In New Orleans, it is daytime and some students are already starting their school day.

3. Explain In Seattle, the sun seems to be rising. What is really happening as a result of rotation?

....

....

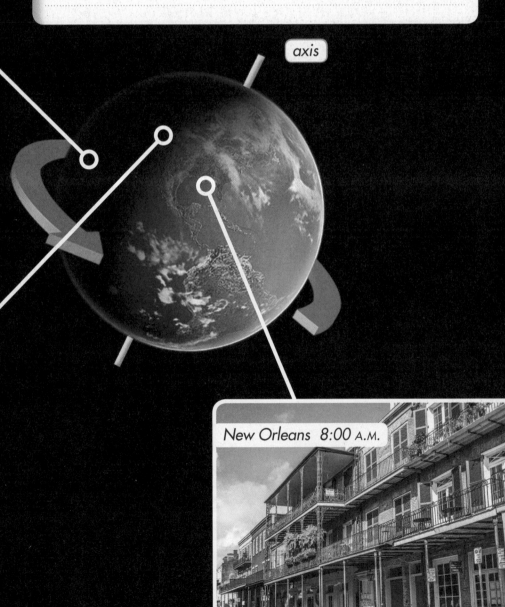

axis

New Orleans 8:00 A.M.

4. Recall About how long does it take Earth to revolve around the sun?

Revolution Around the Sun

You know that Earth rotates on its axis. Earth also moves, or revolves, around the sun. Earth makes one **revolution** when it makes one complete trip around the sun. One revolution takes about one year. As Earth revolves around the sun, Earth's tilted axis always points in the same direction in space.

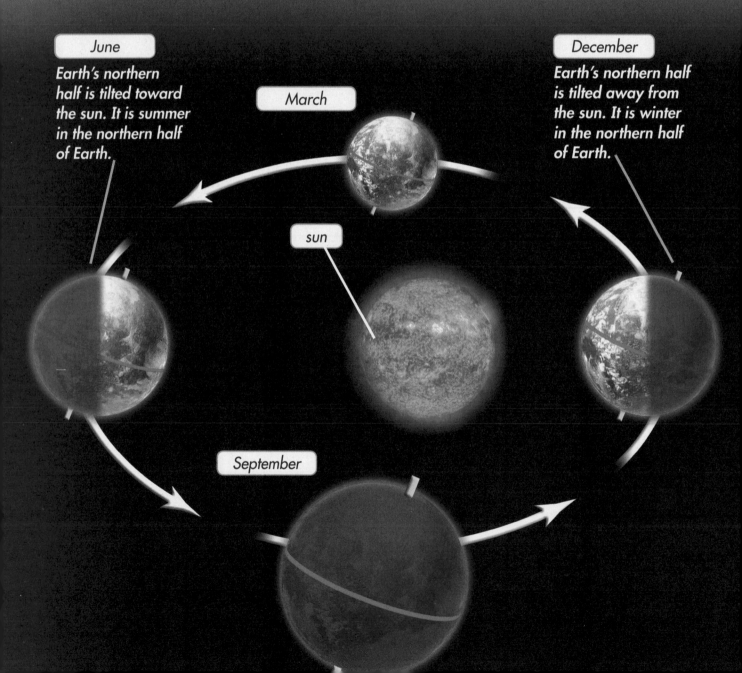

June

Earth's northern half is tilted toward the sun. It is summer in the northern half of Earth.

March

December

Earth's northern half is tilted away from the sun. It is winter in the northern half of Earth.

sun

September

Seasons

A year is divided into four seasons—spring, summer, fall, and winter. The seasons are caused by the tilt of Earth's axis and the planet's revolution around the sun.

As Earth moves around the sun, different parts of the planet tilt toward the sun. Look at the position of Earth in June. The northern half of Earth is tilted toward the sun. The northern half receives more direct rays of sunlight than the southern half and heats up more. It is summer in the northern half and winter in the southern half.

Now look at Earth's position in December. The northern half of Earth is tilted away from the sun. The northern half gets less sunlight and has colder temperatures than the southern half. It is winter in the northern half and summer in the southern half.

In March and September, neither end of Earth's axis points toward the sun. Both halves of Earth get about the same amounts of sunlight.

Lightning Lab

Angle of Light
Shine a reading lamp on black paper from directly overhead. After one minute, feel the temperature of the paper. Repeat with another sheet of paper, this time positioning the lamp above the paper at a 45-degree angle. Compare the temperatures. Explain the differences.

5. **Identify** Draw an ✗ on the position of Earth where the northern half receives the most direct sunlight.

6. **Predict** In September, the northern United States gets about 12 hours of daylight each day. About how many hours of daylight do you think the northern United States gets each day in March?

7. **Explain** What is the result of the revolution of Earth?

morning

midday

afternoon

Shadows During the Day

On a hot summer day, you might escape the heat by standing in the shade of a tree. Did you know you are standing in a shadow?

A shadow forms when an object blocks the light that hits it. The shadow has about the same shape as the object that blocks the light.

The length and direction of shadows change during the day. Find the shadows made by the tree in the pictures. Notice that the morning shadow is long. The shadow stretches in the opposite direction from the sun in the eastern sky.

As the sun appears to move higher in the sky, the shadow becomes shorter. Around midday the sun is at its highest point in the sky. The shadow is very short.

As the sun continues moving across the sky, the shadow becomes longer. Look at the length of the shadow in the third picture. The afternoon shadow stretches in a different direction than the morning shadow did. As the sun moves toward the horizon in the west, the shadow stretches toward the east.

8. **Predict** In each picture, predict the correct position of the sun. Draw a small circle on each picture to show where the sun would be.

myscienceonline.com | Got it? 60-Second Video

Shadow Length During the Year

The length of a shadow changes during the year. This is because the sun's position in the sky changes with the seasons. In the northern half of Earth, the sun is higher in the sky in summer. The sun is lower in the sky in winter. The pictures below show the shadow of a building at noon.

9. Compare How is the building's shadow different in winter than in summer?

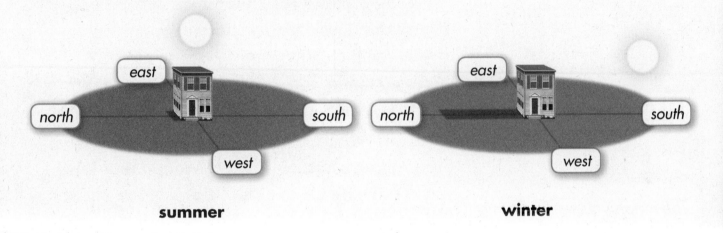

summer

winter

Got it?

10. Explain Name the patterns on Earth that are caused by the planet's rotation and revolution.

11. Compare Compare the length and direction of shadows in the morning and in the afternoon.

⬛ **Stop!** I need help with

❙❙ **Wait!** I have a question about

▶ **Go!** Now I know

What is known about the moon?

Draw an ✗ on the full moon. **Tell** how the moon's shape seems to change.

my pLaneT DiaRY   DISCOVERY

Asaph Hall

Deimos

Phobos

The moon you see in the night sky is not the only moon in our solar system. Scientists have identified at least 170 moons, and there may be more!

Mars has two moons, Phobos and Deimos. The astronomer Asaph Hall discovered the moons in 1877. Phobos and Deimos are much smaller than Earth's moon. When seen from the surface of Mars, they look like tiny dots in the sky. Phobos orbits Mars in less than eight hours. Earth's moon takes almost a month to complete one orbit.

List two ways Phobos is different from Earth's moon.

....

....

....

I will know that the moon orbits Earth. I will know what causes the phases of the moon.

Words to Know

moon phase
crater

Motions of the Moon

If you go outside on a clear night, you can usually see the moon. The moon is Earth's closest neighbor. You know that Earth orbits the sun. But did you know that as Earth moves around the sun, the moon travels along with it?

The moon revolves around Earth while Earth revolves around the sun. The moon takes about 27 days to complete one revolution around Earth. The moon also rotates on its axis about once every 27 days. Because these two motions happen at the same rate, the same side of the moon always faces Earth.

1. Develop Write a caption for this diagram.

....

....

....

....

moon

Earth

sun

Diagrams in this lesson are not to scale.

new moon

None of the moon appears lit.

first quarter phase

About a week after the new moon, the moon looks like a half circle.

Moon Phases

The moon is the brightest object in the night sky. But the moon does not make light. It reflects light from the sun. When you see the moon shining, you are seeing reflected sunlight.

Half of the moon is always lit by the sun. But the moon's lit half cannot always be seen from Earth. Every day, you can see different amounts of the lit half. These changes are caused by the movements of Earth and the moon.

The shape the moon seems to have at a given time is called a **moon phase.** The moon's phases change in a cycle that repeats every 29 $\frac{1}{2}$ days. At first, no part of the moon's lit half is visible. This is called a new moon. During the next two weeks, more of the moon's lit half becomes visible. The full moon phase is when the moon looks like a complete circle. During the weeks after the full moon, you see less and less of the moon's lit half. Then there is another new moon.

2. **Infer** The moon does not make its own light. Why is it the brightest object in the night sky?

3. CHALLENGE The moon reflects sunlight during the daytime too. Why is the moon harder to see during the day?

THE BIG

full moon phase

A full moon happens about two weeks after the new moon. You see all of the lit half of the moon.

third quarter phase

Three-fourths of the moon's cycle is complete. In a week, there will be a new moon again.

Half of the moon is always lit by the sun. A person standing on Earth sees different parts of the sunlit half as the moon moves in its orbit.

first quarter

new moon

full moon

third quarter

4. **Identify** Look at the diagram. Find the position of the moon where its sunlit side faces away from Earth.

Draw an ✗ on it. What is this moon phase?

....

Characteristics of the Moon

The moon is the closest natural object to Earth. It is 384,000 kilometers (239,000 miles) away. The moon is smaller and has much less mass than Earth. In fact, Earth's volume is 49 times greater than the moon's. Earth has 81 times more mass.

The moon's surface has many craters. A **crater** is a bowl-shaped hole on the surface of an object in space. Most of the moon's craters formed when large objects, such as asteroids, smashed into the moon. When you look at the moon, you see that there are light and dark areas on it. The light areas are mountains and highlands. There are many craters in these areas. The dark parts of the moon are flat areas with some craters. Billions of years ago, volcanoes erupted on the moon. Lava from these eruptions spread out and hardened. It formed the dark areas.

The temperature on the moon's surface varies. During the day, the temperature can rise as high as 127°C (260°F). At night, it can get as cold as -173°C (-280°F).

5. **Conclude** Look at the area of the moon in the picture. Do you think this area is part of the highlands? Explain how you know.

....

....

Telescopes

You can use tools to help you see the moon better. One tool is a telescope. A telescope makes objects that are far away look like they are nearer and larger. You can use a telescope to see more details of the light and dark areas on the moon's surface.

People have used spacecrafts to put telescopes in outer space. For example, the Hubble Space Telescope began orbiting Earth in 1990. Scientists use it to observe and take pictures of planets, stars, moons, and other space objects.

You can see much more with a telescope than you can with your eyes alone.

6. ◉ **Main Idea and Details** Tell what the main idea of this page is.

Got it?

7. **UNLOCK THE BIG ?** How do the movements of Earth and the moon cause the moon's appearance to change?

....

....

8. **Explain** What are the dark areas on the moon's surface?

....

....

⬛ **Stop!** I need help with ....

⏸ **Wait!** I have a question about ....

▶ **Go!** Now I know ....

Why do you see phases of the moon?

Follow a Procedure

☑ 1. **Make a model** of the night sky. Glue black paper to the inside of the box and lid.

☑ 2. Poke holes in the paper where there are holes in the box. Use crayons to label the small holes.

☑ 3. Push the flashlight into the large hole in the side. Tape it in place.

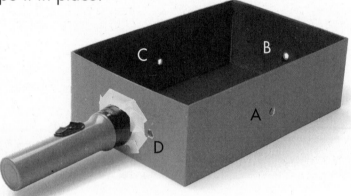

☑ 4. Attach the thread to the ball with the tack. Tape the thread in the center of the lid.

about 4 cm

Materials

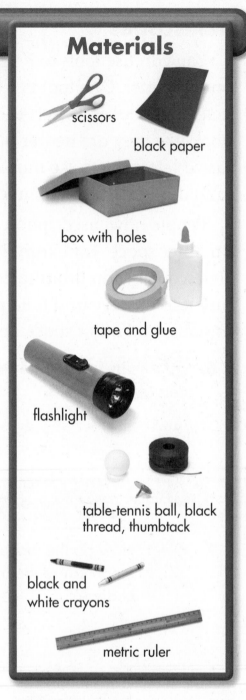

scissors

black paper

box with holes

tape and glue

flashlight

table-tennis ball, black thread, thumbtack

black and white crayons

metric ruler

Inquiry Skill
Scientists sometimes **make a model** to help them observe and understand events.

5. Put the lid on the box. Turn on the flashlight. Look through each hole. **Record** your **observations.**

Phases of the Moon		
Hole	Drawing of Moon Phase	Name of Moon Phase
A		
B		
C		
D		

Analyze and Conclude

6. Your **model** sun always lights half the moon. Why does the moon sometimes appear to be completely lit?

....

....

....

7. **UNLOCK THE BIG ?** **Draw a Conclusion** Why does the moon sometimes not appear lit?

....

....

....

....

Galileo was born in Italy in 1564.

Biography
Galileo

Galileo was a mathematician and astronomer. During his life, Galileo did many science experiments. He also invented science tools. Galileo heard that someone invented a tool that could magnify distant objects. Galileo used this new tool to invent a better telescope. Galileo's telescope could magnify distant objects twenty times better.

Galileo pointed his telescope into the sky and made many discoveries. He saw that the moon has craters. He saw four moons that move around Jupiter. He saw that Venus has different phases. Galileo used his observations about Venus's phases to infer that Earth moves around the sun. These observations helped explain some natural events. For example, Galileo inferred that the sun is the center of the solar system.

Since Galileo, scientists have used telescopes to see objects in space. Look at the picture of Galileo's telescope. Tell how it is similar to and different from the telescopes used today.

APPLY THE BIG ? How did Galileo use a telescope to help us understand the solar system?

....

....

....

Vocabulary Smart Cards

star
light-year
planet
solar system
axis
rotation
revolution
moon phase
crater

Play a Game!

Cut out the Vocabulary Smart Cards.

Work with a partner. Choose a Vocabulary Smart Card.

Say as many words as you can think of to describe the vocabulary word.

Have your partner guess the word.

Have your partner repeat with another vocabulary card.

solar system

sistema solar

star

estrella

axis

eje

light-year

año luz

rotation

rotación

planet

planeta

a giant ball of hot, glowing gases that release energy

What is another meaning of this word?

....

....

....

bola gigante de gases calientes y brillantes que emiten energía

---

the sun, the eight planets and their moons, and other objects that revolve around the sun

Use a dictionary. Find a meaning of *solar*.

....

....

el Sol, los ocho planetas con sus satélites y otros objetos que giran alrededor del Sol

---

the distance light travels in one year

Write a sentence using this word.

....

....

....

....

distancia que la luz viaja en un año

---

an imaginary line around which Earth spins

Draw Earth's axis.

línea imaginaria alrededor de la cual gira la Tierra

---

a large, ball-shaped body that revolves, or travels around, the sun

Name two examples.

....

....

....

cuerpo de gran tamaño, con forma de bola, que se mueve alrededor del Sol

---

one complete spin on an axis

Write the verb form of this word.

....

....

vuelta completa alrededor de un eje

Interactive Vocabulary

Make a Word Question!

Choose a vocabulary word and write a question about it in the center box. Identify the word in the box above. Give examples in the boxes below. Write some facts about the word in the boxes to the right.

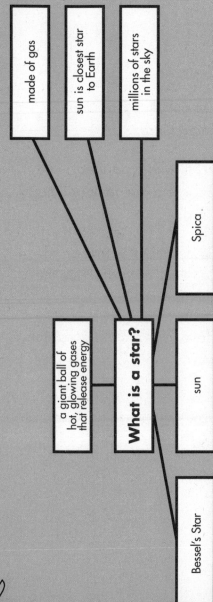

made of gas

sun is closest star to Earth

millions of stars in the sky

Spica

a giant ball of hot, glowing gases that release energy

What is a star?

sun

Bessel's Star

306

revolution

traslación

moon phase

fase de la Luna

crater

cráter

one complete trip around the sun

Write a sentence using this word.

....

....

....

....

vuelta completa alrededor del Sol

the shape the moon seems to have at a given time

Give two examples of this word.

....

....

....

forma que la Luna parece tener en un momento dado

a bowl-shaped hole on the surface of an object in space

Draw an example.

agujero con forma de tazón en la superficie de un objeto del espacio

REVIEW THE BIG **?** How do objects in space affect one another?

Lesson 1

What is a star?

- A star is a ball of hot, glowing gases that release energy.
- Stars can be larger or smaller than our sun.
- A group of stars can make a pattern in the sky.

Lesson 2

What do you know about our solar system?

- A planet is a large, ball-shaped body that orbits the sun.
- The solar system is made up of the sun, the eight planets and their moons, and other objects that orbit the sun.

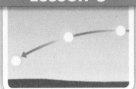

Lesson 3

What are Earth's patterns?

- Earth's rotation causes night and day.
- The seasons are caused by the tilt of Earth's axis and the planet's revolution around the sun.

Lesson 4

What is known about the moon?

- The moon revolves around Earth and rotates on its axis about once every 27 days.
- The moon's phases change in a cycle.

Chapter Review

APPLY
THE BIG
?

How do objects in space affect one another?

Lesson 1

What is a star?

1. **Vocabulary** A hot, glowing ball of gases is a _____.
   A. planet
   B. gravity
   C. telescope
   D. star

2. **Infer** How does a star's distance from Earth affect the time it takes light from that star to reach Earth?

Lesson 2

What do you know about our solar system?

3. **Write About It** Explain how the inner planets are different from the outer planets.

Lesson 3

What are Earth's patterns?

4. **Predict** The picture below shows the shadow of a bike at noon on a summer day. How would the bike's shadow look different at noon on a winter day? Explain.

5. **Vocabulary** Earth makes one _____ every 24 hours.
   A. revolution
   B. circle
   C. rotation
   D. orbit

6. **Describe** Why does the sun appear to change position in the sky?

Lesson 4

What is known about the moon?

7. ◎ **Main Idea and Details** What is the main idea of the following passage?

> The temperature on the moon's surface varies. During the day, the temperature can rise as high as 127°C (260°F). At night, it can get as cold as -173°C (-280°F). At the bottom of craters, the temperature stays around -240°C (-400°F) all the time.

....

....

....

8. **Vocabulary** The shape the moon seems to have at a given time is called a _____.
   A. crater
   B. moon phase
   C. orbit
   D. revolution

9. **Explain** Why is only one side of the moon visible from Earth?

....

....

....

....

....

10. **APPLY THE BIG ?** **How do objects in space affect one another?**

....

Give an example of how the sun affects Earth. Then give an example of how the sun affects the moon.

....

....

....

....

....

Fill in the bubble next to the answer choice you think is correct for each multiple-choice question.

1 You can see a full moon in the sky about once every _____.

Ⓐ week
Ⓑ 14 days
Ⓒ 29 days
Ⓓ year

2 How would you describe our sun?

Ⓐ It is larger than all other stars.
Ⓑ It is larger than some stars and smaller than other stars.
Ⓒ It is smaller than all other stars.
Ⓓ There are no other stars like our sun.

3 Which of these planets is farthest from the sun?

Ⓐ Venus
Ⓑ Saturn
Ⓒ Mercury
Ⓓ Neptune

4 Look at the picture.

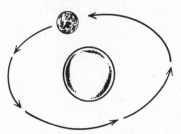

What is the path shown in the picture?

Ⓐ the rotation of a planet
Ⓑ the rotation of the sun
Ⓒ a planet's orbit around the sun
Ⓓ the sun's orbit around a planet

5 Earth is the only planet in our solar system known to support life. Explain what makes life on Earth possible.

....

....

....

....

....

STEM

New Horizons

The *New Horizons* spacecraft can travel 60,000 kilometers per hour! That's fast! *New Horizons* is traveling on a mission to Pluto and a region of the solar system called the Kuiper Belt. *New Horizons* was launched in January 2006.

It is expected to reach Pluto in July 2015. Its purpose is to help scientists learn more about Pluto and objects in the Kuiper Belt. This information will help scientists understand how Pluto and these objects fit into our solar system.

To help scientists study these objects up close, they worked with engineers to develop a new kind of spacecraft that is small and agile. The scientists and engineers used math to calculate the correct speed and path of the spacecraft.

Justify *New Horizons* has a student-built instrument: Student Dust Counter (SDC). Why do you think students want to know about dust in our solar system?

Materials

Big Dipper Model Pattern

Big Dipper Drawing

marker

7 straws

tape

metric ruler

scissors

7 pieces of foil

clay

Can viewpoint affect the appearance of star patterns?

The Big Dipper is the pattern formed by several stars as seen from Earth.

Ask a question.

How would the Big Dipper appear if observed from a distant part of the galaxy?

State a hypothesis.

1. Write a **hypothesis** by circling one choice and finishing the sentence.
   If the stars in the Big Dipper are viewed from another part of the galaxy, then they will form
   (a) *the same*
   (b) *a different*
   pattern because

....

....

Identify and control variables.

2. In an **experiment** you change only one **variable.** Everything else must remain the same. What must stay the same? Give one example.

....

....

3. Tell the one change you will make.

....

....

....

Design your test.

☑ 4. Draw how you will set up your **model.**

☑ 5. List your steps in the order you will do them.

Do your test.

☑ **6.** Follow the steps you wrote.

☑ **7. Record** your results in the table.

Collect and record your data.

☑ **8.** Draw what you see. Fill in the chart.

Interpret your data.

☑ **9.** Compare your drawings. Describe how they are alike or different. Explain.

....

....

....

....

Work Like a Scientist
Communication among scientists is important. Talk with your classmates. Question, discuss, and check one another's evidence and explanations.

State your conclusion.

10. Communicate your conclusion about the appearance of star patterns away from Earth. Did your results support your **hypothesis**? Compare your results with others.

....

....

....

....

....

....

....

....

Model a Solar System

Use a large sheet of paper and colored markers to make a model of the solar system. Describe the parts of the solar system and the patterns your model shows. Make sure the model includes the sun and eight planets.

- How does your model help explain how the solar system works?
- Why is your model solar system not a perfect model of the solar system?

Rock Fantasy

Write a fantasy, which is a made-up story, about how an igneous rock changes into a metamorphic rock. Include a description of the environment the rock is in and how the rock looks and feels. Make sure your fantasy has a beginning, middle, and end.

Brightness of Stars

Stars differ in brightness. Stars also differ in their distance from Earth.

Experiment with flashlights to test how the distance of a light source from the viewer affects its brightness. Predict what will happen when the light source is moved. Use your results to make inferences about the brightness of stars.

- Do your observations support your prediction?
- What can you infer about the brightness of stars?

Using Scientific Methods

1. Ask a question.
2. State your hypothesis.
3. Identify and control variables.
4. Test your hypothesis.
5. Collect and record your data.
6. Interpret your data.
7. State your conclusion.
8. Go further.

Physical Science

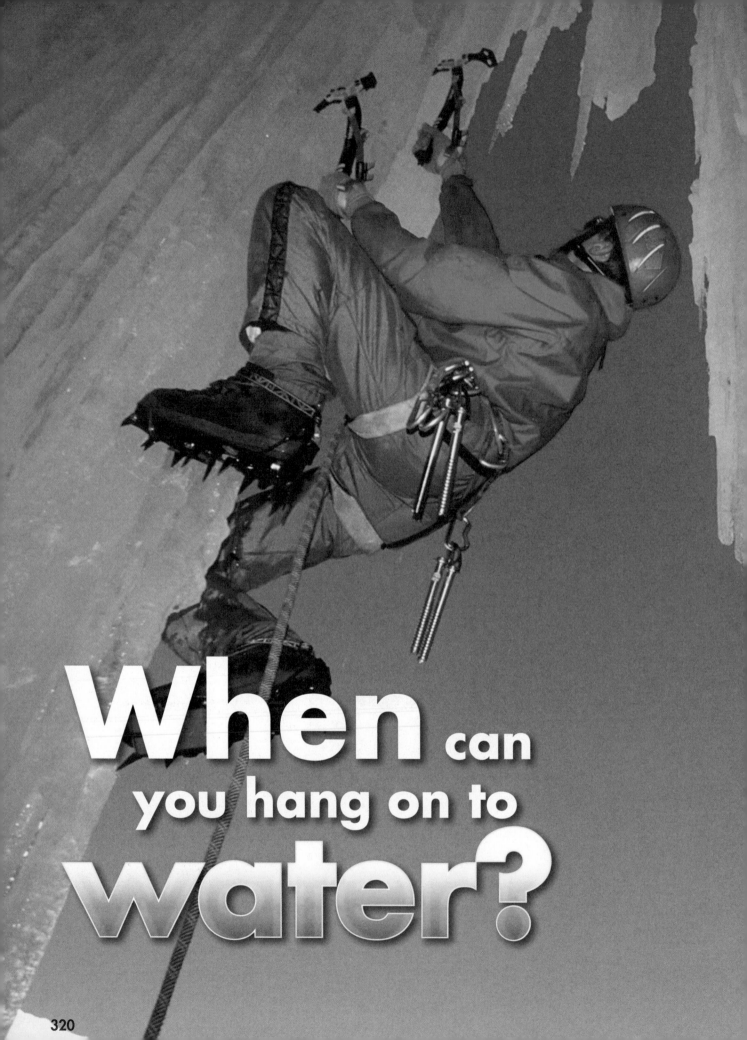

When can you hang on to water?

Matter

Chapter 8

Vertical ice climbing is challenging. Vertical ice climbing requires a lot of safety equipment. People climb ice in mountainous regions around the world, including the Rockies.

Predict What properties do you think allow climbers to climb ice? Why?

....

....

....

THE BIG ? How can matter be described?

How can you classify objects?

Objects can be classified by listening to the sound they make when dropped.

☐ **1. Observe** Drop each object. Listen to the sound.

☐ **2.** Have one member of your group hold up a folder. Drop an object behind the folder so that others in your group cannot see it.

☐ **3.** Ask them to identify the object that made the sound. Repeat with each object.

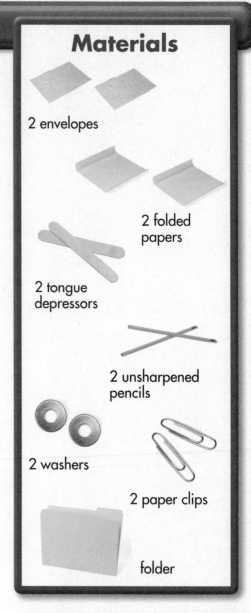

Materials

2 envelopes

2 folded papers

2 tongue depressors

2 unsharpened pencils

2 washers

2 paper clips

folder

☐ **4. Classify** Group the objects with similar sounds.

Explain Your Results

5. Classify Some objects make similar sounds. How are the objects alike?

6. UNLOCK THE BIG ? **Communicate** How can you use sound to classify objects?

Inquiry Skill
Observing objects carefully can help you **classify** them.

Compare and Contrast

- When you **compare** things, you tell how they are alike.
- When you **contrast** things, you tell how they are different.

Rock Collectors

Ben and Misha both collect rocks. Ben likes brightly colored rocks. He is a member of a rock hunters club. This club goes on collecting trips. Misha has a different way of collecting her favorite kinds of rocks—rocks that have fossils. Misha's uncle sends her rocks that have fossils from all around the world. Unlike Ben, Misha just has to make the trip to her mailbox to add to her collection.

Practice It!

Complete the graphic organizer to compare and contrast Ben's and Misha's favorite rocks and the way they collect rocks.

Ben   Misha

What is matter?

Envision It!

Tell how you can describe these objects.

MY PLANET DiARY

FunFact

Have you heard people tell you to drink milk? Did you know that milk contains a metal? Calcium is in milk. Calcium is the most common metal in your body. A substance that contains calcium is in your bones and teeth. In nature, it is also in seashells and coral. This substance that contains calcium gives bones, teeth, and seashells their strength.

Why do you think your body contains a lot of calcium?

What do you think might happen if your body did not get enough calcium?

bone—a substance that contains calcium and other elements

pure calcium

Matter Everywhere

Everything you can see, smell, or touch is matter. Many things that you cannot see, smell, or touch are matter too. Air is an example of matter you sometimes cannot see, smell, or touch. **Matter** is anything that takes up space and has mass. You can feel the mass of objects as weight when you pick them up. When you blow up a balloon, you see that even air takes up space.

Look at the hockey puck and volleyball. The puck is small and hard. The volleyball is large and soft. The puck and volleyball look different, but they are both matter.

1. ◉ **Compare and Contrast** How are the hockey puck and the volleyball alike and different?

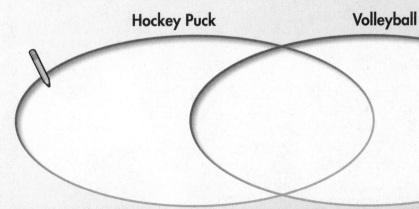

Hockey Puck   Volleyball

Properties of Matter

A **property** is something about matter that you can observe with one or more of your senses. Some properties of matter are size, shape, color, texture, and hardness. A basketball might be large, round, orange, bumpy, and hard. *Bumpy* and *smooth* describe an object's texture. **Texture** is how an object feels to the touch. **Hardness** describes how firm an object, such as an inflated basketball, is.

The properties of an object depend in part on the materials it is made from. Wood, plastic, rubber, and metals are examples of materials. A tennis ball and a basketball make different sounds when they bounce. This is partly because they are made from different materials with different properties. Your sense of smell tells you about another property—odor.

2. Identify Name two materials your shoes are made from. Compare the texture of the materials.

....

....

....

....

3. Tell Which properties of matter best describe this flower?

Lightning Lab

Float or Sink

The ability to float is a property of some matter. Put ten small objects into a large bowl of water one at a time. Record which items float and which sink. Classify the objects by their ability to float.

4. **Determine** Look around your classroom. Write the names of four more objects. Use a different property of matter to describe each object.

Object	Property	Description
globe	shape	round
	size	
	color	
	texture	
	hardness	

Got it?

5. **Define** What is matter?

....

....

6. **Compare** Name two common objects and identify what they are made of. Use properties to tell how they are alike.

....

....

⬜ **Stop!** I need help with ....

⏸ **Wait!** I have a question about ....

▶ **Go!** Now I know ....

Lesson 2

What are states of matter?

Tell what you think the black rock around the flowing lava is.

Inquiry **Explore It!**

What makes water change states?

☐ **1.** Put an ice cube in the cup.
Put the cup into the bag. Seal the bag.

☐ **2.** Tape the bag to a sunny window.
Predict what will happen over the next day.

☐ **3.** **Record** your **observations**. Discuss.
Try to explain the changes you observed.

Materials

cup   ice cube

plastic bag   tape

Data Table

Time	Prediction	Observation
After 2 hours		
After 24 hours		

Explain Your Results

4. Infer What made the ice change?

....

mYscienceonLine.com | **Explore It!** Animation

Words to Know

states of matter	boil
freeze	evaporation
melt	condensation

States of Matter

All matter is made of small particles. These particles are so small that you cannot see them, even under a magnifying lens. The particles are always moving. In some kinds of matter, the particles are held tightly together. In other kinds of matter, they are held less tightly.

States of matter are the forms that matter can take. Three states of matter are solids, liquids, and gases. In solids, particles are packed tightly together. In liquids, particles are packed together less tightly. In gases, particles move about freely.

Your science book is a solid. Like other solids, the book does not change shape. The particles of solids are held tightly together.

1. Circle the words that name three states of matter.

2. **Explain** Which objects in your backpack are solids? How do you know?

....

....

....

....

At-Home Lab

Change of States

Get two plastic cups. Fill each cup with the same amount of water. Mark the water level. Put one cup in a freezer. Put the other cup on a shelf. Observe what happens to the level of water in each cup after three hours.

Solids

Solids are made of tightly packed particles. Solids have their own shape. You can easily measure both the mass and the volume of solids. Like your science book, the fabric of the balloons and balloon baskets in the picture are also solids. The particles in the fabric of the balloons and baskets are tightly packed together.

3. **Identify** Tell two other solids you see in the picture.

Liquids

Particles in liquids are held together less tightly. The particles in a liquid flow past one another. Liquids take the shape of their containers. If you pour a liquid from one container to another, the liquid will take the shape of the new container. You can easily measure the mass and volume of liquids.

Gases

The tiny particles that make up gases are far apart compared to solids and liquids. The particles of a gas move freely and take up the space of their container. The particles of a gas bounce off one another as they move freely. All matter has mass, so gas has mass too. You can measure the mass and volume of a gas.

The air in the balloon is a gas. The air takes the shape of this balloon. The particles of air move freely in the balloon.

4. **CHALLENGE** Other than balloons, what objects give gases a different shape? Explain.

Changes in Water

Matter can change states through heating or cooling. When water heats up, the space between the water particles becomes greater. When water cools down, the space between the water particles becomes less.

When liquid water cools to 0°C (32°F), it **freezes,** or changes from a liquid to a solid. It changes to ice, solid water. When ice is heated, it **melts,** or changes from a solid to a liquid. Ice melts at 0°C (32°F).

You can see water as a liquid and as a solid. You cannot see water as a gas. Water as a gas is called *water vapor.* When water is heated to 100°C, it **boils,** or changes from liquid water into bubbles of water vapor. Water vapor and steam are not the same. Steam is droplets of liquid water in the air.

When water boils, it evaporates. **Evaporation** is the change from liquid water to water vapor. Evaporation can also happen slowly at the water's surface.

5. **Explain** Tell what state of matter water changes into when it evaporates.

6. [CHALLENGE] What do the melting temperature and freezing temperature of water have in common?

condensation

myscienceonline.com | Got *it?* 60-Second Video

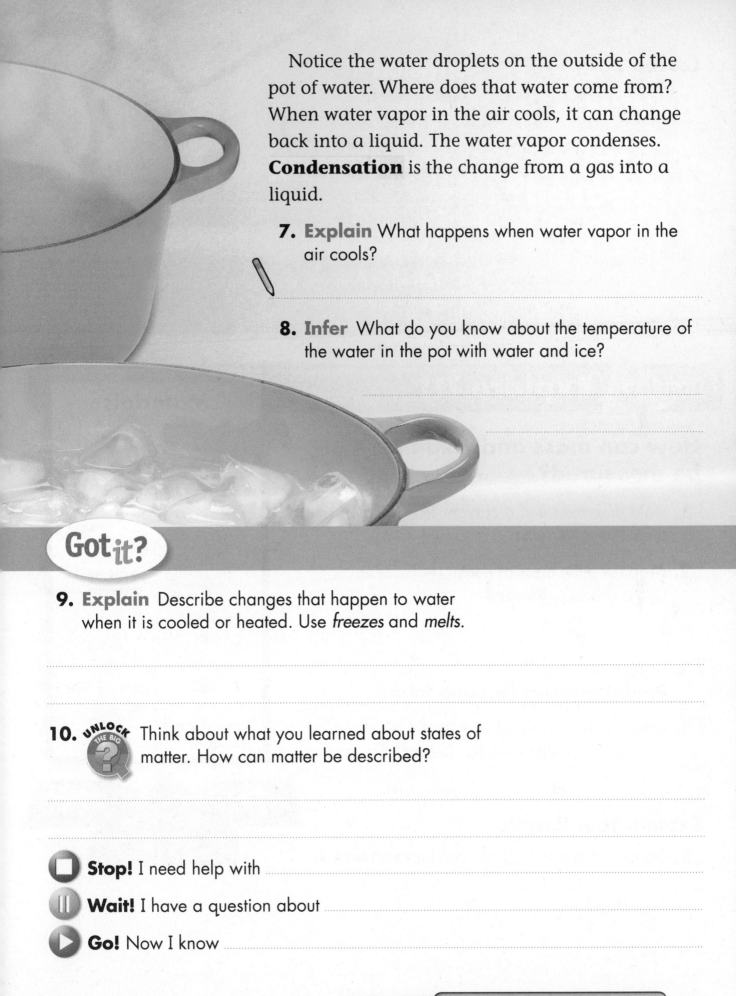

Notice the water droplets on the outside of the pot of water. Where does that water come from? When water vapor in the air cools, it can change back into a liquid. The water vapor condenses. **Condensation** is the change from a gas into a liquid.

7. **Explain** What happens when water vapor in the air cools?

8. **Infer** What do you know about the temperature of the water in the pot with water and ice?

Got it?

9. **Explain** Describe changes that happen to water when it is cooled or heated. Use *freezes* and *melts*.

10. **UNLOCK THE BIG ?** Think about what you learned about states of matter. How can matter be described?

⬛ **Stop!** I need help with

⏸ **Wait!** I have a question about

▶ **Go!** Now I know

How is matter measured?

Envision It!

Tell what tools you could use to measure the art supplies.

Inquiry **Explore It!**

How can mass and volume be measured?

☑ **1.** Hold an eraser and a crayon. Tell which you think has more mass.

☑ **2.** **Measure** the mass of each.
Use a balance. **Record.**

.... g   .... g

☑ **3.** Look at each liquid.
Predict which has the greater volume.

☑ **4.** Measure the volume of each liquid.
Use the graduated cylinder. Record.

.... mL   .... mL

Explain Your Results

5. Tell how mass and volume can be **measured.**

....

....

....

Materials

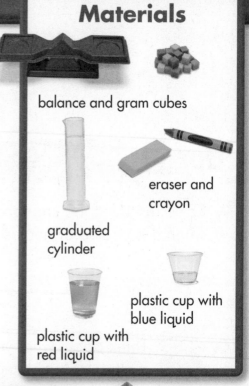

balance and gram cubes

graduated cylinder

eraser and crayon

plastic cup with blue liquid

plastic cup with red liquid

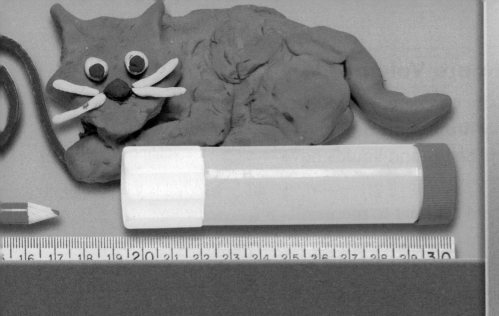

I will know how to measure and compare properties of matter.

Words to Know

volume

mass

Measure Length

Matter is anything that has mass and takes up space. Length is one property of matter that can be measured. Length is the distance from one end of an object to the other end. To measure length, you can use metric rulers and metersticks. You can use these lengths to compare objects. For example, you can measure and compare the length of a pillbug and a beetle to determine which one is longer.

The basic metric unit of length is the meter (m). Shorter lengths are measured in centimeters (cm) or millimeters (mm). There are 100 cm in a meter. There are 1,000 mm in a meter. Longer distances are measured in kilometers (km). There are 1,000 m in a kilometer.

1. **Solve** Some objects are too small to see easily. A hand lens or magnifying glass makes this pillbug easier to measure. Measure about how long this pillbug is in centimeters.

....

....

Measure and Compare Volume

Another way to measure and compare matter is by volume. An object's **volume** is the amount of space the object takes up. Solids and liquids have volume.

You can use a graduated cylinder to measure the volume of a liquid. The basic metric unit for measuring liquid volume is the liter (L). Graduated cylinders mark smaller parts of a liter called milliliters (mL). There are 1,000 milliliters in a liter.

You can measure the volume of a solid, like a rock, using water. A rock keeps its shape in water. A rock pushes water out of its way when it sinks.

2. Solve Compare the volume of the toy to the volume of the rock.

What is the volume of the toy?

What is the volume of the rock?

Which object has a greater volume?

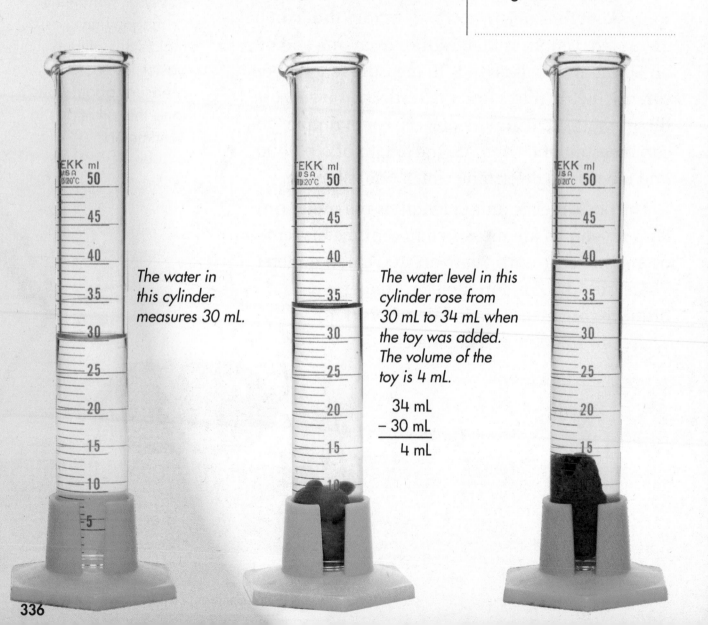

The water in this cylinder measures 30 mL.

The water level in this cylinder rose from 30 mL to 34 mL when the toy was added. The volume of the toy is 4 mL.

$$\begin{array}{r} 34\text{ mL} \\ -\ 30\text{ mL} \\ \hline 4\text{ mL} \end{array}$$

Measure and Compare Mass

You can also measure an object's mass. An object's **mass** is the amount of matter it has. Solids, liquids, and gases all have mass. A balance is a tool used to measure mass.

A metric unit for mass is the gram (g). Larger matter is measured in kilograms (kg). There are 1,000 grams in a kilogram.

3. Solve What is the mass of the crayon?

Each cube has a mass of 1 g.

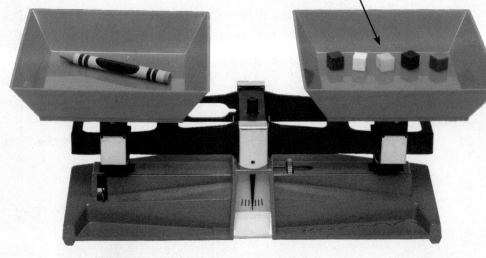

4. Solve The balance pans containing the robot and gram cubes below are even. There are 52 cubes on one pan. What is the mass of the robot?

5. Compare Which has greater mass— the crayon or robot?

Problem Solving

Common Objects	Mass (g)
stapler	500
paper clip	1
pencil	5
dime	2

1 List the objects in the chart in order from least mass to greatest mass.

For exercises **2** through **6,** write and solve a number sentence.

2 How many dimes are needed to equal the mass of 6 pencils?

3 A lime has a mass of 80 grams. How many pencils are needed to equal the mass of one lime?

4 A mug has a mass of 400 grams. How many more grams does a stapler have than a mug?

5 You have nine dimes for a total mass of 18 grams. How many more grams do nine dimes have than seven paper clips?

6 An adult male killer whale has a mass of about 4,500 kg. A dictionary has a mass of 1 kg. How many dictionaries are needed to equal the mass of an adult male killer whale?

myscienceonLine.com | Got it? | 60-Second Video

Measure and Compare Temperature

You can use different scales to measure temperature. The Celsius scale is often used in science. Degrees Celsius is written as °C. The Fahrenheit scale is often used in everyday life in the United States. For example, the outside temperature is reported in degrees Fahrenheit. Degrees Fahrenheit is written as °F. Sometimes both scales are used.

6. Measure What is the temperature of the ice water in the top glass in degrees Celsius? Record the temperature next to the glass.

7. Compute The temperature of the ice in the bottom glass is 0°C (32°F). What is the temperature difference between the water in the two glasses? Show your work.

Got it?

8. Select Which metric unit would you use to measure length and width, temperature, volume, and mass?

....

....

....

9. Analyze What are you measuring when you measure an object's mass?

....

□ **Stop!** I need help with ....

❚❚ **Wait!** I have a question about ....

▶ **Go!** Now I know ....

Inquiry Investigate It!

Does the method you use to measure affect your results?

Follow a Procedure

Using a Metric Ruler

☑ **1.** Stack ten cubes.

☑ **2. Measure** the height, length, and width of the stack. **Record** your **data** below.

☑ **3.** Multiply to find the volume. Record.

  volume = height × length × width

☑ **4.** Repeat with the clay block.

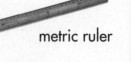

Inquiry Skill Scientists **measure** carefully and record data accurately.

volume = (height) × (length) × (width)

Measuring Volume Using a Metric Ruler				
	Height (cm)	**Length** (cm)	**Width** (cm)	**Volume** (cm³)
Stack of gram cubes	_____	_____	_____	_____
Clay block	_____	_____	_____	_____

Using a Graduated Cylinder

☑ **5.** Pour 30 mL water into the cylinder.

☑ **6.** Drop in 10 cubes one by one. Measure the volume. Record.

volume of water and object (Step 6)	_____ mL
− volume of water (Step 5)	− 30 mL
volume of object (Step 7)	_____ mL

☑ **7.** Subtract to find the volume of the cubes. Record.

☑ **8.** Repeat with the clay block.

Measuring Volume Using a Graduated Cylinder				
Object	Volume of Water with Object	Volume of Water	Volume of Object (mL)	Volume of Object (cm³) (1 cm³ = mL)
Stack of gram cubes	_____ mL	30 mL	_____ mL	_____ cm³
Clay block	_____ mL	30 mL	_____ mL	_____ cm³

Analyze and Conclude

9. You **measured** the volume of the stack of cubes two ways. Compare your results. Were they the same? Explain.

....

....

....

10. UNLOCK THE BIG ? What are some **measurements** that can be used to describe matter.

....

....

STEM

Paint

Technology such as this mixer is used to mix and develop new paint colors.

Paint is all around you! Paint can make surfaces more colorful. What is paint? Some paint is solid coloring matter mixed with two types of liquids. The solid coloring matter is called pigment.

Who develops new paint colors? Many new paint colors are developed by scientists called chemists. Chemists study the properties of substances. These properties include size, color, and texture. Chemists also study how these substances can be mixed. For example, more red pigment makes the paint redder. Chemists change paint in other ways, too. Sometimes they make paint safer for the environment. They also make paint that does not separate into the pigment and liquids when brushed on a wall.

Determine Why do you think that math is an important skill for anyone who makes paint?

Vocabulary Smart Cards

matter
property
texture
hardness
states of matter
freeze
melt
boil
evaporation
condensation
volume
mass

Play a Game!

Choose a Vocabulary Smart Card.

Work with a partner. Write several sentences using the vocabulary word.

Have your partner repeat with another Vocabulary Smart Card.

hardness

dureza

matter

materia

states of matter

estados de la materia

property

propiedad

freeze

congelarse

texture

textura

anything that takes up space and has mass

Write a sentence using this word.

....
....
....

todo lo que ocupa espacio y tiene masa

---

a description of how firm an object is

Write the adjective form of this word. Use it in a sentence.

....
....
....

descripción de la firmeza de un objeto

---

matter | solid
gas | liquid

Make a Word Wheel!

Choose a vocabulary word and write it in the center of the Word Wheel graphic organizer. Write synonyms or related words on the wheel spokes.

---

something about matter that you can observe with one or more of your senses

What is another meaning of this word?

....
....
....

algo en la materia que puedes percibir con uno o más de tus sentidos

---

forms that matter can take

Draw an example.

formas que la materia puede tener

---

how an object feels to the touch

Write a sentence using this word.

....
....
....

cómo se siente un objeto al tocarlo

---

to change from a liquid to a solid

Write a sentence using this word.

....
....
....

cambiar de líquido a sólido

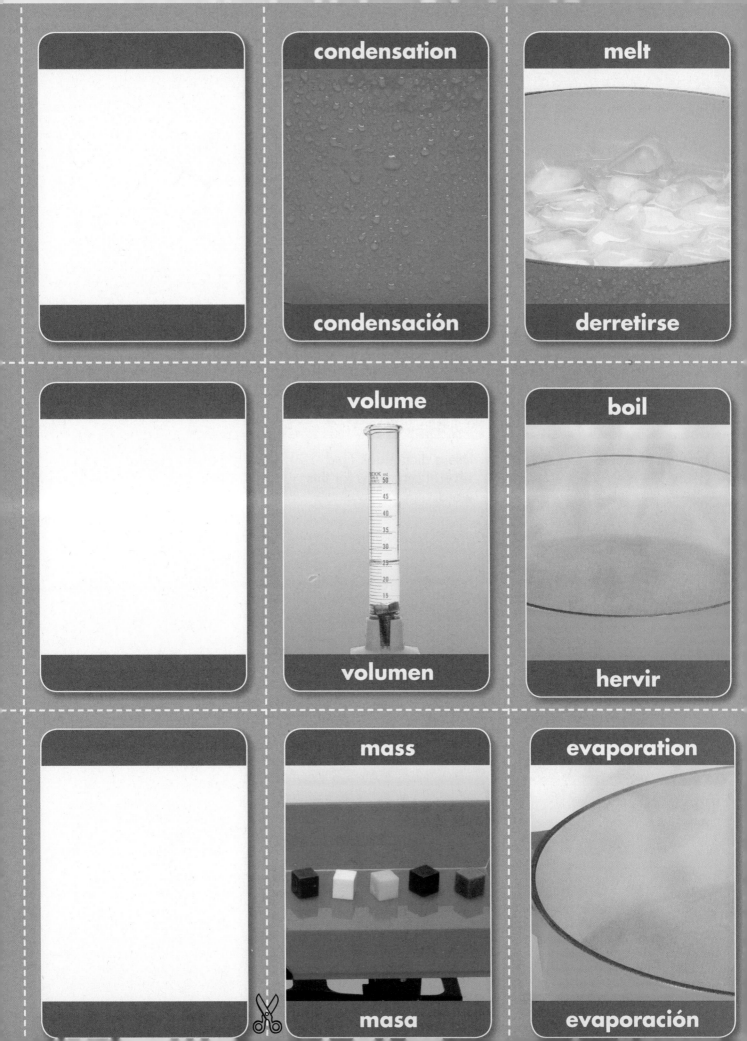

	condensation	**melt**
	condensación	derretirse
	volume	**boil**
	volumen	hervir
	mass	**evaporation**
	masa	evaporación

to change from a solid to a
liquid

Draw an example.

cambiar de sólido a líquido

the change from a gas into
a liquid

Write a sentence using
this word.

cambio de un gas a líquido

to change from liquid water
into bubbles of water vapor

Draw an example.

cambiar de agua en estado
líquido a burbujas de vapor

the amount of space an
object takes up

Use a dictionary. Find
several synonyms for this
word.

espacio que ocupa un
objeto

the change from liquid
water to water vapor

Use the verb form in a
sentence.

cambio del agua en estado
líquido a vapor de agua

the amount of matter an
object has

Write a sentence using
this word.

cantidad de materia que un
objeto tiene

Lesson 1

What is matter?

- Matter is anything that takes up space and has mass.
- Properties of matter include size, shape, color, texture, and hardness.

Lesson 2

What are states of matter?

- Three states of matter are solids, liquids, and gases.
- Water melts, freezes, boils, evaporates, and condenses.

Lesson 3

How is matter measured?

- Properties of matter, such as mass, volume, length, and temperature, can be measured and compared using tools.

Lesson 1

What is matter?

1. **Vocabulary** Anything that takes up space and has mass is called

   _____.

   A. water
   B. air
   C. solid
   D. matter

2. **Contrast** A puzzle piece and checker pieces have different properties. Use some properties of matter to contrast them.

   ....

   ....

   ....

3. **Determine** You are given several small objects. How can you classify them by their ability to float?

   ....

   ....

   ....

Lesson 2

What are states of matter?

4. **Summarize** What terms did you learn that describe the changes water undergoes when it changes states through heating?

   ....

   ....

   ....

   ....

5. **Describe** What happens when water vapor comes in contact with a cold surface?

   ....

   ....

   ....

   ....

6. ◎ **Compare and Contrast** Compare and contrast water as a liquid and water as a gas.

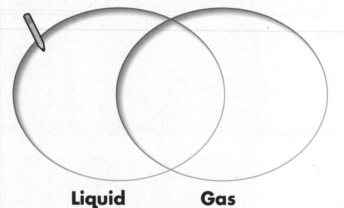

Liquid   **Gas**

Lesson 3

How is matter measured?

7. Analyze Which tool and unit of measure would you use to measure the length of a book?

....

....

....

....

Do the math!

8. A drink comes in a bottle with a volume of 473 mL. The serving size on each bottle is 240 mL. Is 473 mL enough for you and your friend to each have a full serving? If not, how many milliliters short of two full servings is the bottle?

....

....

....

Do the math!

9. Use the two cylinders to answer the question. What is the volume of the bolt in milliliters?

....

....

10. APPLY THE BIG **How can matter be described?**

....

Think about a calculator. How would you describe and measure it? Use the terms *state of matter* and *mass*.

....

....

....

....

Fill in the bubble next to the answer choice you think is correct for each multiple-choice question.

1 Which word can be used to describe the texture of an object?

Ⓐ big
Ⓑ red
Ⓒ smooth
Ⓓ folding

2 What are solids, liquids, and gases?

Ⓐ masses of matter
Ⓑ states of matter
Ⓒ volumes of matter
Ⓓ measurements of matter

3 Look at the picture of the ball in water. What can you conclude about the ball's properties?

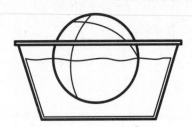

Ⓐ The ball is hard.
Ⓑ The ball is made of plastic.
Ⓒ The ball has a smooth texture.
Ⓓ The ball floats.

4 What tool would you use to measure the amount of space that a liquid takes up?

Ⓐ thermometer
Ⓑ meter stick
Ⓒ graduated cylinder
Ⓓ balance

5 Ice melting into water is a change between which two states of matter?

Ⓐ liquid to gas
Ⓑ solid to liquid
Ⓒ gas to liquid
Ⓓ liquid to solid

6 Explain what happens to water vapor when it condenses.

....

....

....

....

Rubber

Did you know that some or all of the rubber used to make the basketball you play with comes from as far away as Brazil or Malaysia?

Farmers collect rubber from rubber trees on farms. First, a small piece of tree bark is cut off. Then rubber flows out of the tree and is collected in containers. When rubber is first collected from trees, it is called latex. At factories, the latex is used to make sheets of rubber. Sheets of rubber are made by adding acid. Then the water is pressed out. After pressing, the sheets of rubber are sent to companies all over the world to make different things. One item made from rubber is a basketball. Most basketballs are made of both rubber and leather.

Big World

My World

APPLY THE BIG ? What is one property you think rubber has? How do you think this property helps a basketball bounce?

....

....

....

351

How can energy keep you running?

Energy and Its Forms

Try It! How can energy of motion change?

Investigate It! How does heat cause motion?

When was the last time you took a long run? Running on sand takes a lot of energy. It takes more energy to run on sand than to run on a paved surface.

 Predict How does this runner use energy?

....

....

....

THE BIG ? How can energy change?

Inquiry Try It!

How can energy of motion change?

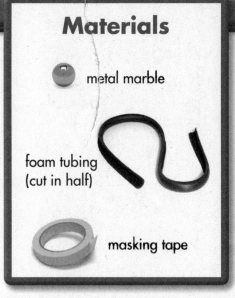

Materials

metal marble

foam tubing
(cut in half)

masking tape

☑ **1. Make a model** of a roller coaster.
Drop in the marble. **Observe.**

☑ **2.** Design your own roller coaster.
Test your model.

Explain Your Results

3. Communicate Describe the motion of
the marble.

....

....

4. Where did the marble move fastest?

....

....

5. UNLOCK THE BIG ? How did the energy of motion change?

....

....

....

....

> **Inquiry Skill**
> You **communicate** when
> you clearly describe what
> you observe in a model.

⊙ Cause and Effect

- A **cause** makes something happen.
- An **effect** is what happens.
- Science writers often use clue words and phrases such as *makes, if,* and *as a result* to signal cause and effect.

Boiling Water

If enough energy is added to liquid water, it boils. It becomes the invisible gas called water vapor. At a temperature of 100°C (212°F), liquid water boils. Energy added at the bottom of a container makes water at the bottom change into a gas. The gas forms bubbles that are lighter than the water around them. As a result, the bubbles of gas float to the water's surface. These bubbles break open and release hot water vapor into the air.

Practice It!

Complete the graphic organizer. Use it to identify a cause and effect in the above paragraph.

Cause

Effect

Lesson 1

What are some forms of energy?

Circle any place you see energy in this picture.

my planet diary

by Maddie
Wesley Chapel,
Florida

I use a lot of energy because it makes my life easier. However, I try to be responsible and use less energy.

I also turn off the lights when I leave a room. Sometimes I want the lights on. Instead, I open the blinds, so I do not waste energy.

by Jordyn
Daytona Beach,
Florida

Hi, Maddie. My family and I are also committed to using less energy. I turn off my fan and my radio before I go to school.

I save more energy at school. Whenever our class leaves the room, we turn off the lights. It would save a lot of energy if every class in the school did that!

Let's Blog!

If you could blog back to Maddie and Jordyn, what would you blog about saving energy?

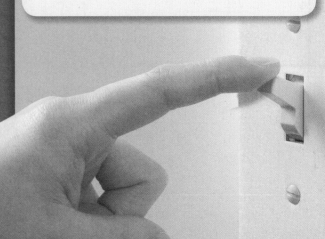

I will know energy takes
many forms, causes motion,
and creates change.

Words to Know

energy   potential
electrical   energy
    energy   kinetic
sound energy   energy

Energy

The ability to do work or to cause change is
called **energy.** Work is done when a force moves
an object. The sun is the main source of energy at
Earth's surface. Energy from the sun causes many
effects. Energy from the sun makes Earth a place
where we can live. Light from the sun helps
plants grow. Energy from the sun causes
winds to blow and water to move
through the water cycle.

*Energy from the sun
causes lettuce to grow.*

1. ◉ **Cause and Effect** Complete
   the graphic organizer below. Write
   three effects of the sun's energy.

Cause	Effects
energy from the sun →	1. Plants grow. 2. A E B 3. wind

Energy at Home

You use many forms of energy every day in your home. The living and nonliving things in the home below use many forms of energy.

Electrical energy is the movement of electric charges. It powers things that use electricity, such as a lamp.

2. **Circle** things that use electrical energy.

Light energy is energy we can see. Light energy comes through windows and brightens rooms.

Heat is the transfer of energy from a warmer object to a colder object. Heat is used to cook food in the kitchen.

3. **Draw** Look at the house. Draw another item in the house and label the form of energy it uses.

mYscienceonLine.com | THE BIG ? | I Will Know...

Mechanical energy is energy that motion or position gives to an object. You use mechanical energy every time you move or lift an object, or use a machine with moving parts.

Sound energy is energy we can hear. Musical instruments produce sound energy.

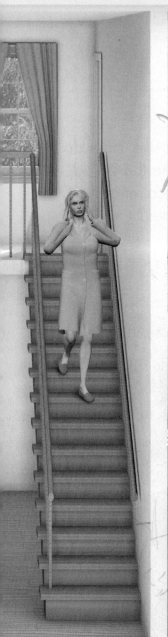

4. **Label** Place an X on things that produce sound energy.

5. **List** What machines in the home use mechanical energy?

6. **Compare and Describe** List some common forms of energy in your school. How are these forms of energy alike?

light energey, heat Eletrical energey

Stored Energy

Energy can be stored. As you stand ready to jump, run, or snowboard, your body has stored energy. Stored energy makes movement possible. Stored energy is **potential energy.** Potential energy changes into another kind of energy if you use it to do work or cause a change.

A raised object has potential energy due to gravity. For example, the snowboarder at the top of the hill in the photo below has potential energy because of his high position. Potential energy is also gained from stretching or compressing objects. For example, you can stretch or compress a spring to store potential energy.

The stored energy in food, fuels, and batteries is chemical energy. Stored chemical energy can change into a form that can do work. For example, the stored energy in food is released to help you move. It can also keep your body warm.

7. **List** Look again at the illustration on the previous pages. List two examples of potential energy in the home.

....

....

....

8. **Describe** How do you use the stored chemical energy in batteries?

....

At-Home Lab

Make Motion
Get a bowl and a table-tennis ball. Put the ball in the bowl. Move the bowl around. Tell how the ball moves. Tell where the ball has the most potential energy. Tell where it has the least potential energy.

Energy of Motion

Potential energy can change to **kinetic energy**, or the energy of motion. A car moves when the chemical energy stored in gasoline changes to kinetic energy. Potential energy changes to kinetic energy when you release a stretched spring. The potential energy the snowboarder has at the top of the hill in the photo at right changes to kinetic energy as he moves down the hill. He moves down the hill because gravity pulls him.

Energy can be used to lift objects. When a snowboarder carries a snowboard to the top of a hill, he and the snowboard gain potential energy. They now have the potential to slide to the bottom of the hill. At the bottom of the hill the snowboarder may have enough kinetic energy to lift him and his snowboard to the top of the next hill.

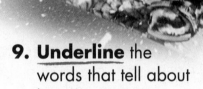

The snowboarder's potential energy due to gravity changes to kinetic energy.

9. Underline the words that tell about kinetic energy.

Got it?

10. Explain Write one way each type of energy is used in everyday life.

Electrical ....

Mechanical ....

Sound ....

11. Give an Example How can energy be used to move or lift objects?

....

....

⬛ **Stop!** I need help with ....

⏸ **Wait!** I have a question about ....

▶ **Go!** Now I know ....

Lesson 2

How does energy change form?

Envision It!

Tell how you think energy changes form as this electric train travels.

Inquiry Explore It!

What can produce potential energy?

☑ **1.** Tape one end of a 60 cm string to the edge of a table. Hang five washers from the other end.

☑ **2.** Pull the washers sideways about 30 cm. Let them go. **Describe** their motion.

....

....

Materials

60 cm string

5 washers

Explain Your Results

3. Infer   When do the washers have the most potential energy? Why?

....

....

4. Infer   When do the washers have the least potential energy? Why?

....

....

5. Hypothesize   The washers lose potential energy and get it back with each swing. How do you think they get it back?

....

I will know energy can change into many forms.

Word to Know

wave

Changing Forms of Energy

There are different forms of energy. Energy can change from one form to another. People change energy into forms they can easily use. For example, a music player changes electrical energy into sound energy.

Your body changes energy into forms that are useful for you. For example, your body stores potential energy from food as chemical energy. The chemical energy stored in your body changes to kinetic energy as you move objects or lift them.

1. **Circle** five forms of energy in the paragraphs above.

2. **Predict** Into what form of energy does this robot dog change electrical energy?

_____

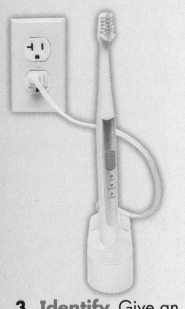

Using Energy

Sometimes people use machines to change forms of energy. You use kinetic energy to turn on a light switch, a common machine. When the light switch is turned on, electrical energy changes to light energy. A cable car, another machine, changes potential energy to kinetic energy.

An electric toothbrush is another machine. It has an electric cord that plugs into an outlet. Electrical energy is stored as chemical energy in the battery of the toothbrush. The chemical energy changes back to electrical energy when the toothbrush is turned on. The electrical energy then changes to kinetic energy as the toothbrush moves.

Energy does not change completely from one form to another. Energy does not go away, either. Some energy always produces heat. After you turn on a light bulb, it becomes warm. This is because some of the energy produces heat.

3. Identify Give an example of how energy is used to lift an object.

....

....

....

4. Hypothesize How do you think the cable car gains potential energy?

....

....

Go Green

Reduce Energy Usage

Gasoline contains a form of stored energy. It is made from oil. There is a limited supply of oil on Earth. Think of some ways people use gasoline. Tell three ways people could use less gasoline.

cable car

How Energy Travels

Energy can travel from one place to another. Suppose a moving object strikes another object. Some kinetic energy passes to the second object. Have you ever gone bowling? When the bowling ball hits the group of pins, the ball slows down and the pins begin moving. Before hitting the pins, the bowling ball has all of the kinetic energy. The pins have no kinetic energy. When the ball hits the pins, some kinetic energy transfers to the pins. Heat is also produced, which causes some energy to be lost. The total amount of energy does not change.

5. Underline one cause and (circle) one effect in the paragraph.

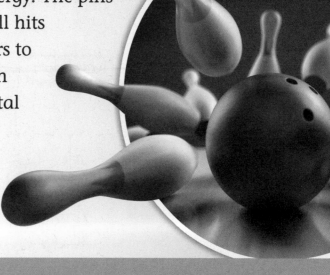

Do the math!

Model and Apply Division

In bowling, you roll a ball about 18 meters down the lane to hit the pins. If a bowling ball is thrown at 6 meters per second, how long does it take to hit the pins?

Rule: Time = Distance ÷ Speed

You can use repeated subtraction to find how many groups of 6 are in 18.

18 − 6 = 12
12 − 6 = 6
6 − 6 = 0

You can subtract 6 three times. There are three groups of 6 in 18.

The ball takes 3 seconds to hit the pins.

1 Solve If you throw the bowling ball at 3 meters per second, about how long will it take for the ball to hit the pins?

2 Hypothesize When a bowling ball hits the pins, energy transfers from the ball to the pins. If you roll the ball too slowly, what might happen when it reaches the pins?

Waves

Energy can travel as waves. For example, light and sound travel as waves. A **wave** is a disturbance that carries energy from one point to another point. Waves of energy can look like the wave of moving rope below. The rope goes from one side of the dotted line to the other. Energy causes this effect as it travels from one end of the rope to the other.

6. ⊙ **Main Idea and Details** Read the paragraph. Write the main idea.

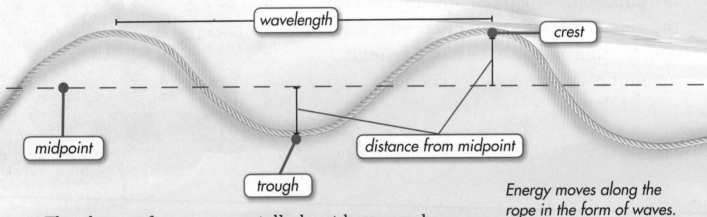

wavelength

crest

midpoint

distance from midpoint

trough

Energy moves along the rope in the form of waves.

The shape of a wave can tell about how much energy it carries. The wavelength and the distance from the midpoint to the crest or trough can indicate about how much energy a wave carries.

The bottom of a wave is called a trough. The top of a wave is called a crest. Waves with greater distance from the midpoint to a crest or trough have more energy than waves with less distance.

Wavelength is the distance between one crest and the next crest or one trough and the next trough. Waves with shorter wavelengths have more energy than waves with longer wavelengths.

7. **Produce** Draw a wave that carries less energy than the rope above.

myscienceonline.com | Got it? ⊙ 60-Second Video

Waves in water can be small, like the ripples in the bucket below. Waves caused by hurricanes can be huge! The size of a wave depends on how much energy it carries. The energy a wave carries can change. Look at the bucket. First, the energy from the falling drop disturbs the water surface. Then, as the waves move away from the source, they carry less energy.

Got it?

8. **Compare** Some toys get their energy from batteries, and some from a windup key. What are some advantages of each method?

....

9. **UNLOCK THE BIG ?** Think about what you learned in this lesson. How can energy change?

....

....

⬜ **Stop!** I need help with ....

⏸ **Wait!** I have a question about ....

▶ **Go!** Now I know ....

How do light and matter interact?

Envision It!

Tell where you think light is coming from in these sea jellies.

What happens when light is reflected in many directions?

Materials

flashlight

milk

spoon

clear plastic cup with water

☐ **1.** Shine the flashlight through the water. **Observe** the water from all directions. **Record** what you see.

....

....

☐ **2.** Add $\frac{1}{3}$ spoonful of milk. Stir. Repeat Step 1. Does the color of the water look the same from all directions?

....

....

Explain Your Results

3. Compare your **observations** before and after the milk was added.

....

....

UNLOCK THE BIG ?

I will know how objects reflect, refract, and absorb light. I will know how light forms shadows.

Words to Know

light energy   refract
reflect   absorb

Path of Light

You can see objects because of light energy. **Light energy** is energy we can see. Light travels outward from its source in all directions. Light travels in straight lines until it strikes an object or travels from one medium to another. For example, light from a light bulb can brighten a whole room. The light from the spotlights below does not travel in all directions. The sides of the spotlight direct the light to travel in one direction. Light can pass through some of the objects it strikes. For example, light can pass through a window or a glass of water. These objects do not block all light that passes through them.

1. **List** Write three objects that do not block all light.

....

....

....

How Light Changes

The path of light can change in different ways. Light can be reflected, refracted, or absorbed.

Reflect

You can see an object because light **reflects,** or bounces off the object. Some objects reflect light better than others. Flat, smooth surfaces reflect light evenly. A mirror or a smooth lake reflects light evenly. Other objects do not reflect light evenly. A rough lake does not reflect light evenly.

Refract

What happens to light in an ice cube? The ice cube **refracts,** or bends, light. Refracted light changes direction. The ice cube below refracts light that reflects off the strawberry. The refracted light forms images of the strawberry.

Light refracts when it passes through different materials at different speeds. Light passing through air slows down when it enters water. This causes the straw in the glass at left to look broken.

2. Explain Why can you see the reflection of the insect?

....

....

refraction

3. Draw an ✗ where you see the strawberry reflected or refracted inside the ice cube.

Absorb

Have you ever wondered why you see colors? You see colors because of what happens to light when it hits different materials.

Light is made up of different colors. An object **absorbs,** or takes in, some of the light that hits it. The object reflects the rest. Most objects reflect light. Different objects absorb and reflect different colors of light. For example, red flowers reflect the color red. Red flowers absorb other colors of light. The reflected color red is what your eyes see. White light is made up of all colors of light. If an object looks white, it reflects all colors of light. If an object looks black, it absorbs all colors of light.

4. [CHALLENGE] Will you be cooler on a hot day in a light-colored shirt or a dark-colored shirt? Explain.

Light and Objects

Some materials refract light. Water and air are two materials that refract light.

5. **State** How does each water droplet change the image of the flower?

refract

Objects such as these hot-air balloons absorb some colors of light and reflect other colors.

6. **Explain** Why do you see the color blue on a hot-air balloon?

absorb

The rocks and lake reflect light. The rocks do not have a smooth surface. They reflect light from the sky in many directions. This is why you do not see an image of the sky on the rocks.

7. **Draw** Finish drawing the reflection on the water on the next page.

reflect

Shadows

During a sunny day, you might use an umbrella to shade yourself from the hot sun. The shade the umbrella creates is a shadow.

Light travels outward from its source in all directions until it strikes an object. When light is blocked by an object, a shadow is formed. A shadow is a dark area made when an object blocks light between a light source and a surface. You can see shadows on surfaces. The length of the shadow depends on the angle of the light. For example, the length and direction of shadows caused by sunlight change during the day.

8. **Analyze** Why do these tables and chairs make shadows in the sunlight?

....

....

....

....

At-Home Lab

Make Shadows
Stand in a place with bright sunlight. Make a shape with your hand. Look at the shadow it makes. Make the shadow look sharper. Make the shadow look fuzzier.

myscienceonline.com | Got it? ⏱ 60-Second Video

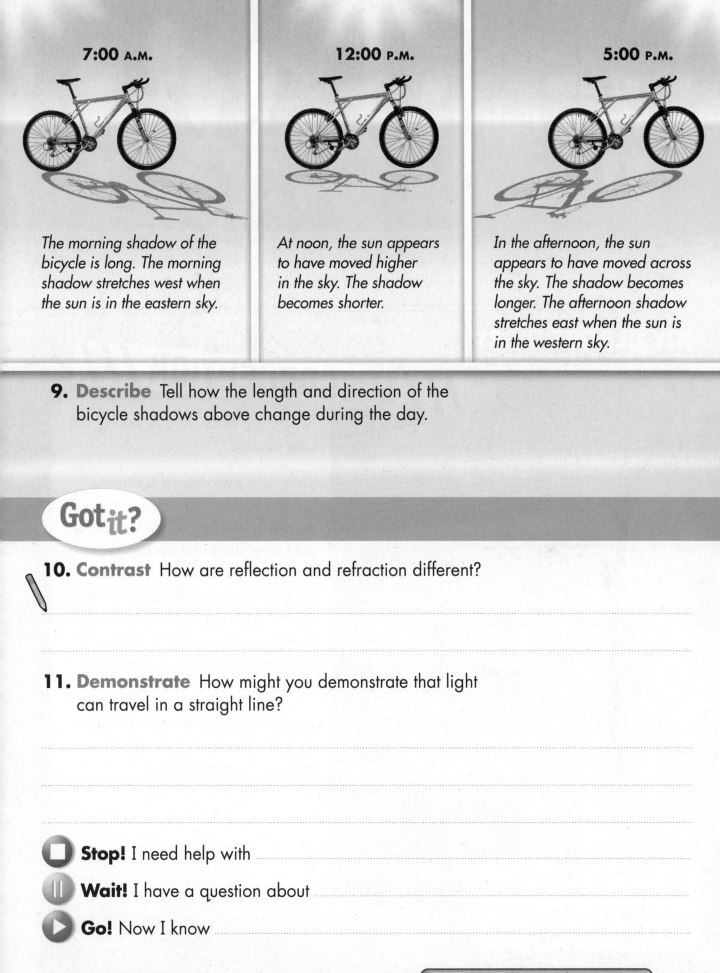

7:00 A.M.

The morning shadow of the bicycle is long. The morning shadow stretches west when the sun is in the eastern sky.

12:00 P.M.

At noon, the sun appears to have moved higher in the sky. The shadow becomes shorter.

5:00 P.M.

In the afternoon, the sun appears to have moved across the sky. The shadow becomes longer. The afternoon shadow stretches east when the sun is in the western sky.

9. **Describe** Tell how the length and direction of the bicycle shadows above change during the day.

Got it?

10. **Contrast** How are reflection and refraction different?

....

....

11. **Demonstrate** How might you demonstrate that light can travel in a straight line?

....

....

....

⬛ **Stop!** I need help with ....

⏸ **Wait!** I have a question about ....

▶ **Go!** Now I know ....

What are heat and light energy?

Envision It!

Tell how you think light affects this picture.

my planet Diary

/// MISCONCEPTION ////

"Close the door. You're letting the heat escape!"

Have you ever heard someone say this? In fact, it's true that heat moves from place to place. On a cold day, heat will transfer from the warm air inside a house to the cooler air outside. But closing a door won't completely stop this from happening. On a cold day, heat inside a house is constantly moving to the air outside.

Look at the picture and read the caption. From what parts of the house is heat escaping?

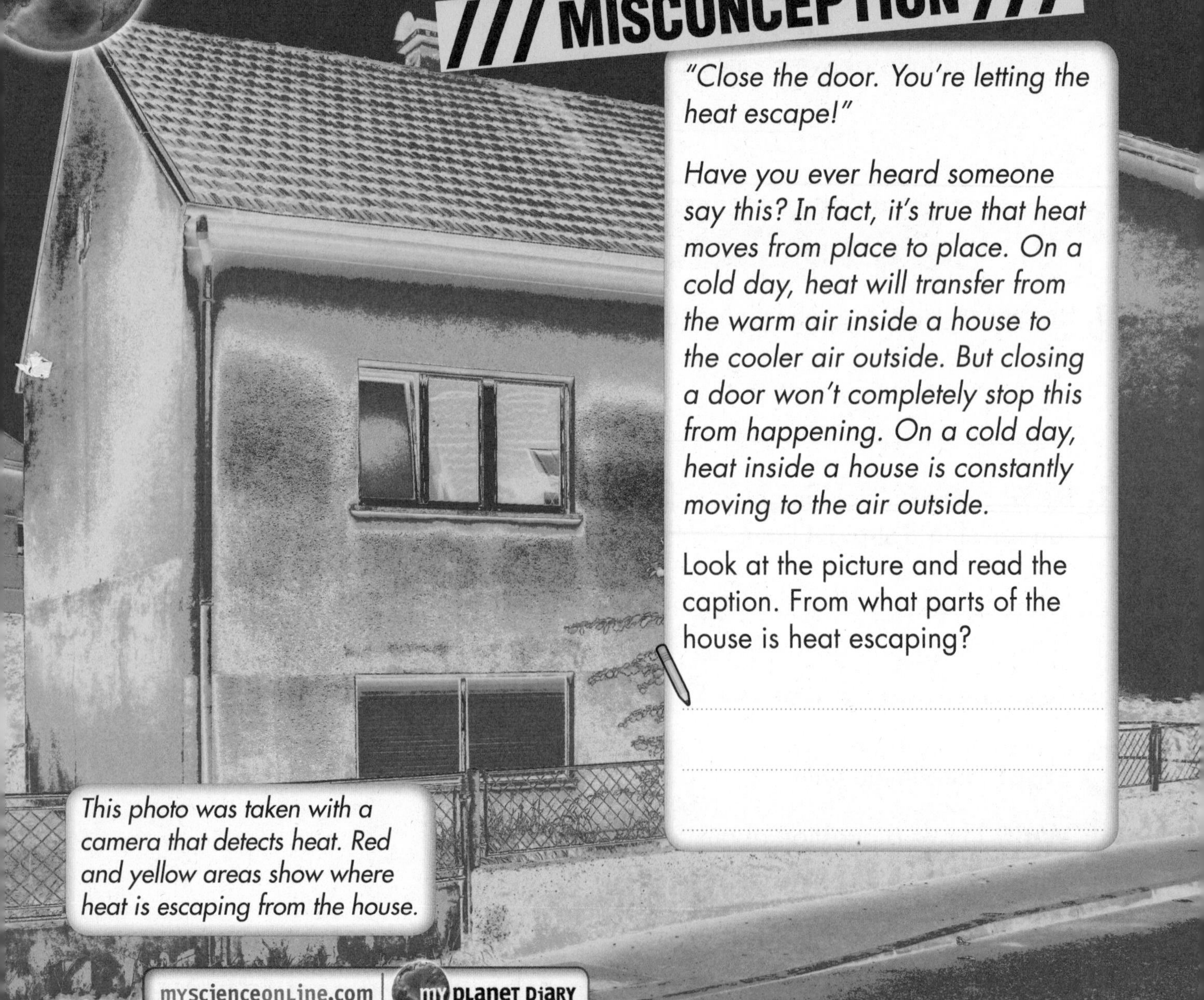

....

....

....

This photo was taken with a camera that detects heat. Red and yellow areas show where heat is escaping from the house.

I will know how heat and light energy affect matter and can be produced.

Words to Know

thermal energy

Thermal Energy and Heat

Matter is made of very small moving particles. Each particle of matter moves because it has energy. The energy of moving particles is called **thermal energy.** Thermal energy is the kinetic energy and potential energy of particles in matter. Energy from the sun makes the particles in objects move faster. The object becomes warmer. That is why sunlight feels warm on your skin. When the sun's energy no longer reaches the matter, its particles slow down and the matter cools. That is why you feel cooler when you are in the shade.

Heat is the transfer of energy from one place to another. Heat can take the form of thermal energy traveling from warmer objects to cooler objects. When you place a metal spoon into a pot of cooking food, heat travels from the warmer pot through the cooler spoon. In a short time, the top of the spoon will feel warm.

1. **Predict** What would happen to the hot spoon if it was placed in a pot of cool water?

....

....

....

When the warm pot and the spoon reach the same temperature, the flow of energy stops.

Heat and Light

When energy changes form, one result is heat. For example, heat is produced when you rub two objects together. You can investigate heat by rubbing your hands together. Your hands warm up because kinetic energy is transferred.

Energy heats your home. Some people heat their homes with natural gas. Some people use electricity. Other people use solar panels that collect energy from the sun.

When energy changes form, some energy is always given off in the form of heat. Think about light. Energy changes form when light is produced. This means that sources of light are also sources of heat.

Burning is a chemical change that can produce light and heat. For example, candles, campfires, and matches give off light that helps heat the space around them as they burn.

2. **Infer** Why might people rub their hands together when they are cold?

....

....

3. **Analyze** List three things you use that produce both light and heat.

....

....

....

Electricity can also be a source of light and heat. Electricity makes the wire in a light bulb get so hot that it gives off light. Bulbs in heat lamps can be used to keep food warm.

Lightning Lab

Heat and Colors
Find a sunny place. Get a sheet of white paper. Get a sheet of black paper. Tell if the sheets of paper feel warm. Place them in the sunlight. Wait five minutes. Feel the sheets. Tell how the sheets of paper feel.

Got it?

4. **Infer** What happens when two liquids of different temperatures are mixed? Explain.

....

....

5. **Understand** What are two ways heat can be produced?

....

....

◻ **Stop!** I need help with ....

⏸ **Wait!** I have a question about ....

▷ **Go!** Now I know ....

Lesson 5

What is sound energy?

Write words to describe the sound you think this party blower makes.

Inquiry ## Explore It!

What can affect the sound made by a rubber band?

☐ **1.** Stretch a thick rubber band and a thin rubber band around a box.

☐ **2. Observe** Pluck each band. How does each sound? **Record.**

....

....

☐ **3.** Slide a ruler under the bands. Turn the edge up. Pluck each band. How does each sound?

Materials

safety goggles

thick rubber band

plastic tub (or shoebox)

thin rubber band

ruler

Be careful! Wear safety goggles. Be careful not to snap the rubber bands.

Explain Your Results

4. Draw Conclusions How does a rubber band's thickness affect its sound?

....

....

myscienceonline.com | **Explore It!** Animation

Words to Know

volume
pitch

Sound

At a party, you hear loud music and noisemakers. In a field, you hear crickets chirp quietly. You hear many different sounds every day. Some sounds are loud, and others are soft. You hear high sounds and low sounds. Yet all sounds are made in the same way. Sound happens when matter vibrates. *Vibrate* means to move quickly back and forth.

Any matter that vibrates can make sound. You can even make sound with a ruler. Hold one end of a ruler tightly against a table. Press the other end down so the ruler bends, then let it go. The ruler vibrates and makes sound.

1. ◉ **Cause and Effect** Complete the graphic organizer to show an effect.

Cause

The ruler vibrates.

→ **Effect**

....

2. (Circle) the areas in the diagram where air particles are squeezed together.

3. [CHALLENGE] Suppose you build a chain of dominoes and knock over the first one. As each domino falls, it knocks over the one next to it. In what way is this a good model for the way sound energy moves through air?

....

....

....

....

How Sound Travels

When you hit a drum, the drumhead vibrates and makes sound. But how does the sound move through the air from the drum to your ear? All sounds travel in waves. These waves form when matter vibrates. Vibrations in matter cause the particles that make up air to vibrate too.

Think about the vibrating drumhead. As the drumhead vibrates, it causes the air particles around it to move. The moving particles form waves. In some areas, the air particles are squeezed together. In other areas, the particles spread apart. This pattern repeats as the drumhead continues to vibrate.

As a sound wave travels, the air particles that make up the wave do not move along with it. They vibrate in place and bump into each other. When they bump, energy transfers from one particle to the next. In this way, the sound energy moves through the air from particle to particle until it reaches your ear.

Volume

Sound waves can have different properties. Because of this, the sounds we hear have different properties.

Think about the siren on a fire truck. The first thing you might notice about a siren is its **volume,** or how loud or soft a sound is. Volume is a property of sound. Volume is related to how much energy a sound has.

When you whisper, you make a soft sound. The sound waves you create have little energy. When you shout, you use more energy to make a sound. The sound waves you create have more energy. The sound is louder.

A siren sounds very loud if you are standing near the siren.

Volume also depends on how far away a listener is from the source of the sound. Suppose you are near a siren when it goes off. The sound would not have to travel far to get to your ears. But if you are far away, the siren would not seem as loud. The sound waves do not lose energy as they travel away from the siren. But the energy spreads out in all directions over a larger area.

4. **Illustrate** Draw a picture to show how sound spreads out as it moves away from a roaring lion.

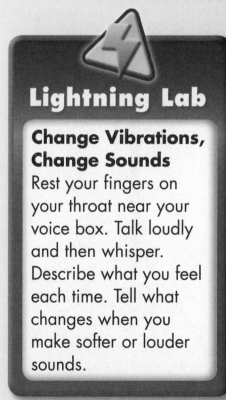

Lightning Lab

Change Vibrations, Change Sounds

Rest your fingers on your throat near your voice box. Talk loudly and then whisper. Describe what you feel each time. Tell what changes when you make softer or louder sounds.

Pitch

How is the song of a bird different from the roar of a lion? It certainly is softer than the lion's roar. It is different in another way too.

A bird makes a higher sound than a lion. **Pitch** is how high or low a sound is. The bird makes a high-pitched sound. The lion makes a low-pitched sound.

A sound's pitch depends on its frequency. Frequency is the number of sound waves made in a certain amount of time. Objects that vibrate quickly have a high frequency. High-frequency sounds have a high pitch. Objects that vibrate slowly have a low frequency and a low pitch.

The material an object is made of affects its pitch. The size and shape of an object also affect pitch. For example, a small drum will usually have a higher pitch than a big drum.

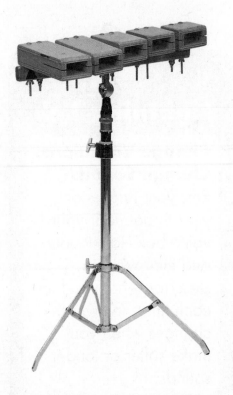

This songbird can make sounds of many different pitches. Its voice sounds musical.

5. **Compare** A mouse and a lion make different sounds. Use the words *high* and *low* to compare their pitch.

....

....

....

6. **Apply** The wooden blocks at left make sound when hit with a rubber hammer. **Circle** the block that you think has the highest pitch.

Pitch in Stringed Instruments

Guitars, violins, cellos, and harps are kinds of stringed instruments. Stringed instruments make sound when you pluck their strings or rub a bow across their strings. Each string's pitch depends on the string's properties. A thin string vibrates faster than a thick string, so a thin string has higher pitch. In the same way, a short or tight string vibrates faster than a long or loose string. So the string that is shorter or tighter makes a sound with a higher pitch.

Each string of a guitar has a different pitch.

7. **Infer** When you stretch a rubber band and pluck it, it vibrates and makes a sound. How could you change the pitch of the vibrating rubber band?

....

....

Got it?

8. **Compare** Use the words *loud* and *soft* to compare the sounds of a bicycle and a large truck.

....

....

9. **Predict** A guitar has thick strings and thin strings. Would you expect the thick strings to sound higher or lower than the thin strings? Explain why.

....

....

⬛ **Stop!** I need help with ....

⏸ **Wait!** I have a question about ....

▶ **Go!** Now I know ....

Lesson 6

What is electrical energy?

Envision It!

Circle two examples of electrical energy in this picture.

Inquiry **Explore It!**

How can you control electrical energy?

Be careful! Wear safety goggles.

☑ **1.** Connect the wires.
   Observe and **record** what happens.

☑ **2.** Turn the light on and off.

Explain Your Results

3. Communicate How did you turn the light off?

....

....

4. Infer How does a light switch work?

....

....

....

Materials

light bulb and holder

2 wires

battery and holder

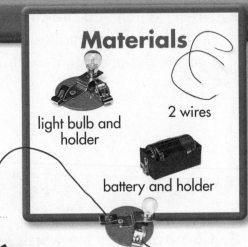

I will know how electricity moves through circuits. I will know some materials that conduct electricity.

Words to Know

closed circuit
open circuit

Electric Charges

All matter is made up of small particles that have electric charges. An electric charge is a property of some particles that causes them to attract or repel each other. Particles of matter have both positive (+) and negative (-) electric charges. When particles have an equal number of positive and negative charges, the charges balance each other. The matter has no overall charge. Matter with more negative charges than positive charges has an overall negative charge. Matter with more positive charges than negative charges has an overall positive charge.

Put two objects with the same charge near each other. They push away from each other. Two objects with opposite charges attract each other. If you rub the girl's hair with the balloon, the balloon picks up negative charges from the hair. The girl's hair then has an overall positive charge. The balloon has a negative charge. The balloon and the hair have opposite charges, so they attract each other.

1. **Label** Write the symbols + and − on the girl's hair and the balloon to show their electric charges.

Electric Currents and Circuits

The movement of electric charge from one place to another is electric current. Lightning is an uncontrolled electric current. Lightning can travel in any direction. To be useful, an electric current must travel in a controlled path through wires and other materials. This way, electric current can provide the energy needed to turn on lights or make a CD player work.

The path that a controlled electric current flows through is an electric circuit. The path must be unbroken for electric current to flow through it. Every circuit needs a source of energy, such as a battery or an outlet that you can plug a cord into. The diagram below shows a circuit made from a battery, wires, and a light bulb.

2. Demonstrate Draw arrows to show the direction electric current flows in the diagram below.

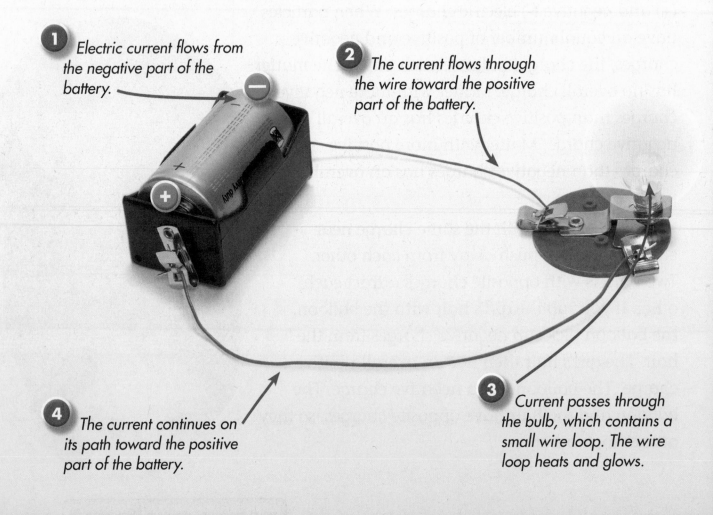

1 Electric current flows from the negative part of the battery.

2 The current flows through the wire toward the positive part of the battery.

3 Current passes through the bulb, which contains a small wire loop. The wire loop heats and glows.

4 The current continues on its path toward the positive part of the battery.

Closed Circuits and Open Circuits

A circuit with no gaps or breaks is called a **closed circuit.** Electric current will continue to flow through a closed circuit until it is broken. A circuit with a broken path is called an **open circuit.** Current will not flow through an open circuit.

You can create a break in a circuit by disconnecting a wire from a battery or light bulb. Most circuits have a device called a switch. A switch allows you to open and close the circuit without disconnecting a wire. When you lift the lever on the switch, the circuit is open. The light turns off. When you lower the lever, the circuit is closed. The light turns on.

an open switch

3. **Explain** What happens to the movement of electric current when you open a switch?

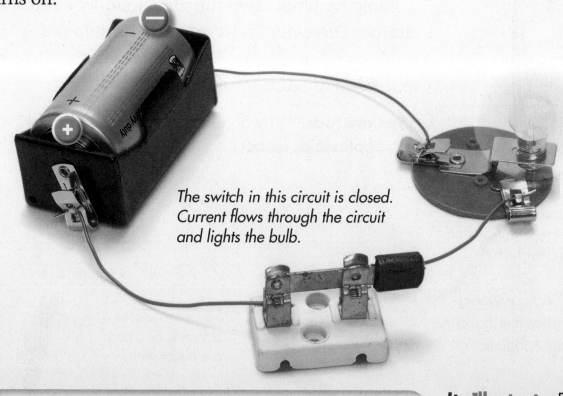

The switch in this circuit is closed. Current flows through the circuit and lights the bulb.

4. **Illustrate** Draw an open circuit. Draw an arrow to show where there is a break in the circuit.

Conductors and Insulators

Why are wires used to build electric circuits? Wires are usually made of metal with a covering of plastic or rubber. Electric charge moves easily through metals such as copper, gold, silver, and aluminum. The metal part of wire carries electric current throughout a circuit.

A material through which electric charge moves easily is called a conductor. Metals are not the only conductors. For example, the mineral graphite is a conductor. Graphite is the material you write with in a pencil. Most of the water around us is also a strong conductor.

Some materials stop the movement of electric charge. These materials are called insulators. Rubber and plastic are kinds of insulators. Glass and wood are also insulators.

5. Conclude Why do electric wires have a covering of plastic or rubber?

....

....

....

Pure water is a weak conductor. When chemicals such as salt are added to water, it becomes a strong conductor. Most water around us is a strong conductor.

6. Infer Where would you find water that is a strong conductor?

....

7. Compare Tell why metals, such as copper and silver, are good conductors.

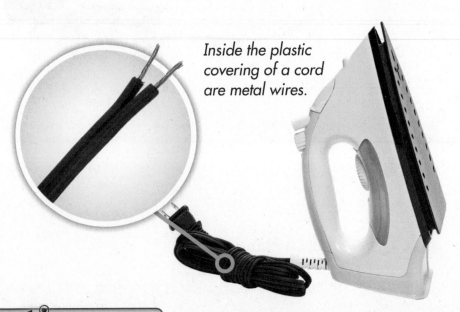

Inside the plastic covering of a cord are metal wires.

myscienceonline.com | Got it? | 60-Second Video

Classify Conductors

You can use a circuit like the one below to investigate whether an object is a conductor. You touch the bare ends of the wires to the object. Does the bulb light up? If so, electric charge is moving through the object.

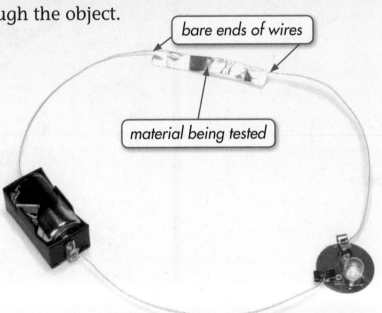

bare ends of wires

material being tested

8. Classify Suppose you tested a penny, a rubber eraser, and a paper clip. Which objects do you think are conductors? Why?

....

....

....

....

....

Got it?

9. Infer Workers who fix electrical equipment often use tools with parts made of plastic, rubber, or other insulators. Why does this make sense?

....

10. Explain When you turn on the switch on your classroom wall, the overhead lights go on. Explain why this happens. Use the term *closed circuit* or *open circuit*.

....

....

Stop! I need help with ....

Wait! I have a question about ....

Go! Now I know ....

Materials

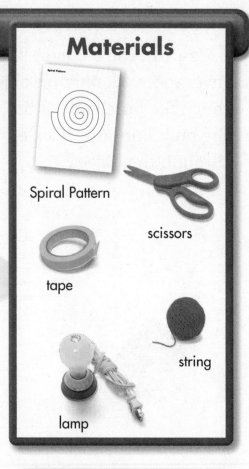

Spiral Pattern

scissors

tape

string

lamp

How does heat cause motion?

Follow a Procedure

☑ **1.** Cut out the spiral.

☑ **2.** Tape one end of the string to the middle of the spiral.

☑ **3.** **Predict** what will happen if you hold the spiral over the lamp before the bulb is turned on. **Record.**

☑ **4.** Predict what will happen if the bulb is turned on. Record.

> **Inquiry Skill**
> A **prediction** can be based on what you already know or what you observe.

Motion of Spiral

	Predictions	Observations
Lamp off		
Lamp on		

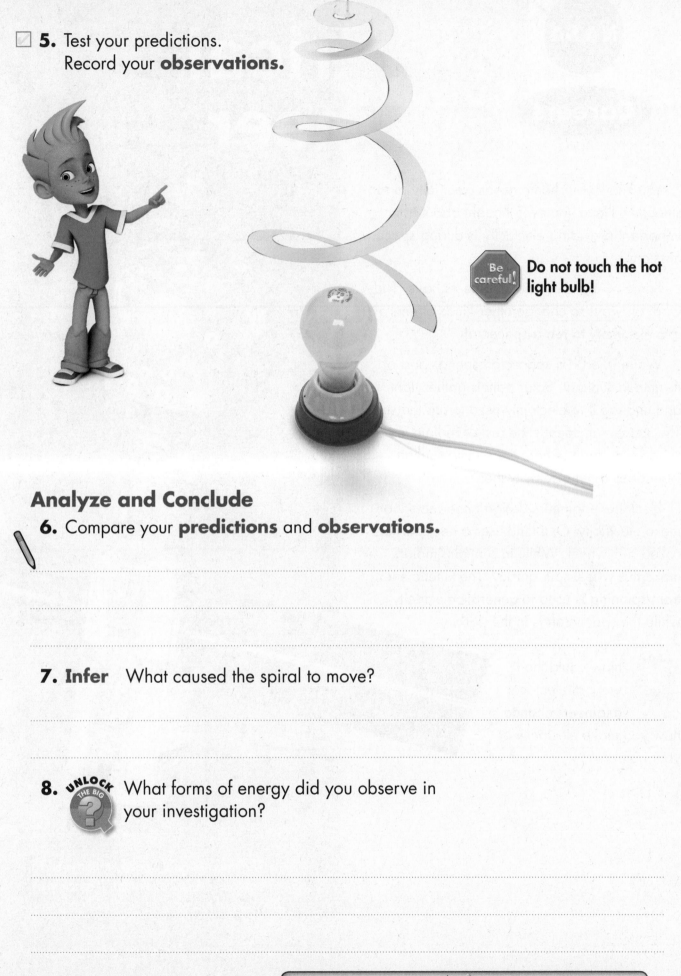

☐ **5.** Test your predictions.
Record your **observations.**

Be careful! **Do not touch the hot light bulb!**

Analyze and Conclude

6. Compare your **predictions** and **observations.**

....

....

....

7. Infer What caused the spiral to move?

....

....

8. UNLOCK THE BIG ? What forms of energy did you observe in your investigation?

....

....

....

NASA Careers

Electrical Engineer

You know your home needs electricity to run smoothly. Have you ever thought about how important providing electricity is during space missions?

Some NASA electrical engineers have. They work on ways to change other kinds of energy into electricity to run a spacecraft.

While in orbit a spacecraft spends part of its time in sunlight. Solar panels gather light and change it to electricity used to run the ship. The spacecraft spends the rest of its time in the shadow of Earth, where there is no sunlight. How does it get electricity then?

Electrical engineers design generators that make electricity. One kind uses a heavy wheel called a flywheel. While in sunlight, motors make this wheel spin quickly. The kinetic energy from spinning is used to generate electricity while the spacecraft is in the dark.

UNLOCK THE BIG ? How could the work of electrical engineers change how you make electricity at your home?

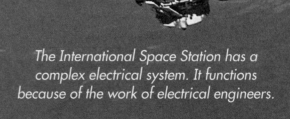

The International Space Station has a complex electrical system. It functions because of the work of electrical engineers.

Vocabulary Smart Cards

energy
electrical energy
sound energy
potential energy
kinetic energy
wave
light energy
reflect
refract
absorb
thermal energy
volume
pitch
closed circuit
open circuit

Play a Game!

Choose a Vocabulary Smart Card.

Write a sentence using the vocabulary word. Draw a blank where the vocabulary word should be.

Have a partner fill in the blank with the correct vocabulary word.

Have your partner repeat with another card.

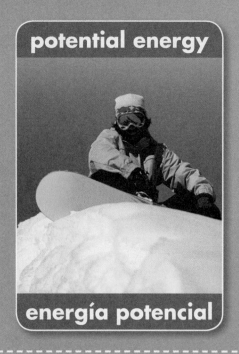

potential energy

energía potencial

energy

energía

kinetic energy

energía cinética

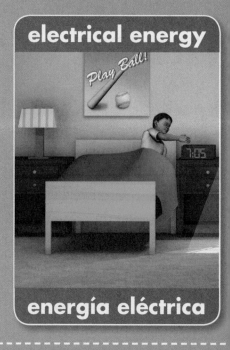

electrical energy

energía eléctrica

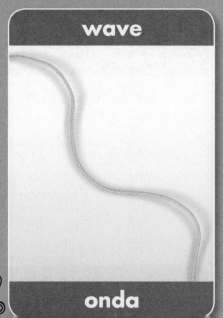

wave

onda

sound energy

energía sonora

the ability to do work or to cause change

Write three other forms of this word.

....

....

....

capacidad de hacer trabajo o causar cambios

stored energy

Write two examples.

....

....

....

....

energía almacenada

Interactive Vocabulary

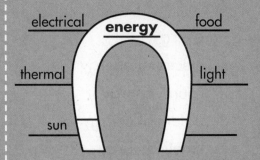

electrical   energy   food

thermal   light

sun

Make a Word Magnet!

Choose a vocabulary word and write it in the Word Magnet. Write the words that are related to it on the lines.

the movement of electric charges

Draw an example.

el movimiento de cargas eléctricas

energy of motion

Write a sentence using this term.

....

....

....

....

energía de movimiento

energy we can hear

Draw an example.

energía que podemos oír

a disturbance that carries energy from one point to another point

Write another meaning of this word.

....

....

....

perturbación que lleva energía de un punto a otro

pitch	absorb	light energy
	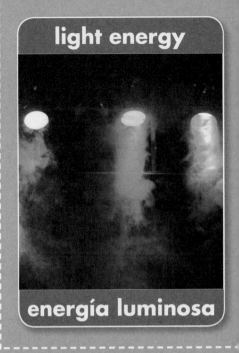	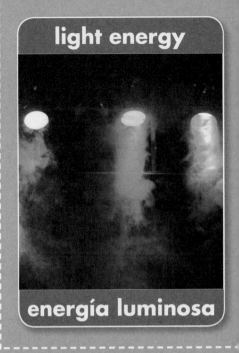
tono	absorber	energía luminosa

closed circuit	thermal energy	reflect
	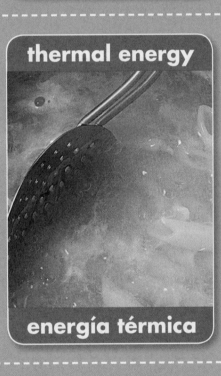	
circuito cerrado	energía térmica	reflejar

open circuit	volume	refract

circuito abierto	volumen	refractar

energy we can see

Write two examples.

....

....

....

....

....

energía que podemos ver

to take in

Write a sentence using this word.

....

....

....

....

....

retener

how high or low a sound is

Write an example of a sound with a high pitch.

....

....

....

....

cuán agudo o grave es un sonido

to bounce off

Write a sentence using the noun form of this word.

....

....

....

....

....

hacer rebotar algo

the kinetic energy and potential energy of particles in matter

Write a sentence using this term.

....

....

....

....

energía cinética y energía potencial de las partículas que forman la materia

a circuit with no gaps or breaks

Write a sentence using this term.

....

....

....

....

....

circuito que no tiene rupturas ni interrupciones

to bend

Write three other forms of this word.

....

....

....

....

....

desviar o inclinar

how loud or soft a sound is

Write a sentence using this word.

....

....

....

....

....

cuán fuerte o suave es un sonido

a circuit with a broken path

Write a sentence using this term.

....

....

....

....

....

circuito que tiene una ruptura en su ruta

Lesson 1 	### What are some forms of energy? • Energy is the ability to do work and cause change. • Energy makes things move, change, or grow. • People use many forms of energy every day.
Lesson 2 	### How does energy change form? • Energy can change from one form to another. • Energy of motion can be transferred. • Some energy travels as waves.
Lesson 3 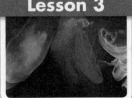	### How do light and matter interact? • Objects can reflect light evenly or unevenly. • Some objects refract light. • Some objects absorb some of the colors of light that hit them.
Lesson 4 	### What are heat and light energy? • Things that give off light also give off heat. • Heat affects the temperature of matter. • Heat is produced when objects rub against each other.
Lesson 5 	### What is sound energy? • Sound happens when matter vibrates. • A sound's energy determines how loud or soft the volume is. • A sound's pitch is how high or low the sound is.
Lesson 6 	### What is electrical energy? • An electric charge can attract or repel. • Electric current is the movement of an electric charge. • An electric circuit is a path for electric current.

Lesson 1

What are some forms of energy?

1. **Determine** (Circle) the image that best shows kinetic energy.

2. **Analyze** What is one way that stored energy can change to become energy of motion?

Lesson 2

How does energy change form?

3. ⊙ **Cause and Effect** When you turn on an electric toothbrush, chemical energy in the battery changes to electrical energy. List two additional energy changes that happen as a result.

Lesson 3

How do light and matter interact?

4. **Vocabulary** A blue book _____ blue light that strikes it.
   A. colors
   B. absorbs
   C. reflects
   D. shadows

5. **Describe** Why do shadows form behind some objects?

Lesson 4

What are heat and light energy?

6. **Communicate** How are the sun, a campfire, and a street lamp alike?

....

....

....

7. **Describe** How could you use two objects to produce heat?

....

....

....

Lesson 5

What is sound energy?

8. **Predict** A bell vibrates quickly when you ring it. Will the bell have a high pitch or a low pitch? Explain.

....

....

....

....

....

Lesson 6

What is electrical energy?

9. **Write About It** Explain the movement of electricity through a closed electric circuit made of a battery, wire, and a bulb.

....

....

....

....

....

....

10. **APPLY THE BIG ?** How can energy change?

....

Think about a trip to the grocery store. What forms of energy can you experience? Explain how this energy can change form.

....

....

....

....

....

Fill in the bubble next to the answer choice you think is correct
for each multiple-choice question.

1 A car moves when the stored
energy in gasoline changes
to kinetic energy. What is this
stored energy called?

Ⓐ gravity
Ⓑ chemical energy
Ⓒ thermal energy
Ⓓ light energy

2 Which word describes the pitch
of a guitar string vibrating
slowly?

Ⓐ loud
Ⓑ low
Ⓒ high
Ⓓ soft

3 What is an electric circuit?

Ⓐ movement of electric energy
Ⓑ an outlet you plug a cord into
Ⓒ the path that electric current
flows through
Ⓓ a machine used to change
sunlight into electricity

4 Jack's mom lit some candles for
the dinner table. Which form
of energy does the fire from a
candle release?

Ⓐ mechanical
Ⓑ sound
Ⓒ light
Ⓓ chemical

5 A banana is the color yellow
because _____.

Ⓐ it absorbs the color yellow
Ⓑ it refracts the color yellow
Ⓒ it reflects all colors except
yellow
Ⓓ it absorbs all colors except
yellow

6 How is the path of light hitting
a mirror different from the path
of light going through a water
droplet?

....

....

....

Electrical Energy Conservation

We use electrical energy every day. We use electrical energy to light our homes and run appliances, such as televisions and refrigerators. Most electrical energy comes from nonrenewable sources. After a nonrenewable source of energy is used up, it cannot be replaced. Most electricity in the United States is made from the burning of coal. Coal is a nonrenewable source of energy.

Scientists are developing different sources of energy to use instead of nonrenewable sources. For example, scientists are working to develop solar energy and wind energy. Meanwhile, we can reduce the amount of energy we use by following the tips on this page.

Use a thermostat with a timer.

Use compact fluorescent light bulbs.

Turn off lights when leaving a room.

Suggest Write two more ways you can conserve electrical energy in your home.

....

....

Is the world **in motion** or are you?

Forces and Motion

Chapter 10

Try It!   What can magnetic force move?

Lesson 1 What is motion?

Lesson 2 How does force affect motion?

Lesson 3 What is gravity?

Investigate It! How can you describe motion?

The boy pedals hard down the path. The world around him becomes a blur. The trees seem to fly by.

Predict How do you know that it is the biker who is moving, and not the trees?

....

....

....

THE BIG ? What forces cause motion?

What can magnetic force move?

Magnetic force can make objects move.

Materials

magnet

rubber band   metal marble

penny   paper clip   plastic paper clip

☐ **1.** Place the objects in the circle.

☐ **2.** Bring the magnet close to the edges of the circle. **Observe** which objects move.

☐ **3. Record** List the objects that the magnet moved.

☐ **4.** List the objects that the magnet did not move outside the circle.

Inquiry Skill
You use what you observe to **infer.**

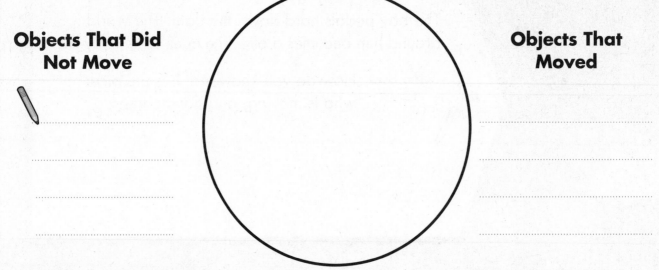

Objects That Did Not Move

Objects That Moved

Explain Your Results

5. **UNLOCK THE BIG ?** **Infer** Use what you **observed** to describe magnetic force.

◉ Draw Conclusions

- Learning to **draw conclusions** can help you evaluate what you read and observe.
- The conclusions that you draw should make sense and be supported by facts.

Walking Home

Jamal and Eric both walk home from school. They decide to do an experiment to see who gets home the quickest. They both leave school at the same time. Jamal walks faster than Eric. Eric lives farther away from school than Jamal. Jamal has fewer hills to climb.

Apply It!

Use the graphic organizer. List facts from the paragraph and draw a conclusion.

Fact

Fact

Fact

Conclusion

What is motion?

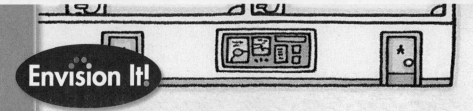

Draw a path from the classroom to the cafeteria.
Tell how to walk the path.

my PLANET DiARY VOICES FROM History

Isaac Newton (1642–1727)

When you learn how forces affect motion, you have Isaac Newton to thank. Even in his own day, Newton was considered one of history's greatest scientists. He had a deep curiosity about the natural world. He looked for clear and logical ways to explain everything he noticed. He put together ideas from all different areas of science in very creative ways. Among the results were his famous laws of motion. These laws, including his definition of force, caused people to think about science in a new way. Newton once said, "If I have ever made any valuable discoveries, it has been owing more to patient attention than to any other talent."

Isaac Newton stated the scientific laws of motion in his book Principia Mathematica.

How do you think patient attention could help you make scientific discoveries?

....

....

....

According to Newton's third law of motion, these balls exert a force on each other when they collide.

When Objects Move

Look at the picture of the students playing. How would you describe the position of the girl? **Position** is an object's location, or where something is. You might say the girl's position is on the ladder or beside the slide.

Now look at the boy sliding down the slide. The boy is in motion. **Motion** is a change in the position of an object. Motion describes the boy's movement from the top of the slide toward the bottom.

1. **Describe** Observe a classmate walking from one side of the room to the other. Describe the classmate's new position.

....

....

2. ◎ **Draw Conclusions** After reading the paragraphs, what can you conclude about the boy's position?

....

At-Home Lab

Observe and Describe Motion
On a sunny day, find an object with a shadow. Use pictures and position words to describe the shadow at three different times during the day. Then write a sentence that analyzes the change in the shadow's position over time.

4. CHALLENGE Sometimes a car near your car will move with the same speed and in the same direction as your car. What happens to your position compared to that car?

An Object's Position

The position of an object often depends on how a person looks at it. Suppose you wanted to tell a friend about the boat in the picture. How would you describe its position? You could use numbers to describe distances. You could also use position words, such as *in front of, behind, left, right,* and *beside.* The words you use might change if you were riding in the boat.

You could also draw a map. A map models the position of objects in relation to each other.

3. Illustrate Draw a map to show the position of the boat and cars in the picture after a few seconds.

Positions of Moving Objects

Objects on a map are fixed in place. How do you describe the position of moving objects? The cars and the boat in the picture are in motion. The way you describe their position may change depending on the position and motion of other objects.

5. Analyze How would the position of the boat seem to change as the white car moves along the road?

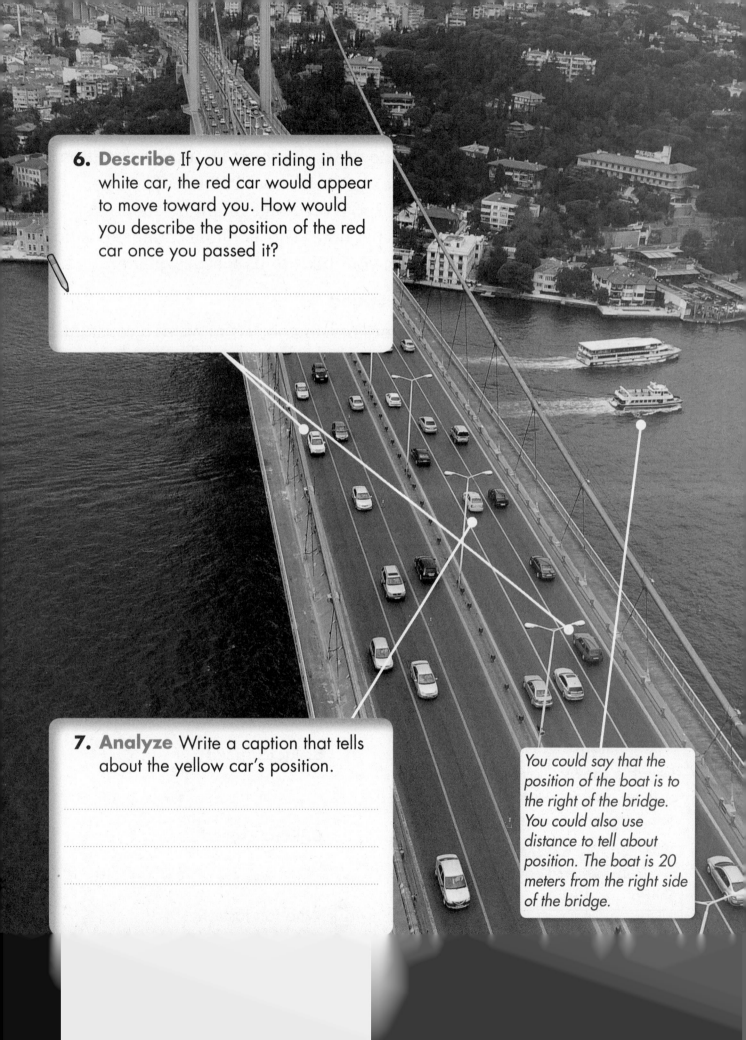

6. Describe If you were riding in the white car, the red car would appear to move toward you. How would you describe the position of the red car once you passed it?

....

....

7. Analyze Write a caption that tells about the yellow car's position.

....

....

....

You could say that the position of the boat is to the right of the bridge. You could also use distance to tell about position. The boat is 20 meters from the right side of the bridge.

How Fast Objects Move

How can you describe how fast objects move? You can tell their speed. **Speed** is the rate at which, or how fast, an object changes its position. A jet plane's speed is about 900 kilometers per hour. Your speed on a bike might be about 15 kilometers per hour. The jet plane changes position faster than your bike, so its speed is greater.

Constant Speed

Sometimes moving objects move at a constant speed. A plane that flies steadily at 900 kilometers per hour is moving at a constant speed. The plane does not change how fast it moves.

8. ◉ **Main Idea and Details**
Underline the main idea of the first paragraph.

Do the math!

Find an Object's Speed

You can find the speed of an object if you know the distance it moved and how much time it took to move that distance. To find speed, divide distance by time.

distance ÷ time = speed

The table shows distances and times for three runners. Distances are in meters (m) and times are in seconds (s).

Runner	Distance	Time
Sheela	100 m	25 s
Jack	40 m	8 s
Kara	200 m	50 s

1 Write number sentences to show each runner's speed in meters per second ($\frac{m}{s}$).

A. Sheela's speed

.... m ÷ .... s = ... $\frac{m}{s}$

B. Jack's speed

.... m ÷ .... s = ... $\frac{m}{s}$

C. Kara's speed

.... m ÷ .... s = ... $\frac{m}{s}$

2 Who ran fastest?

....

myscienceonline.com | Got it? 60-Second Video

Variable Speed

A roller coaster would not be fun if it moved at a constant speed. The thrill of the ride comes from slowly climbing up and then quickly moving down the steep track. The roller coaster moves at a variable speed. It changes speed as it moves.

9. **Exemplify** Give two examples of objects that move at a variable speed.

10. **Exemplify** Describe three examples of motion you might see on a playground.

11. **Analyze** How does the motion and position of each roller skate change as a person skates down a sidewalk?

⬛ **Stop!** I need help with

⏸ **Wait!** I have a question about

▶ **Go!** Now I know

How does force affect motion?

Tell which way you think the leash will move.

How does mass affect motion?

☑ **1.** Compare the mass of the two balls.

☑ **2.** Place the table tennis ball at the bottom of the ramp. Roll the rubber ball down the ramp. **Record** the distance the table tennis ball rolls.

....

3. Predict What will happen if the balls switch places?

....
....

☑ **4.** Test your prediction.

Explain Your Results

5. Draw a Conclusion How did mass affect motion?

....
....
....

Materials

2 stacked books with ruler

table tennis ball

rubber ball

meterstick

mYscienceonLine.com | **Explore It!** Animation

Words to Know

force   magnetism
friction

Causes of Motion

Crack! A baseball player hits the ball. The bat pushes against the ball. The bat has all the power of the player's swing. A force causes the motion, speed, and direction of the ball to change. A **force** is a push or a pull.

Most of the forces you use are contact forces. When you hit a baseball with a bat, the bat's force changes the speed and direction of the ball. If the bat does not make contact with the ball, these changes cannot occur.

A bat needs contact to apply force.

1. ◉ **Draw Conclusions** Complete the graphic organizer. List facts that support the conclusion.

Fact	
Fact	
Fact	**Conclusion**

A bat's push is a contact force.

2. Classify (Circle) the picture where the girl is pushing more mass. Put an ✗ on the picture where she must use more force to change the motion.

Effects of Mass and Friction

A force can change an object's position or the direction of its motion. A push by the girl can cause the shopping cart to start moving. If she then pushes to the right, the moving cart will change direction to the right.

How much an object changes its direction and speed depends on how much force is used. A large force will cause a greater change in motion than a smaller force. The cart will go faster if the girl pushes harder.

How an object moves also depends on its mass. When the girl starts shopping, her cart is empty. She does not need much force to push it. As the girl shops, she stops and puts objects in the cart. Each time she does, the cart's mass gets larger. The girl must then use more force to push the cart or change its direction.

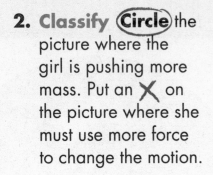

Lightning Lab

Varying Mass and Force

Slide a plastic bin along the floor. Fill the bin with books. Push the bin again using the same amount of force. Describe what happens.

3. Explain You need to move a chair to another place in the classroom. How does the amount and direction of force determine how much the chair will move?

....

4. ◉ **Main Idea and Details** What is the main idea of this page?

....

While the girl's grocery cart moves down the aisle, its wheels rub against the floor. This causes friction. **Friction** is a contact force that opposes the motion of an object. Friction can cause a moving object to slow down or to stop.

The amount of friction between two objects depends on their surfaces. Pushing a grocery cart over smooth tiles in a store is pretty easy. You need more force to push a cart across the asphalt parking lot. The smooth tile produces less friction on the wheels than the asphalt does.

5. List Write two places in the picture where friction is acting.

....

....

6. [CHALLENGE] Why do bowling alley owners keep the surface of the lanes smooth and polished?

....

....

....

....

....

Motion and Combined Forces

As a kite flies through the air, it dips and it dives. What forces act on the kite? The force of the wind pushes it up. Weight is one of the forces pulling it down. The boy also pulls down on the string. Each push or pull has its own amount of force. Each force also acts in its own direction. An object's motion depends on all the forces that act together.

Balanced Forces

Sometimes a kite hangs in the air. It is almost motionless. This is because the forces acting on the kite balance each other. Forces that work together and make no change in motion are called balanced forces.

You can see balanced forces all around you. Think of two strong football players pushing against each other. If they each push with the same force but in opposite directions, neither player moves.

7. Illustrate Draw and label arrows on the picture to show the forces acting on the kite.

8. Explain Each player is applying force. The two players do not move. What is happening?

9. Illustrate Draw arrows to show the balanced forces.

Unbalanced Forces

If the forces acting on an object are not balanced, the motion of the object will change. Unbalanced forces can cause an object at rest to move. They can also change the speed or direction of a moving object.

You might compare the forces acting on an object to a game of tug-of-war. In tug-of-war, two teams pull a rope in opposite directions. If the forces are equal, the rope does not move. To win, one team must pull with greater force than the other team. One team must unbalance the forces acting on the rope. The rope will then move in the direction of the greater pull.

10. Apply Complete the sentence.

.... forces cause the rope in tug-of-war to move in a certain direction.

11. Infer Look at the picture below. Which way do you think the rope is moving? Why?

....

....

....

....

....

More force

Less force

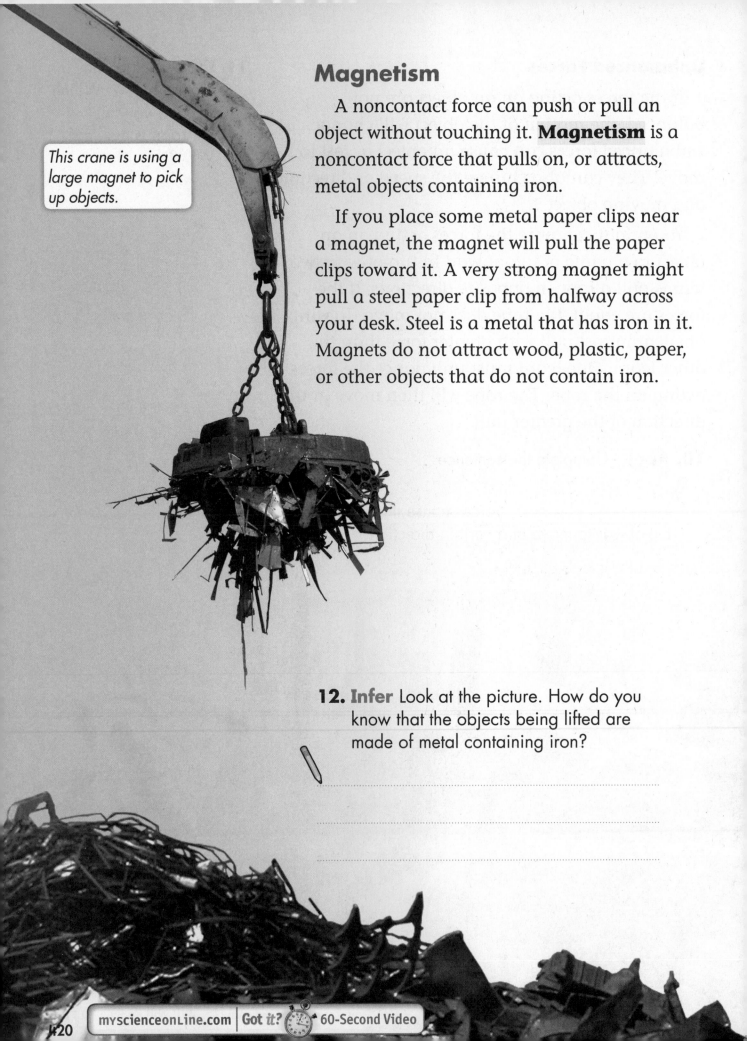

This crane is using a large magnet to pick up objects.

Magnetism

A noncontact force can push or pull an object without touching it. **Magnetism** is a noncontact force that pulls on, or attracts, metal objects containing iron.

If you place some metal paper clips near a magnet, the magnet will pull the paper clips toward it. A very strong magnet might pull a steel paper clip from halfway across your desk. Steel is a metal that has iron in it. Magnets do not attract wood, plastic, paper, or other objects that do not contain iron.

12. **Infer** Look at the picture. How do you know that the objects being lifted are made of metal containing iron?

Magnets work because they have a magnetic field around them. The field is strongest near the magnet's poles. Each magnet has a north pole and a south pole. The north pole of one magnet will attract the south pole of another magnet. Poles that are the same will push away from each other.

13. Infer Why is magnetism a noncontact force?

The magnetic field's force pulls the paper clips toward the magnet.

Got it?

14. Explain What happens if you hit a baseball hard? softly? Why?

15. UNLOCK THE BIG ? How can the force of magnetism cause objects to move?

⬜ **Stop!** I need help with ....

⏸ **Wait!** I have a question about ....

▶ **Go!** Now I know ....

What is gravity?

Envision It!

Why do you think the skydivers fall back to Earth?

Inquiry **Explore It!**

How does gravity pull an object?

☑ **1.** Place a ball in the smaller cup.
Raise the free end of the meterstick about 80 cm.

☑ **2.** Release the stick. Gently push it down.

☑ **3.** **Observe** and **record** where the ball lands.

Materials

meterstick with cups

rubber ball

goggles

folding meterstick

Explain Your Results

4. Communicate Describe the path of the ball.

....

....

....

5. Interpret Data Explain your results using what you know about gravity.

....

....

....

....

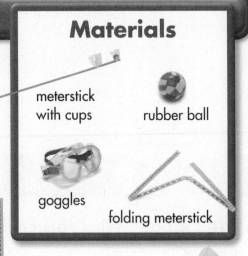

Word to Know

gravity

Law of Gravity

There are different forces acting on people all of the time. A force is any push or pull. One kind of force is a noncontact force. A noncontact force is a push or pull that affects an object without touching it. **Gravity** is a noncontact force that pulls objects toward one another. The law of gravity states that all objects are pulled toward one another by gravity. Skydivers and water from this fountain are pulled toward Earth by gravity. Without gravity, they would float away. Gravity pulls you and everything else on Earth toward Earth's center.

1. **Compare** Tell how tossing a coin is like water flowing from this fountain.

Gravity and Weight

The pull of gravity on an object gives an object its weight. An object's weight depends on where it is. When the pull of gravity is weaker, the object's weight is less. For example, the moon has less gravity than Earth. So, you weigh less on the moon. The pull of gravity is also less the farther you are from Earth's center. So, you weigh less on a mountaintop than in a valley.

An object's weight also depends on the amount of matter in an object. Objects with more matter have more mass. So, the pull of gravity is greater on an object with more mass. For example, the pull of gravity is greater on an elephant than on an apple. Even if the pull of gravity changes, the object's mass stays the same. Your mass on Earth and on the moon is the same, but your weight is different.

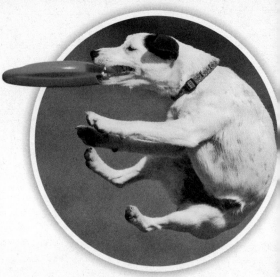

2. Apply Compare the pull of gravity on the dog to the pull of gravity on the frisbee.

....

....

....

Do the math!

Multiplication

You learned that the mass of any matter is the same everywhere. The weight of an object depends on the pull of gravity.

Example

The pull of gravity on Earth is 6 times as strong as the pull of gravity on the moon. If a cat weighs 3 pounds on the moon, how much would the same cat weigh on Earth?

3 pounds × 6 = 18 pounds

The cat weighs 3 pounds on the moon but 18 pounds on Earth.

1 Solve The pull of gravity on Earth is 3 times as strong as the pull of gravity on Mars. If a bike weighed 9 pounds on Mars, how much would that bike weigh on Earth? Show your work.

2 Solve If a dog weighed 9 pounds on the moon, how much would the same dog weigh on Earth? Show your work.

myscienceonline.com | Got it? | 60-Second Video

Gravity is a force that can be overcome. For example, when you toss a ball in the air, the ball overcomes gravity for a few moments. Then it falls back to Earth. If your push is stronger than the pull of gravity, the ball will go up. Gravity pulls the ball back down. It is easier to overcome gravity with a light object than with a heavy object.

3. **Determine** How does gravity affect juggling?

Lightning Lab

Overcoming Gravity

Get a light object and a heavy object. Hold them up. Describe what resists the force of gravity. Drop them at the same time. Describe how they fell.

Got it?

4. **Determine** What makes it easier to carry an object down stairs than up stairs?

5. **Predict** How would throwing a ball on the moon be different than throwing a ball on Earth?

⬛ **Stop!** I need help with

⏸ **Wait!** I have a question about

▶ **Go!** Now I know

How can you describe motion?

Follow a Procedure

☐ **1.** **Measure** 2 meters from a wall and place one end of the chute there.

☐ **2.** Place 2 books under the other end of the chute.

☐ **3.** Release the ball at the top of the chute. Start timing when the ball reaches the floor.

☐ **4.** **Record** the time when the ball hits the wall.

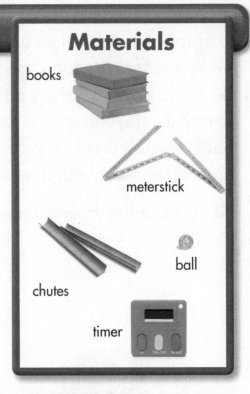

Materials

books

meterstick

chutes

ball

timer

Inquiry Skill
Scientists **measure** carefully and record their measurements.

2 m

5. Stop the timer when the ball comes back to the bottom of the chute. Record.

Ball Movement Results			
Time (seconds)			
Number of Books	From Bottom of Chute to Wall (Time A)	From Bottom of Chute to Wall and Back (Time B)	From Wall to Bottom of Chute (Time C = Time B – Time A)
2 books			
4 books			

6. Stack 4 books and repeat steps 2 to 5.

Analyze and Conclude

7. Interpret Data When did the ball move faster?

....

....

....

....

8. UNLOCK THE BIG ? What effect did the wall have on the motion of the ball?

....

....

....

....

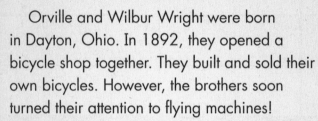

The Wright Brothers

Orville and Wilbur Wright were born in Dayton, Ohio. In 1892, they opened a bicycle shop together. They built and sold their own bicycles. However, the brothers soon turned their attention to flying machines!

The Wright brothers studied the motion of aircraft. They examined the forces that keep a craft in the air or pull it down. They examined the forces that move the craft forward or slow its motion.

Orville and Wilbur tested their ideas on gliders. Success came in 1902. They built a glider that a pilot could control in the air.

Their next step was to design and build an engine-powered aircraft. They needed a gasoline engine that did not weigh too much. Yet it had to provide enough force to move the craft in the air. In 1903, Orville and Wilbur made the first controlled flight in an aircraft with an engine.

REVIEW THE BIG ? How might building bicycles have helped the brothers build airplanes?

....

....

....

Vocabulary Smart Cards

position
motion
speed
force
friction
magnetism
gravity

Play a Game!

Cut out the Vocabulary Smart Cards.

Work with a partner. Choose a Vocabulary Smart Card.

Write a sentence using the vocabulary word. Draw a blank where the vocabulary word should be.

Have your partner fill in the blank with the correct vocabulary word.

force

fuerza

position

posición

friction

fricción

motion

movimiento

magnetism

magnetismo

speed

rapidez

the location of an object

Use a dictionary. Write as many synonyms for this word as you can.

ubicación de un objeto

---

a push or a pull

Write a sentence using this word.

empujón o jalón

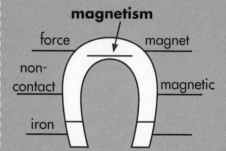

force — **magnetism** — magnet

non-contact

magnetic

iron

Make a Word Magnet!

Choose a vocabulary word and write it in the Word Magnet. Write words that are related to it on the lines.

---

a change in the position of an object

Write a sentence using this word.

cambio en la posición de un objeto

---

a contact force that opposes the motion of an object

Make a drawing that shows what this word means.

fuerza de contacto que se opone al movimiento de un objeto

---

the rate at which an object changes position

Write the definition as a formula.

tasa a la cual un objeto cambia de posición

---

a non-contact force that pulls objects containing iron

Draw an example of this word.

fuerza sin contacto que atrae objetos que contienen hierro

gravity

gravedad

a noncontact force that pulls objects toward one another

Draw an example.

fuerza sin contacto que hace que los objetos se atraigan entre sí

Lesson 1

What is motion?

- Motion is a change in position.
- Position is the location of an object, or its place.
- Speed is the rate at which an object changes its position.

Lesson 2

How does force affect motion?

- A force is a push or a pull.
- The amount of force used affects an object's motions.
- Mass and friction affect an object's motion.

Lesson 3

What is gravity?

- Gravity is a noncontact force that pulls objects toward one another.
- The pull of gravity on an object gives the object its weight.

Lesson 1

What is motion?

1. **Vocabulary** Which word means the same as *position*? Circle the correct answer.
   A. motion
   B. location
   C. direction
   D. speed

Do the
math!

2. **Calculate** The caterpillar crossed this leaf in 5 seconds. Use the formula for speed to find out exactly how fast the caterpillar traveled.

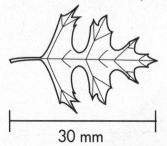

30 mm

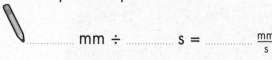
distance ÷ time = speed

caterpillar's speed =

_____ mm ÷ _____ s = _____ $\frac{mm}{s}$

3. **Explain** How do you know when an object is in motion?

....

....

Lesson 2

How does force affect motion?

4. **Predict** What would happen if more force were applied to a moving cart? The force acts in the same direction in which the cart is moving.

....

....

5. **Write About It** Describe friction and give an example of it.

....

....

....

....

....

....

6. ◉ **Draw Conclusions** A volleyball is headed toward you. You hit the ball back in the direction from which it came. What can you conclude about force?

....

....

....

Lesson 3

What is gravity?

7. Infer Why would a crayon roll down a ramp but need force to move up a ramp?

....

....

....

....

....

8. Analyze Without gravity, what would happen if you threw a ball straight up in the air?

....

....

....

....

9. Justify How could you show that gravity affects an apple?

....

....

....

....

10. APPLY THE BIG **? What forces cause motion?**

....

Describe what happens when you open a door. Use the terms *force*, *motion*, and *position*.

....

....

....

....

....

....

....

....

....

....

....

....

....

....

Benchmark Practice

Fill in the bubble next to the answer choice you think is correct for each multiple-choice question.

1 What **always** changes when an object is in motion?

  Ⓐ its direction
  Ⓑ its speed
  Ⓒ its mass
  Ⓓ its position

2 Look closely at the bicycles. What force would cause the wheels to slow down?

  Ⓐ gravity
  Ⓑ position
  Ⓒ magnetism
  Ⓓ friction

3 Which will make a bowling ball roll faster?

  Ⓐ Increase the distance it rolls.
  Ⓑ Apply a greater force.
  Ⓒ Increase the ball's weight.
  Ⓓ Increase the ball's mass.

4 Jake and Maria are playing catch. Jake misses catching the ball. What causes the ball to fall to Earth?

  Ⓐ friction
  Ⓑ speed
  Ⓒ gravity
  Ⓓ mass

5 Which of the following would **not** affect the motion of an object?

  Ⓐ a change in mass
  Ⓑ balanced forces
  Ⓒ a greater force
  Ⓓ more friction

6 Would a person's weight on one planet be different from the same person's weight on another planet? Explain.

....

....

....

STEM

Roller Coasters

Roller coasters can be fun! If you have been on a roller coaster, did you move right or left? Did you move up or down? What forces did you feel? Engineers use science, technology, and math to design roller coasters. Roller coasters test the limits of technology! Engineers test different materials for strength before building a roller coaster. Steel is very strong. Steel allows engineers to build taller hills and tighter loops. Engineers use math to calculate how fast the cars will travel. Roller coasters use science, technology, engineering, and math to make the ride more fun!

During a roller coaster ride, energy is constantly changing. Potential energy is greatest at the top of hills. It is the least at the bottom of hills.

Illustrate Roller coasters use both potential and kinetic energy. Potential energy is stored energy. Kinetic energy is energy of motion. In this image, circle where the roller coaster has the most kinetic energy. Draw an ✗ where the roller coaster has the most potential energy.

457

Materials

masking tape

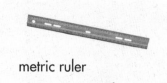

metric ruler

marker

meterstick

pullback toy car

Inquiry Skill
You **experiment** when you design a way to answer a scientific question.

How does energy affect the distance a toy car travels?

Potential energy is stored energy. The more you pull back a toy car, the more potential energy it has.

Ask a question.

How does a car's potential energy affect the distance it travels?

State a hypothesis.

1. Write a **hypothesis** by circling one choice and finishing the sentence.
   If a car's potential energy increases, then the distance it travels will
   (a) *increase*
   (b) *decrease*
   (c) *stay the same*
   because

....

....

Identify and control variables.

2. When you **experiment,** you need to change just one **variable.** Everything else must remain the same. What should stay the same? List two examples.

....

....

3. Tell the one change you will make.

....

....

Design your test.

4. Draw how you will set up your test.

5. List your steps in the order you will do them.

Do your test.

First see how far the car travels. Then decide if you will measure with a metric ruler or a meterstick.

- ☑ **6.** Follow the steps you wrote.

- ☑ **7.** Make sure to **measure** carefully. **Record** your results in the table.

- ☑ **8.** Scientists repeat their tests to improve their accuracy. Repeat your test if time allows.

Work Like a Scientist
Scientists work with other scientists. They compare their methods and results. Talk with your classmates. Compare your methods and results.

Collect and record your data.

- ☑ **9.** Fill in the chart.

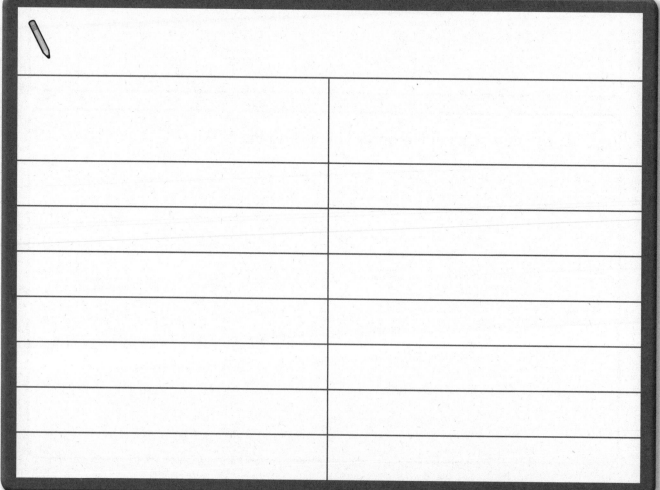

Interpret your data.

☐ **10.** Use your data to make a bar graph.

<table>
<tr><td></td><td></td><td></td><td></td><td></td><td></td><td></td></tr>
<tr><td></td><td></td><td></td><td></td><td></td><td></td><td></td></tr>
<tr><td></td><td></td><td></td><td></td><td></td><td></td><td></td></tr>
<tr><td></td><td></td><td></td><td></td><td></td><td></td><td></td></tr>
<tr><td></td><td></td><td></td><td></td><td></td><td></td><td></td></tr>
<tr><td></td><td></td><td></td><td></td><td></td><td></td><td></td></tr>
<tr><td></td><td></td><td></td><td></td><td></td><td></td><td></td></tr>
<tr><td></td><td></td><td></td><td></td><td></td><td></td><td></td></tr>
</table>

☐ **11.** Look at your graph closely. Did the distance you pulled the car back affect the distance it traveled? Identify the evidence you used to answer the question.

....

....

State your conclusion.

12. Communicate your conclusion. How does increasing the toy car's potential energy affect the distance it travels? Compare your **hypothesis** with your results. Compare your results with others.

> **Technology Tools**
> Your teacher may wish you to use a computer (with the right software) or a graphing calculator to help collect, organize, analyze, and present your data. These tools can help you make tables, charts, and graphs.

....

....

....

....

Use Light Energy

Use a shallow pan filled with water and a piece of clear plastic wrap to show how the energy from sunlight can change matter. Set the pan in a place that receives direct sunlight. Cover the pan with the clear plastic wrap. Write a prediction of how the energy of the sun will affect the liquid water.

After an hour, observe the pan. Write a description of what you see.

• Do your observations support your prediction?

• What would happen if you removed the clear plastic wrap from the pan?

Toy Power

Choose a wind-up toy. Observe the toy as it works. Look for ways the toy transfers energy from one part to another.

• How does your wind-up affect the distance the toy travels?

• How might some kinetic energy be transferred from one part to another?

Using Scientific Methods

1. Ask a question.
2. State your hypothesis.
3. Identify and control variables.
4. Test your hypothesis.
5. Collect and record your data.
6. Interpret your data.
7. State your conclusion.
8. Go further.

Write a Poem

Write a poem about matter. Include at least four properties of matter. You may want to select some objects and describe them in your poem. Here are some tips to help you write your poem.

• A poem is written in lines.

• A poem may rhyme or have a rhythm.

Measurements

Metric and Customary Measurements

The metric system is the measurement system most commonly used in science. Metric units are sometimes called SI units. SI stands for International System. It is called that because these units are used around the world.

These prefixes are used in the metric system:

kilo- means *thousand*
1 kilometer = 1,000 meters

milli- means *one thousandth*
1,000 millimeters = 1 meter, or 1 millimeter = 0.001 meter

centi- means *one hundredth*
100 centimeters = 1 meter, or 1 centimeter = 0.01 meter

1 liter

1 cup

Temperature
Water freezes at 0°C, or 32°F.
Water boils at 100°C, or 212°F.

Volume
One liter is greater than 4 cups.

1 pound

1 kilogram

Mass
One kilogram is greater than 2 pounds.

1 meter

1 yard

Length and Distance
One meter is longer than 1 yard.

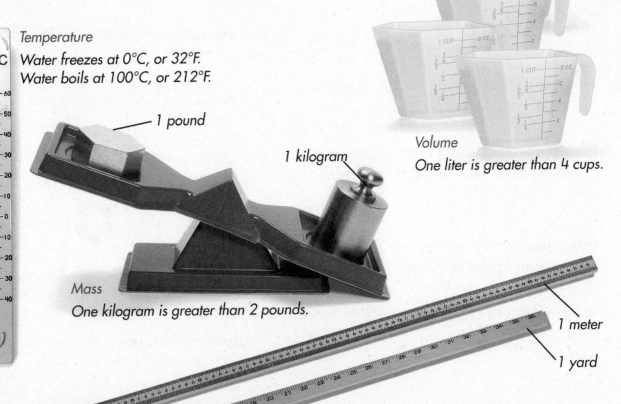

Glossary

The glossary uses letters and signs to show how words are pronounced. The mark ′ is placed after a syllable with a primary or heavy accent. The mark ′ is placed after a syllable with a secondary or lighter accent.

To hear these vocabulary words and definitions, you can refer to the AudioText CD, or log on to the digital path's Vocabulary Smart Cards.

A

absorb (ab sôrb′) to take in

absorber retener

adaptation (ad′ ap tā′ shən) a trait that helps a living thing survive in its environment

adaptación rasgo de los seres vivos que los ayuda a sobrevivir en su medio ambiente

arthropod (är′ thrə pod) an animal that has a hard covering outside its body

artrópodo animal que tiene el cuerpo envuelto por una cubierta dura

atmosphere (at′ mə sfir) the blanket of air that surrounds Earth

atmósfera capa de aire que rodea la Tierra

axis (ak′ sis) an imaginary line around which Earth spins

eje línea imaginaria alrededor de la cual gira la Tierra

B

bar graph (bär graf) a graph that helps you compare data and see patterns

gráfica de barras gráfica que ayuda a comparar datos y ver patrones

boil (boil) to change from liquid water into bubbles of water vapor

hervir cambiar de agua en estado líquido aburbujas de vapor

C

carbon dioxide (kär′ bən dī ok′ sīd) a gas in air that is absorbed by most plants

dióxido de carbono gas en el aire que la mayoría de las plantas absorben

chart (chärt) a kind of list

tabla tipo de lista

climate (klī′ mit) the pattern of weather in a place over many years

clima patrón que sigue el tiempo atmosférico de un lugar a lo largo de muchos años

closed circuit (klōzd′ sėr′ kit) a circuit with no gaps or breaks

circuito cerrado circuito que no tiene rupturas ni interrupciones

community (kə myü′ nə tē) all the populations that live in the same place

comunidad todas las poblaciones que conviven en el mismo lugar

condensation (kon′ den sā′ shən) the change from a gas to a liquid

condensación cambio de un gas a líquido

consumer (kən sü′ mər) a living thing that eats other organisms

consumidor ser vivo que se alimenta de otros organismos

crater (krā′ tər) a bowl-shaped hole on the surface of an object in space

cráter agujero con forma de tazón en la superficie de un objeto del espacio

D

decomposer (dē′ kəm pō′ zər) a living thing that breaks down waste and dead plant and animal matter

descomponedor ser vivo que destruye residuos y materia de animales y vegetales muertos

design process (di zīn′ pros′ es) a step-by-step method used to solve a problem

proceso de diseño método que sigue pasos y que se usa para resolver un problema

E

ecosystem (ē′ kō sis′ təm) the living and nonliving things that interact in an environment

ecosistema todos los seres vivos y las cosas sin vida que interactúan en un área determinada

electrical energy (i lek′ trə kəl en′ ər jē) the movement of electric charges

energía eléctrica el movimiento de cargas eléctricas

energy (en′ ər jē) the ability to do work or to cause change

energía capacidad de hacer trabajo o causar cambios

erosion (i rō′ zhən) the movement of weathered materials

erosión el movimiento de materiales que han sufrido meteorización

evaporation (i vap′ ə rā′ shən) the change from liquid water to water vapor, a gas

evaporación cambio de agua en estado líquido a vapor

F

flowering plant (flou′ ər ing plant) a plant with seeds that grows flowers

angiosperma planta con semillas que produce flores

food chain (füd chān) the transfer of energy from one living thing to another

cadena alimentaria transmisión de energía de un ser vivo a otro

force (fôrs) a push or a pull

fuerza empujón o jalón

freeze (frēz) to change from a liquid to a solid

congelarse cambiar de líquido a sólido

friction (frik′ shən) a contact force that opposes the motion of an object

fricción fuerza de contacto que se opone al movimiento de un objeto

G

germinate (jėr′ mə nāt) to begin to grow

germinar empezar a crecer

gravity (grav′ ə tē) a noncontact force that pulls objects toward one another

gravedad fuerza sin contacto que hace que los objetos se atraigan entre sí

H

habitat (hab′ ə tat) the place where a living thing makes its home

hábitat el lugar donde un ser vivo establece su hogar

hardness (härd′ nis) a description of how firm an object is

dureza descripción de la firmeza de un objeto

humidity (hyü mid′ ə tē) the amount of water vapor in the air

humedad cantidad de vapor de agua que hay en el aire

I

igneous rock (ig′ nē əs rok) rock that forms when melted rock cools and hardens

roca ígnea roca que se forma cuando las rocas derretidas se enfrían y endurecen

inclined plane (in klīnd′ plān) a slanting surface that connects a lower level to a higher level

plano inclinado superficie inclinada que conecta un nivel bajo con un nivel más alto

infer (in fėr′) to draw a conclusion

inferir sacar una conclusión

inherit (in her′ it) to receive from a parent

heredar recibir de un progenitor

inquiry (in kwī′ rē) the process of asking questions

indagación proceso de hacer preguntas

instinct (in′ stingkt) a behavior an animal is born able to do

instinto conducta que tiene un animal desde que nace

invertebrate (in vėr′ tə brit) an animal without a backbone

invertebrado animal que no tiene columna vertebral

investigate (in ves′ tə gāt) to look for answers

investigar buscar respuestas

K

kinetic energy (ki net′ ik en′ ər jē) energy of motion

energía cinética energía de movimiento

L

landform (land′ fôrm′) a solid feature of Earth's crust

accidente geográfico formación sólida de la corteza terrestre

larva (lär′ və) second stage of the life cycle of some insects

larva segunda etapa del ciclo de vida de algunos insectos

lava (lä′ və) magma that flows onto Earth's surface

lava magma que fluye a la superficie terrestre

lever (lev′ ər) a simple machine to lift and move things by using a stiff bar that rests on a support

palanca máquina simple que se usa para levantar y mover cosas mediante una barra rígida que tiene un punto de apoyo

life cycle (līf sī′ kəl) the stages through which a living thing passes during its life

ciclo de vida estados por los que pasa un ser vivo durante su vida

light energy (līt′ en′ ər jē) energy we can see

energía luminosa energía que podemos ver

light-year (līt′ yir′) the distance light travels in one year

año luz distancia que la luz viaja en un año

loam (lōm) soil that contains a mixture of humus and mineral materials of sand, silt, and clay

marga suelo que contiene una mezcla de humus y minerales de la arena, cieno y arcilla

magnetism (mag′ nə tiz′ əm) a non-contact force that pulls objects containing iron

magnetismo fuerza sin contacto que atrae objetos que contienen hierro

mass (mas) the amount of matter an object has

masa cantidad de materia que un objeto tiene

matter (mat′ ər) anything that takes up space and has mass

materia todo lo que ocupa espacio y tiene masa

melt (melt) to change from a solid to a liquid

derretirse cambiar de sólido a líquido

metamorphic rock (met′ ə môr′ fik rok) rock that forms when existing rock is changed by heat and pressure

roca metamórfica roca que se forma cuando las rocas existentes cambian debido al calor y la presión

metamorphosis (met′ ə môr′ fə sis) a change in form during an animal's life cycle

metamorfosis cambio de la forma de un animal durante su ciclo de vida

mineral (min′ ər əl) natural, nonliving material that makes up rocks

mineral material natural y sin vida del que se componen las rocas

model (mod′ l) a copy of something

modelo copia de algo

moon phase (mün fāz) the shape the moon seems to have at a given time

fase de la Luna forma que la Luna parece tener en un momento dado

motion (mō′ shən) a change in the position of an object

movimiento cambio en la posición de un objeto

nutrient (nü′ trē ənt) any material needed by living things for energy, growth, and repair

nutriente cualquier sustancia que los seres vivos necesitan para obtener energía, crecer y reponerse

open circuit (ō′ pən sėr′ kit) a circuit with a broken path

circuito abierto circuito que tiene una ruptura en su ruta

oxygen (ok′ sə jən) a gas in the air that plants and animals need

oxígeno gas en el aire que las plantas y los animales necesitan para vivir

P

photosynthesis (fō′ tō sin′ thə sis) the process by which plants use air, water, and energy from sunlight to make food

fotosíntesis proceso por el cual las plantas usan el aire, el agua y la energía del sol para producir alimento

pitch (pich) how high or low a sound is

tono cuán agudo o grave es un sonido

planet (plan′ it) a large, ball-shaped body that revolves, or travels around, the sun

planeta cuerpo de gran tamaño, con forma de bola, que se mueve alrededor del Sol

pollinate (pol′ ə nāt) to carry pollen to

polinizar llevar polen de un lugar a otro

population (pop′ yə lā′ shən) all the living things of the same kind that live in the same place

población todos los seres vivos de la misma especie que viven en el mismo lugar

position (pə zish′ ən) the location of an object

posición ubicación de un objeto

potential energy (pə ten′ shəl en′ ər jē) stored energy

energía potencial energía almacenada

precipitation (pri sip′ ə tā′ shən) water that falls to Earth

precipitación agua que cae a la Tierra

procedure (prə sē′ jər) a plan for testing a hypothesis

procedimiento plan que se usa para poner a prueba una hipótesis

producer (prə dü′ sər) a living thing that makes, or produces, its own food

productor ser vivo que genera, o produce, su propio alimento

property (prop′ ər tē) something about matter that you can observe with one or more of your senses

propiedad algo en la materia que puedes percibir con uno o más de tus sentidos

prototype (prō′ tə tīp) the first working product that uses a design

prototipo el primer producto que funciona y que sique un diseño

pulley (pul′ ē) a machine that can change the direction or amount of force needed to move an object

polea máquina que puede cambiar la dirección o la cantidad de fuerza necesaria para mover un objeto

pupa (pyü′ pə) stage of an insect's life cycle between larva and adult

pupa etapa de la vida de un insecto entre larva y adulto

R

reflect (ri flekt′) to bounce off

reflejar hacer rebotar algo

refract (ri frakt′) to bend

refractar desviar o inclinar

reproduce (rē′ prə düs′) to make more of the same kind

reproducir hacer más de una misma cosa

research (ri serch′) to look for facts about something

hacer una investigación buscar datos sobre algo

revolution (rev′ ə lü′ shən) one complete trip around the sun

traslación vuelta completa alrededor del Sol

rock (rok) natural, solid, nonliving material made from one or more minerals

roca material natural, sólido sin vida, compuesto por uno o más minerales

rotation (rō tā′ shən) one complete spin on an axis

rotación vuelta completa alrededor de un eje

S

scientist (sī′ ən tist) person who asks questions about the natural world

científico persona cuyo trabajo implica hacer preguntas sobre el mundo y la naturaleza

....

screw (skrü) an inclined plane wrapped around a center post

tornillo plano inclinado enrollado alrededor de un eje central

....

sedimentary rock (sed′ ə men′ tər ē rok) rock that forms when sediments are pressed together and cemented

roca sedimentaria roca que se forma por la acumulación de sedimentos unidos a gran presión

....

soil (soil) the layer of loose material that covers Earth's land

suelo capa de material suelto que cubre la superficie de la Tierra

....

solar system (sō′ lər sis′ təm) the sun, the eight planets and their moons, and other objects that revolve around the sun

sistema solar el Sol, los ocho planetas con sus satélites y otros objetos que giran alrededor del Sol

sound energy (sound en′ ər jē) energy we can hear

energía sonora energía que podemos oír

....

speed (spēd) the rate at which an object changes position

rapidez tasa a la cual un objeto cambia de posición

....

spore (spôr) a small cell that grows into a new plant

espora célula pequeña que se convierte en una planta nueva

....

star (stär) a giant ball of hot, glowing gases that release energy

estrella bola gigante de gases calientes y brillantes que emiten energía

....

states of matter (stāts uv mat′ ər) forms that matter can take

estados de la materia formas que la materia puede tener

technology (tek nol′ ə jē) use of science knowledge to invent tools and new ways of doing things

tecnología uso del conocimiento científico para inventar instrumentos y nuevas maneras de hacer las cosas

texture (teks′ chər) how an object feels to the touch

textura cómo se siente un objeto al tocarlo

thermal energy (thėr′ məl en′ ər jē) the kinetic energy and potential energy of particles in matter

energía térmica energía cinética y energía potencial de las partículas que forman la materia

tool (tül) object used to do work

instrumento objeto que se usa para trabajar

trait (trāt) a feature passed on to a living thing from its parents

rasgo característica que pasa de padres a hijos entre los seres vivos

unit of measure (yü′ nit uv mezh′ ər) quantity you use to measure

unidad de medida cantidad que ser usa para medir

vertebrate (vėr′ tə brit) an animal with a backbone

vertebrado animal que tiene columna vertebral

volume (vol′ yəm) the amount of space an object takes up

volumen espacio que ocupa un objeto

volume (vol′ yəm) how loud or soft a sound is

volumen cuán fuerte o suave es un sonido

water cycle (wȯ′ tər sī′ kəl) the movement of water from Earth's surface into the air and back again

ciclo del agua movimiento de ida y vuelta que realiza el agua entre el aire y la superficie de la Tierra

wave (wāv) a disturbance that carries energy from one point to another point

onda perturbación que lleva energía de un punto a otro

weather (weᴛʜ′ ər) what the air is like outside

tiempo atmosférico las condiciones al aire libre

weathering (weᴛʜ′ ər ing) any process that breaks rock into smaller pieces

meteorización todo proceso que rompe la roca en trozos más pequeños

wedge (wej) two slanted sides that end in a sharp edge

cuña dos lados inclinados que terminan con un borde filoso

wheel and axle (wēl and ak′ səl) a round wheel attached to a post

eje y rueda figura circular que gira alrededor de una varilla

work (wėrk) the use of a force to move an object across a distance

trabajo uso de una fuerza para mover un objeto, por cierta distancia

Index

Page numbers for pictures, charts, graphs, maps, and their associated text are printed in *italic type*.

272, 321, 322, 353, 354, 405, 406

Tug-of-war, *419*
Turtles, 141, *144*, *180*, *200*

Unbalanced forces, 419
Understand, *379*
Unit of measure, 29–30, 37–40, 335–339
Uranus, *283, 285*
Ursa Major, *278*

Vaccines, *52*
Valley, *246*
Variable speed, *413*
Variables, *18*
Venus, *282–284, 304*
Vertebrate, 139–141, 165–168
Vibrations, *381–382*
Vines, *107*
Vocabulary
absorb, 369, 371, 395–398
adaptation, 191, 195, 201–204
arthropod, 139, *143*, 165–168
atmosphere, 225, 228, 259–264
axis, 289, 305–308
bar graph, 23, 25, 37–40
boil, 329, 332, 343–346
carbon dioxide, 99, 100, 125–128
chart, 23, 25, 37–40
climate, 225, 226, 259–264
closed circuit, 387, 389, 395–398
community, 179, 182, 201–204
condensation, 221, 222, 259–264, 329, 333, 343–346
consumer, 185, 201–204
crater, 297, 300, 305–308
decomposer, 185, 201–204
design process, 61, 69–72
ecosystem, 179, 180, 201–204
electrical energy, 357, 358, 395–398
energy, 357, 395–398
erosion, 251, 252, 259–264
evaporation, 221, 222, 259–264, 329, 332, 343–346

flowering plant, 91, 92, 125–128
food chain, 185, 186, 201–204
force, 415, 429–432
freeze, 329, 332, 343–346
friction, 415, 417, 429–432
germinate, 111, 113, 125–128
gravity, 423, 429–432
habitat, 179, 182, 201–204
hardness, 325, 326, 343–346
humidity, 225, 230, 259–264
igneous rock, 233, 235, 259–264
inclined plane, 55, 57, 69–72
infer, 11, 13, 37–40
inherit, 147, 148, 165–168
inquiry, 7, 8, 37–40
instinct, 147, 150, 165–168
invertebrate, 139, 142, 165–168
investigate, 7, 37–40
kinetic energy, 357, 361, 395–398
landform, 245, 259–264
larva, 155, 156, 165–168
lava, 245, 248, 259–264
lever, 55, 56, 69–72
life cycle, 117, 125–128
light energy, 369, 395–398
light-year, 275, 305–308
loam, 239, 242, 259–264
magnetism, 415, 420, 429–432
mass, 335, 337, 343–346
matter, 325, 343–346
melt, 329, 332, 343–346
metamorphic rock, 233, 236, 259–264
metamorphosis, 155, 158, 165–168
mineral, 233, 259–264
model, 17, 20, 37–40
moon phase, 297, 298, 305–308
motion, 409, 429–432
nutrient, 105, 125–128
open circuit, 387, 389, 395–398
oxygen, 99, 100, 125–128
photosynthesis, 99–100, 125–128
pitch, 381, 384, 395–398
planet, 281, 305–308
pollinate, 111, 112, 125–128
population, 179, 182, 201–204
position, 409, 429–432
potential energy, 357, 360, 395–398
precipitation, 221, 223, 259–264
procedure, 23, 24, 37–40
producer, 185, 201–204

property, 325, 326, 343–346
prototype, 61, 63, 69–72
pulley, 55, 57, 69–72
pupa, 155, 156, 165–168
reflect, 369, 370, 395–398
refract, 369, 370, 395–398
reproduce, 111, 125–128
research, 61, 62, 69–72
revolution, 289, 292, 305–308
rock, 233, 259–264
rotation, 289–290, 305–308
scientist, 7, 37–40
screw, 55, 57, 69–72
sedimentary rock, 233, 236, 259–264
soil, 239, 259–264
solar system, 281, 282, 305–308
sound energy, 357, 359, 395–398
speed, 409, 412, 429–432
spore, 91, 95, 125–128
star, 275, 305–308
states of matter, 329, 343–346
technology, 51, 69–72
texture, 325, 326, 343–346
thermal energy, 377, 395–398
tool, 29, 37–40
trait, 139, 165–168
unit of measure, 29, 30, 37–40
vertebrate, 139, 140, 165–168
volume, 335, 336, 343–346, 381, 383, 395–398
water cycle, 221, 222, 259–264
wave, 363, 366, 395–398
weather, 225, 259–264
weathering, 251, 259–264
wedge, 55, 56, 69–72
wheel and axle, 55, 56, 69–72
work, 55, 69–72
Vocabulary (Critical Thinking), 42, 74, 131, 170–171, 206, 266, 310–311, 348, 400, 434
Volcanoes, *244, 247–248*
Volume, 334–336, *340–341*, 343–346, 381, 395–398
of sound, *383*
Von Frisch, Karl, *146*

Credits

Staff Credits

The people who made up the *Interactive Science* team — representing composition services, core design digital and multimedia production services, digital product development, editorial, editorial services, manufacturing, and production — are listed below.

Geri Amani, Alisa Anderson, Jose Arrendondo, Amy Austin, David Bailis, Scott Baker, Lindsay Bellino, Charlie Bink, Bridget Binstock, Holly Blessen, Robin Bobo, Craig Bottomley, Jim Brady, Laura Brancky, Chris Budzisz, Odette Calderon, Mary Chingwa, Caroline Chung, Kier Cline, Brandon Cole, Mitch Coulter, AnnMarie Coyne, Fran Curran, Dana Damiano, Michael Di Maria, Nancy Duffner, Amanda Ferguson, David Gall, Mark Geyer, Amy Goodwin, Gerardine Griffin, Chris Haggerty, Margaret Hall, Laura Hancko, Autumn Hickenlooper, Guy Huff, George Jacobson, Marian Jones, Kathi Kalina, Chris Kammer, Sheila Kanitsch, Alyse Kondrat, Mary Kramer, Thea Limpus, Dominique Mariano, Lori McGuire, Melinda Medina, Angelina Mendez, Claudi Mimo, John Moore, Kevin Mork, Chris Niemyjski, Phoebe Novak, Anthony Nuccio, Jeff Osier, Charlene Rimsa, Rebecca Roberts, Camille Salerno, Manuel Sanchez, Carol Schmitz, Amanda Seldera, Jeannine Shelton El, Geri Shulman, Greg Sorenson, Samantha Sparkman, Mindy Spelius, Karen Stockwell, Dee Sunday, Dennis Tarwood, Jennie Teece, Lois Teesdale, Michaela Tudela, Karen Vuchichevich, Tom Wickland, James Yagelski, Tim Yetzina

Illustrations

100, 116, 118, 119, 125, 160, 192, 220, 229, 288, 294, 295 Precision Graphics; **101** Sharon & Joel Harris; **106, 108, 113** Alan Barnard; **226, 259** Studio Liddell; **246, 248, 331** Big Sesh Studios; **280, 281, 282, 284, 285, 292, 297, 305** Paul Oglesby; **289, 291, 305** Robert (Bob) Kayganich; **358, 395** Jeff Grunewald
All other illustrations Chandler Digital Art

Photographs

Every effort has been made to secure permission and provide appropriate credit for photographic material. The publisher deeply regrets any omission and pledges to correct errors called to its attention in subsequent editions.

Unless otherwise acknowledged, all photographs are the property of Pearson Education, Inc.

Photo locators denoted as follows: Top (T), Center (C), Bottom (B), Left (L), Right (R), Background (Bkgd)

COVER: Jill Lang/Shutterstock

vi (TR) ©Chris Johnson/Alamy Images; **vii** (TR) David J. Green/Alamy; **viii** (TR) ©Jan Hopgood/Shutterstock; **ix** (TR) ©EcoPrint/Shutterstock; **x** (TR) ©Kjersti Joergensen/Shutterstock; **xi** (TR) ©Ted Foxx/Alamy; **xii** (TR) ©Charles C. Place/Getty Images; **xiii** (TR) ©Tony Freeman/PhotoEdit; **xiv** (TR) ©Christophe Testi/Shutterstock; **xv** (TR) ©Xavier Pironet/Shutterstock; **1** (Bkgrd) ©niderlander/Shutterstock; **2** (C) ©Kim Karpeles/Alamy Images; **6** (T) ©gary corbett/Alamy Images, (BR) Florida Division of Forestry, Tallahassee; **7** (CR) ©Doug Steley A/Alamy Images; **9** (TR) ©Will & Deni McIntyre/Photo Researchers, Inc.; **10** (T) ©Dennis Hallinan/Alamy Images; **11** (B) ©dmac/Alamy Images; **12** (C) ©forestpath/Shutterstock; **13** (TR) ©matthiasengelien/Alamy; **15** (TR) ©Jeff Greenberg/Alamy Images; **16** (T) ©Science Source/Photo Researchers, Inc.; **17** (BR) ©Aaron Haupt/Photo Researchers, Inc.; **20** (TL) ©Alfred Pasieka/Photo Researchers, Inc.; **22** (TR) ©Images & Stories/Alamy Images; **23** (TR) ©Chris Johnson/Alamy Images, (B) ©Images & Stories/Alamy; **26** (T) ©Ariel Skelley/Blend/Jupiter Images; **28** (TR) ©Rob Walls/Alamy Images; **29** (BR) ©Bob Daemmrich/PhotoEdit, Inc., (TL) ©Jubal Harshaw/Shutterstock; **32** (B) ©Andy Crawford/DK Images; **33** (TR) ©imagebroker/Alamy Images; **36** (C) B. Tristan Denyer; **37** (CR) ©Doug Steley A/Alamy Images, (TC) ©forestpath/Shutterstock, (TR) ©Will & Deni McIntyre/Photo Researchers, Inc.; **39** (BR) ©Bob Daemmrich/PhotoEdit, Inc.; **45** (TL) ©Holmberg/Sipa/NewsCom, (L) Paul Nicklen/National Geographic Image Collection/Alamy; **46** (C) ©Digital Art/Corbis; **49** (R) ©Martin D. Vonka/Shutterstock; **50** (T) ©Idealink Photography/Alamy, (CL) U.S. Patent and Trademark Office; **51** (CR) Getty Images; **52** (BL) ©Monkey Business Images/Shutterstock, (CL) Jupiter Images; **53** (TR) ©Andrey Burmakin/Shutterstock; **54** (T) ©Aflo Foto Agency/Alamy; **55** (CR) ©Photo and Co/Getty Images; **56** (BR) ©Michelle D. Bridwell/PhotoEdit, (CL) DK Images, (TL) Jupiter Images; **57** (BL) ©Bonnie Kamin/PhotoEdit, Inc., (CR) ©Tetra Images/SuperStock, (TR) Wuttichok Painichiwarapun/Shutterstock; **58** (R) Corbis; **59** (T) Philip Gatward/©DK Images; **60** (TR) ©Bettmann/Corbis; **61** (TL) ©axle71/Shutterstock; **62** (T) ©lightpoet/Shutterstock; **63** (B) ©Mny-Jhee/Shutterstock, (TR) ©Patrick Breig/Shutterstock; **64** (TL) David J. Green/Alamy; **65** (TR) ©D. Hurst/Alamy Images, (CR) ©Zakharoff/Shutterstock; **68** ©Jaak Nilson/Alamy Images; **69** (BC) ©Bonnie Kamin/PhotoEdit, Inc., (CC) ©Michelle D. Bridwell/PhotoEdit, (CR) ©Photo and Co/Getty Images, (TC) DK Images, (TR) Getty Images, (BR) Jupiter Images; **71** (TC) ©lightpoet/Shutterstock, (CC) ©Patrick Breig/Shutterstock, (TR) ©Tetra Images/SuperStock, (CR) Wuttichok Painichiwarapun/Shutterstock; **77** (CL) ©Image Source , (C) ©Tara Carlin/Alamy; **83** (B) ©Ilja Masik/Shutterstock; **85** (Bkgd) ©Flirt/Superstock, Inc, (T) ©Mark Newman/Photo Researchers, Inc., (C) Jiri Haureljuk/Shutterstock, (B) ©tbkmedia.de/Alamy Royalty Free; **86** (C) ©Mark Newman/Photo Researchers, Inc.; **90** (BL) ©Andrzej Gibasiewicz/Shutterstock, (TR) ©Lana/Shutterstock, (TC) ©yunus85/Shutterstock; **91** (TC) ©Masterfile Royalty-Free, (TL) Chris Kammer, (BR) Getty Images; **92** (BR) ©Jonathan Larsen/Shutterstock, (L) Thinkstock; **93** (TR) ©Liz Van Steenburgh/Shutterstock, (CR) Image Source; **94** (L) ©prism68/Shutterstock, (BR) Marta Teron/Fotolia; **95** (TC) Tawin Mukdharakosa/Shutterstock, (CL) ©Matthias Spitz/Shutterstock, (R) ©Peter Baker/Getty Images, (BR) ©silver-john/Shutterstock, (BC) Getty Images; **96** (C) ©Masterfile Royalty-Free; **98** (T) ©Elena Yakusheva/Shutterstock; **99** (CR) ©Jan Hopgood/Shutterstock; **102** (R) ©Anne Kitzman/Shutterstock; **103** (TL) ©Steve Brigman/Shutterstock; **104** (T) ©Shannon Matteson/Shutterstock; **105** (CR) Silver Burdett Ginn; **106** (TR) Getty Images, (B) Stockdisc; **107** (T) ©Gary Paul Lewis/

Shutterstock; **108** (B) ©Petros Tsonis/Shutterstock; **109** (TR) DLeonis/Fotolia; **110** (T) Getty Images; **111** (BL) Brian Jackson/ Fotolia; **112** (B) ©Varina and Jay Patel/Shutterstock, (CL) Getty Images; **113** (TL) ©Richard Griffin/Shutterstock; **114** (B) ©Marko Dupalo/Fotolia, (CR) Peter Chadwick/©DK Images, (CL) ©KrystynaSzulecka/Alamy; **115** (TR) ©Richard Griffin/ Shutterstock; **116** (R) ©Paul Marcus/Shutterstock; **117** (CR) ©Kosam/Shutterstock, (BR) ©Marcel Mooij/Shutterstock; **120** (BR) ©Jupiterimages/Thinkstock; **121** (CR) ©Eye-Stock/Alamy; **124** (TC) Cynthia Gehrie, (R) Royal Catchfly, (Silene regia), Watercolor on paper, 16-3/4" x 11"/Published with permission of the artist Heeyoung Kim, All Rights Reserved; **125** (CR) Tawin Mukdharakosa/Shutterstock, (TR) Image Source, (BC) Silver Burdett Ginn; **127** (TC) ©Marcel Mooij/Shutterstock, (BR) ©Richard Griffin/Shutterstock, (CR) ©Varina and Jay Patel/ Shutterstock, (TR, CR) Getty Images; **133** (R) JSC/NASA, (TR) NASA; **134–135** (Bkgd) clabert/Fotolia; **137** (B) Getty Images; **138** (TR) Digital Vision, (TC) Getty Images; **139** (R) ©Purestock/James Urbach/SuperStock, (TL, TC) Digital Vision; **140** (Bkgrd) ©Masterfile Royalty-Free; **141** (CR) ©Christian Musat/Shutterstock, (BR) ©Henk Bentlage/Shutterstock, (TR) Digital Vision; **142** (BR, Bkgrd, BC) Digital Vision; **143** (CR) ©mashe/Shutterstock, (TR) ©Sarah Curran Schaal/Shutterstock, (BR) Getty Images; **144** (B) Getty Images, (TR) Jane Burton/©DK Images; **146** (TC) ©Foto011/Shutterstock, (B) ©Pakhnyushcha/ Shutterstock, (TR) ©Petr Jilek/Shutterstock, (C) Time & Life Pictures/Getty Images; **147** (TC) ©Caryn Becker/Alamy, (BC) ©EcoPrint/Shutterstock, (TL) ©Wheatley/Shutterstock; **148** (BL) ©Clint Farlinger/Alamy Images, (C) Alistair Duncan/©DK Images; **149** (C) ©Kevin Britland/Alamy, (TR) ©Masterfile Royalty-Free; **150** (C) ©Alexsander Isachenko/Shutterstock, (TR) ©Boris Bort/Shutterstock; **151** (BL) ©Blend Images/ SuperStock, (CR) ©James Balog/Getty Images; **152** (TR) ©Eric Isselée/Shutterstock, (CR) ©Rick & Nora Bowers/Alamy Images, (BL) American Society of Mammalogists; **153** (TR) ©David Tipling/Alamy; **154** (TC) ©Ron Niebrugge/Alamy Images, (TR) Frank Greenaway/Courtesy of The National Birds of Prey Centre, Cloucestershire/©DK Images; **155** (CR) ©Suzann Julien/iStockphoto, (TL) Comstock Images/Thinkstock; **156** (Bkgrd) ©Elena Elisseeva/Shutterstock, (TR) ©Rick & Nora Bowers/Alamy Images, (BC) ©Terry Reimink/Shutterstock; **157** (TC, CR) ©Jacob Hamblin/Shutterstock; **158** (BC) ©Malcolm Schuyl/Alamy, (TR) ©Splash/Shutterstock; **159** (C) ©Wolfgang Staib/Shutterstock, (BL) Geoff Brightling/©DK Images; **160** (CL) ©Corbis/SuperStock, (CR) ©Papilio/Alamy Images, (BR) Dan Bannister/©DK Images; **162** (BR) ©Krasowit/ Shutterstock, (BL) ©Photofrenetic/Alamy Images, (CR) ©Royalty-Free/Corbis/Jupiter Images, (CL, BC) Getty Images; **164** (CR, B) ©Mark Conlin/Alamy Images; **165** (BC) ©Boris Bort/ Shutterstock, (CC) ©Clint Farlinger/Alamy Images, (CR) ©Masterfile Royalty-Free, (TR) ©Purestock/James Urbach/ SuperStock, (BR) Digital Vision, (TC) Getty Images; **167** (TR, CR) ©Jacob Hamblin/Shutterstock, (BR) ©Malcolm Schuyl/ Alamy, (BR) Geoff Brightling/©DK Images; **169** (TL) Getty Royalty Free, (TCL) ©Petr Jilek/Shutterstock, (CL) ©Ron Niebrugge/Alamy, (B) Jiri Haureljuk/Shutterstock; **173** (C) ©Eyal Nahamias/Alamy; **174** (C) ©tbkmedia.de/Alamy; **177** (B) ©Andrea Pistolesi/Getty Images; **178** (T) ©bierchen/ Shutterstock, (B) Warren Price Photography/Shutterstock, (CR,

BR) ©Windell Curole and Joe Suhayda; **179** (BR) ©Randy Green/Getty Images; **180** (TR) ©Kjersti Joergensen/ Shutterstock, (C) ©Nancy Carter/PhotoLibrary Group, Inc.; **181** (BR) ©Lisa Dearing/Alamy; **182** (B) ©Georgette Douwma/ Getty Images, (TL) ©Jamie Robinson/Shutterstock; **184** (T) ©imagebroker/Alamy; **185** (BR) ©Lynne Carpenter/ Shutterstock, (CR) ©sfStop/Alamy, (BL) ©Wouter Tolenaars/ Shutterstock; **186** (TR) ©Alexey Stiop/Shutterstock, (T) ©Serg64/Shutterstock, (C, BR) ©TTphoto/Shutterstock; **187** (TR) Michael Lane/123RF, (BR) ©Eric Gevaert/Shutterstock, (TR) ©Serg64/Shutterstock; **188** (TR) ©Clinton Moffat/Shutterstock, (TC) Michael Lane/123RF, (CR) ©Denis Pepin/Shutterstock, (C) ©creativenature.nl/Fotolia, (BR) ©Eric Gevaert/Shutterstock, (B) ©graph/Shutterstock, (B) ©Joel Sartore/National Geographic/ Getty Images, (CR) ©Roberta Olenick/PhotoLibrary Group, Inc., (TL) ©Rusty Dodson/Shutterstock, (CL) ©Viorel Sima/ Shutterstock; **190** (T) ©Design Pics Inc./Alamy; **191** (BR) ©Juniors Bildarchiv/Alamy; **192** (CR) ©Steve McWilliam/ Shutterstock; **193** (TR) ©Cynthia Kidwell/Shutterstock; **194** (B) ©Jim Parkin/Shutterstock; **195** (B) ©Sergey Korotkov/Alamy, (TR, TC) ©Smit/Shutterstock; **196** (B) ©Gary Braasch/Corbis; **197** (CR) ©Phil Schermeister/NGS Image Collection, (TL) ©Philip James Corwin/Corbis; **200** (B) ©Craig Stocks Arts/ Shutterstock, (BR) ©Danita Delimont/Shutterstock, (C) ©Deon Reynolds/PhotoLibrary Group, Inc., (CC) ©Juniors Bildarchiv GmbH/Alamy, (T) ©Joe Mamer Photography/Alamy Images, (TR) ©William Leaman/Alamy; **201** (TC, BR) ©Georgette Douwma/Getty Images, (CR) ©Jamie Robinson/Shutterstock, (CC) ©Lynne Carpenter/Shutterstock, (TR) ©Nancy Carter/ PhotoLibrary Group, Inc., (BC) ©sfStop/Alamy; **203** (CR) Michael Lane/123RF, (BR) ©Sergey Korotkov/Alamy, (TR) ©Wouter Tolenaars/Shutterstock; **209** (L) Darren Green/Fotolia, (CC) ©Masterfile Royalty-Free; **215** (TR) Leonello Calvetti/Getty, (TC) ©John Doornkamp/Design Pics Inc./Alamy, (BC) Jacob W. Frank/Getty Images; **216** (C) ©John Doornkamp/Design Pics Inc./Alamy; **217** (TR) Leonello Calvetti/Getty; **219** (Bkgrd) ©Zastol'skiy Victor Leonidovich/Shutterstock; **220** (T) ©Brand X Pictures/Jupiter Images, (R) ©Taylor S. Kennedy/Getty Images; **221** (CR) The Earth Observatory/NASA; **222** (TR) ©Adisa/Shutterstock, (CR) ©Pavel Cheiko/Shutterstock, (Bkgrd) ©nfsphoto/Fotolia; **223** (TR) ©Allen Stoner/Shutterstock, (TC) ©Mytho/Shutterstock; **224** (T) ©Hill Creek Pictures/Getty Images, (T) ©John Lund/Drew Kelly/PhotoLibrary Group, Inc.; **225** (CR) ©Elena Elisseeva/Shutterstock, (TC) ©MilousSK/ Shutterstock; **228** (R) ©Mike Phillips/Shutterstock; **230** (BC) ©Emil Pozar/Alamy Images, (Bkgrd) ©Serg64/Shutterstock, (BL) ©Ted Foxx/Alamy, (BR) DK Images; **231** (TR) Artur Synenko/Shutterstock; **232** (TR) ©DEA/C.DANI/Getty Images, (TC) Colin Keates/Courtesy of the Natural History Museum, London/©DK Images; **233** (TC) ©DEA/C.BEVILACQUA/Getty Images, (CR) Thinkstock, (BCR) Gontar/Shutterstock; **234** (TR) ©Ted Foxx/Alamy, (BR) ©PULSE/Jupiter Images; **235** (TL) ©M. Claye/Jacana Scientific Control/Photo Researchers, Inc., (BR) Andreas Einsiedel/©DK Images, (CL) DK Images, (TC, CC) Getty Images, (BC) J. D. Griggs/U.S. Geological Survey; **236** (TL) ©George F. Mobley/Getty Images; **237** (CL) ©Andrew J. Martinez/Photo Researchers, Inc., (TR, TL, CR) DK Images; **238** (TR) ©DK Images, (TC) Peter Anderson/©DK Images; **239** (CR) ©Jeff Randall/Getty Images, (TC) Andy

This is your book.

You can write in it.

Take Note

This space is yours. It is great for drawing diagrams and making notes

This is your book.

You can write in it.